The Spiritual Doctrine
of
SISTER ELIZABETH OF THE TRINITY

BY

M. M. PHILIPON, O. P.

Translated by
A BENEDICTINE OF STANBROOK ABBEY

Nihil Obstat

    E. A. Cerney, S. S., D. D.
     Censor Librorum

Imprimatur

    ✠Michael J. Curley
     Archbishop of Baltimore and Washington

March 29, 1947

TO

JANUA CAELI—GATE OF HEAVEN

THROUGH WHOM SOULS ASCEND TO THE

TRINITY

FILIAL HOMAGE

In conformity with the decrees of Pope Urban VIII, and other Sovereign Pontiffs, we declare that, in making use of the word "Saint," we do so only in the sense commonly understood among the faithful, without desiring to anticipate the official judgment of the Church, which alone is competent to pronounce upon the holiness of her children. We unreservedly submit to her judgment in advance.

CONTENTS

	PAGE
PREFACE	
INTRODUCTION	

CHAPTER

I	Spiritual Journey	1
II	The Ascesis of Silence	33
III	The Indwelling of the Blessed Trinity	46
IV	The Praise of Glory	81
V	Conformity to Christ	101
VI	*Janua Coeli*	122
VII	Sister Elizabeth of the Trinity and the Souls of Priests	135
VIII	The Gifts of the Holy Ghost	154
IX	Prayer to the Trinity	189

EPILOGUE

	Her Mission	205

APPENDIX

I	Last Spiritual Counsels	214
II	Heaven on Earth	219
III	Last Retreat of "*Laudem Gloriae*"	232

PREFACE

> *"This mystery of the indwelling of the Blessed Trinity in the depths of her soul was the great reality of her interior life."* (Garrigou-Lagrange)

The most elementary truths of Christian faith, such as those expressed in the *Our Father*, are, we find, the most profound truths when we have meditated upon them long and lovingly; when, through the years, we have lived with them, while carrying our cross, and they have become the object of almost continuous contemplation.

To be led to the heights of sanctity, it would be enough for a soul to live intensely but one of these truths of our Faith.

One of the most important of these truths is that of the special presence of God in the souls of the just, according to the words of Our Lord: *If any one love Me, he will keep My word, and My Father will love him, and We will come to him and will make Our abode with him.* (John XIV, 23) By these words and by the promise of His Holy Spirit, Christ taught us that the most fundamental vocation of every baptized soul is to live in fellowship with the very Persons of the Blessed Trinity. Hence, according to St. Thomas' frequently repeated words, the Christian life even here on earth is, in a sense, eternal life begun: *quaedam inchoatio vitae aeternae.* The grace of Baptism makes us truly partakers of the divine nature even as it subsists in the bosom of the Trinity. God has so loved us in His Son as to will to make us share in the very principle of His intimate life, the principle of the immediate vision He has of Himself, which He communicates to the Word and to the Holy Ghost. Thus the just enter into the family of God and into the life-cycle of the Trinity. Living faith, enlightened by the Gift of Wisdom, assimilates them to the light of the Word;

infused charity assimilates them to the Holy Spirit. In them the Father begets His Word; in them the Father and the Son breathe the Personal Love that unites Them. In each of them the Trinity dwells, whole and entire, as in a living temple; here below It dwells as in a darkened temple, but in heaven in a light that knows no shadow and in an unchanging love.

The servant of God, Elizabeth of the Trinity, was one of those enlightened and heroic souls able to cling to one of these great truths, which are both the simplest and the most important, and, beneath the appearance of an ordinary life, to find therein the secret of a very close union with God. This mystery of the indwelling of the Blessed Trinity in the depths of her soul was the great reality of her interior life. As she herself said: " The Trinity! there is our dwelling, our ' home,' the father's house that we must never leave. . . . It seems to me that I have found my heaven on earth, for heaven is God and God is in my soul. On the day I understood that, everything became clear to me. . . ."

Obviously the foundation of this supernatural life is the practice of the theological virtues. Faith is the supernatural light through which we receive the revelation of this divine world. Our hope, upheld by the omnipotence of God, Whose hand is ever stretched out to help us, enables us to tend surely toward eternal happiness. Charity establishes us permanently in the friendship and fellowship of the Divine Persons, according to the teaching of St. John the Evangelist: " God is charity: and he that abideth in charity, abideth in God, and God in him " (*I John* IV, 16). In essence, there is but the one supernatural life; it begins on earth with our Baptism and it will reach its full development in heaven with the vision of God face to face.

Faith is the root of all this new activity. It is " the substance," the principle, the germ " of things hoped for," things which we shall one day behold unveiled. The least light of faith is thus infinitely superior to the natural intuitions of the greatest genius and the highest angel. It belongs to the same essentially supernatural order as the beatific vision. Living faith, enlightened by the gifts of understanding and wisdom, is, accordingly, the only light proportionate to this life of intimate communion with the Divine Persons.

Hence, above all else, Sister Elizabeth of the Trinity stands before us as a soul of faith, living in ever more perfect communion with the invisible world while, under the hand of God, sense and spirit were being purified through the events of her daily life. Like a true daughter of St. John of the Cross, she was aware of the primary importance of faith in the supernatural life. " In order to draw near to God," she wrote, " we must believe. Faith is the substance of things hoped for, and the evidence of things that appear not. St. John of the Cross says that it serves us as feet to go to God, that it is possession in an obscure manner. It alone can give us real light upon Him Whom we love; our soul should choose it as the means of reaching the blessed union. . . ."

Without neglecting the practice of the moral virtues, she was seen to apply herself more and more to the interior activity of the theological virtues. " My only practice is to enter into myself and lose myself in Those Who are there."

The perfect flowering of faith, hope, and charity demands special assistance from God, and it is precisely by an increasingly predominant activity of the gifts of the Holy Ghost that the mystical life is characterized. Although the theological virtues are actually superior to the gifts that accompany them, they receive a new perfection from the gifts, just as a tree is more perfect with its fruit than without it. According to St. Thomas, a soul that only *imperfectly* possesses a principle of action cannot act as it should unless it is helped by a higher agent. In the spiritual life, the beginner needs the guidance of an experienced master, just as the student of medicine or surgery needs the direction of his professor. Now, by means of the theological and moral virtues, the just man as yet possesses only *imperfectly* this divine life of grace which introduces him into the family of the Trinity. Hence, the Divine Persons must Themselves come to his aid, according to St. Paul's words to the Romans: " Whosoever are led by the Spirit of God, they are the sons of God." (*Rom.* VIII, 14). He must live, not in the manner of a human creature, but *in God's manner*, in the intimacy of the Divine Persons, in order that he may be "perfect as the heavenly Father is perfect." How is anyone to judge of all things, both human and divine, after the manner of God Himself unless divine knowledge and wisdom are specially imparted to him? In the midst of the frequently insoluble situations of human life, how is he to make a swift decision that will coincide with the plan of divine Providence without a special operation of the gift of counsel? Finally, how is he to remain immutably attached to the divine will amid the difficulties—at times, terrible difficulties—of life, without the special assistance of the divine fortitude itself, which alone can triumph over all the powers of evil?

In the manifestation of these gifts of the Holy Ghost in the world of souls, however, the greatest variety is apparent, according to the circumstances in which God places them and according to their mission. The intellectual gifts are more readily discerned in some souls; in others, the gifts of fear, piety, and fortitude. There is an infinite range of subtle distinctions. Even the same gift assumes diverse forms in the different saints. In some, as in St. Augustine, wisdom appears primarily in a contemplative form; in others, as in St. Vincent de Paul, it appears in a practical form, wholly given to works of mercy. To the former, the Holy Ghost gives the ability to penetrate and to savor the deep things of God and to speak of them in glowing terms; He makes the latter see, as in a diffused light, the suffering members of Christ and the means by which they may work effectively for their salvation.

In the case of the servant of God considered in these pages, we are impressed by the high degree of her possession of the gifts of understanding and wisdom by means of which she was able to penetrate so deeply into the mystery of the Trinity and to feel its effects profoundly, and almost continuously. Even before she entered Carmel, it was obvious that she was powerfully gripped by this presence of the Divine Persons in the depths of her soul. Toward the end of her life, on the feast of the Ascension—the last time she celebrated this feast on earth—she felt the Blessed Trinity take possession of her soul to such a degree that she seemed to see the Three Divine Persons holding Their council of love in her. From that day on, whenever any special intention was recommended to her prayers, she would answer: " I will speak of it to my Almighty Council." On the eve of her death, she could write in all truth: " The belief that a Being, Whose name is Love, is dwelling in us at every moment of the day and night, and that He asks us to live in His company, that, I own to you, is what has made my life an anticipated heaven."

We are also deeply struck at seeing the degree to which she had received the gift of fortitude. It is constantly noticeable in the courage with which the servant of God accepted the hardest of trials, particularly during her illness. Unable to practice extraordinary mortifications, which obedience to her Superior forbade throughout her religious life, she bore unflinchingly, during a long and very trying year of novitiate, the painful passive purifications that were inevitable for a still too keenly sensitive character. She bravely walked the road of the dark night, more and more seeking refuge in pure faith, and never ceasing to lift herself up to God, beyond all His graces and all His gifts. But it was particularly during her last illness that her gift of fortitude revealed itself in its splendor. While her physical frame was being destroyed, her soul remained steadfast under the most crucifying divine purifications. She rose above the actual suffering so that, through joy and suffering alike, she might think only of her office of being a " Praise of Glory " of the Trinity. She thought of the majesty with which Christ the King, crowned with thorns, went to Calvary and it is a reflection of that majesty which we find in this valiant Bride of the Savior, who worked with Him, through Him, and in Him, by the same means as He, for the salvation of souls. Truly did God grant her last wish: " To die not only as pure as an angel, but transformed into Jesus Crucified."

Finally, one of the most characteristic features of the spiritual physiognomy of Sister Elizabeth of the Trinity is obviously her doctrinal sense, nourished at the best sources of Christian thought in her two favorite teachers: St. Paul, the Apostle of the Mystery of Christ, and St. John of the Cross, the mystical Doctor of Carmel. Without being a theologian in the formal sense of the word, yet, like a true daughter of St. Teresa, she had a taste for solid doctrine, which she made the substantial food of her interior life, delighting to ponder the great truths of faith in silence and prayer under the light of life which increases in us as we grow in love of God and of souls.

Hence, the author's task was twofold: first, to set forth, in the light of the guiding principles of mystical theology, the essential movements of this contemplative soul and to distinguish the fundamental truths by which the servant of God lived, according to her special grace, under a Carmelite form; secondly, after having noted the principal stages of her ascension, to bring out the points of doctrine which particularly nourished her spiritual life, i. e., the ascesis of silence, the indwelling of the Trinity, the " Praise of Glory," conformity to Christ, her very personal devotion to Our Lady of the Incarnation, the operation of the gifts of the Holy Ghost in her, and finally the profound meaning of her celebrated prayer to the Holy Trinity and of her mission.

Father Marie-Michel Philipon wrote these pages after long meditation on the life and writings of Sister Elizabeth of the Trinity. For several years he has been truly penetrated with them, and he has sought to explain them in the light of the principles of theology, as formulated by St. Thomas and applied to the direction of contemplative souls by St. John of the Cross.

He has fulfilled his task with both reverence and a sense of doctrine that together made it possible for him to combine supernatural enthusiasm with a right moderation—a balance difficult to maintain, especially in cases where the servant of God was called upon to practice simultaneously virtues that appear contrary to one another: fortitude and gentleness, prudence and simplicity, compassion for the erring and sinners and ardent zeal for the glory of God.

The reader will draw great profit from this clear-sighted

PREFACE

profound study, which concretely and vividly reveals the theology of " the grace of the virtues and the gifts " by displaying the riches it contains.

May the Blessed Trinity find in this book a new ray of glory and may those who read it draw from it the true humility that is so closely connected with the theological virtues, which, in turn, reveal to us the meaning of the highest things. So many poor human beings, made for eternal life and the fellowship of the Divine Persons, drag out their lives in the sterile, restless activity of a topsy-turvy world. God grant that some of them may find in these pages the bearings to chart their course and to regain the right road which leads to union with God, to the " light of life," which enlightens everything from on high, by showing us the " one thing necessary," the end for which we are destined.

FR. REGINALD GARRIGOU-LAGRANGE, O.P.

Rome, *The Angelico*,
July 12, 1937.

INTRODUCTION

" A theologian views a soul and a doctrine."

The publication of the *Souvenirs*, containing an account of the life and a number of the writings of Sister Elizabeth of the Trinity, has met with extraordinary success in France. In less than thirty years, and without any flamboyant advertising, more than ninety thousand copies have been sold, not counting a dozen translations into foreign languages. The Chinese version is now nearly finished.

Thousands of letters have been received at the Carmel of Dijon, expressing the gratitude of those who have read the *Souvenirs*. They have come from all over the world and from the most varied sources: from simple Christian folk, from religious and contemplatives in particular, from numerous priests and seminarians, from eminent theologians and from outstanding members of the episcopate.

His Eminence Cardinal Mercier, on his way home from Rome after the canonization of St. Joan of Arc, decided to stop at Dijon and make a pilgrimage to the Carmel. When he was shown a portrait of Elizabeth of the Trinity in the chapter room, he asked: " How long was she in Carmel? "[1] " Five years, Your Eminence," replied the Mother Prioress. And the Cardinal remarked with a smile: " You become holy quickly here! " When he was taken to the cell of the young Carmelite, which had been transformed into an oratory, he expressed the

---

[1] Here are the most important dates in her life: Born at Bourges, July 18, 1880; Baptized, July 22, 1880; First Communion, April 19, 1891; First mystical graces: Retreat in January, 1899; Entered Carmel, August 2, 1901; Clothing: December 8, 1901; Profession: Epiphany, 1903; Admission to the infirmary: March, 1906; Died, November 9, 1906.

same thought once more: "*She* became a saint in no time, while we drag along."

The holy and distinguished prelate often used the *Souvenirs* as his bedside reading. During a meeting with his clergy, he warmly recommended the book to them and expressed the wish that it might find a place in the library of every one of his priests.

How are we to account for such a widespread attraction?

It is for the Church, and the Church alone, to pronounce upon the sanctity of God's servants. In advance, we submit to her judgment unreservedly in a filial spirit.

Our own point of view is a different one. As we read over the correspondence received at the Carmel of Dijon after the publication of the *Souvenirs*, and made endless inquiries in religious communities as to the nature of the influence exercised by Sister Elizabeth of the Trinity, one obvious conclusion was forced upon us: what has most impressed readers of the holy Carmelite's writings is *their doctrinal character*. The Abbe Sauvé struck the right note, and merely voiced the general impression, when he wrote: "It is in that, perhaps, that the *Souvenirs* will do the most good." [2]

Many similar statements could be quoted from the most diverse schools of spirituality.[3] We consider two of them particularly revealing.

The Reverend Father Arintero, O.P. wrote to the Carmel on June 16, 1937: "I am enchanted by this book [the *Souvenirs*] on account of its beautiful *doctrine*, which is sure to do immense good to souls.

"What I most admire in this servant of God is *her profound understanding of the great mysteries of Christian life*: our incorporation in Christ, Whose mission we must continue; the indwelling of the Blessed Trinity in our hearts. . . . Through

[2] Quoted in the *Souvenirs*, p. xxvi, ed. 1935. The *Souvenirs* were translated into English by the Benedictines of Stanbrook Abbey, 1913.

[3] Individuals quoted in the *Souvenirs* include: the Rev. Father Foch, S.J., Dom Vandeur, O.S.B., the Rev. Chas. Sauvé, S.S., the Very Rev. Father Louis of the Trinity, O.C.D., the Very Rev. Father Vallée, O.P., certain Carthusians, etc.

this grasp of the great mysteries, identical with St. Paul's, she became a faithful interpreter of some of the most sublime passages of his profound Epistles. When Sister Elizabeth explains them in her intimate letters, even though only in passing, she sheds floods of life-giving light, thereby drawing innumerable souls to the interior life. . . ."

Again, His Excellency Monsignor Sagot du Vauroux wrote: " What I find most remarkable in the life of Sister Elizabeth of the Trinity is the *absolute conformity of her views,* her inclinations, her interior life and her words *with the surest principles of mystical theology.* She cannot subtilize. Her imagination never carries her beyond the limits ordinarily observed by a sound reason enlightened by faith and quickened by love. Tenuous or vague considerations are foreign to her. The words come easily to her pen, as accurate as the thoughts they express. She thoroughly understands and penetrates the sense of the Scriptures, particularly St. Paul's Epistles; nor are we surprised at the special attraction her eager heart felt for this great saint. In interesting and accurate commentaries she sheds light on the most sublime teachings of St. John of the Cross. Who is this who writes so sublimely, yet with so sure a touch? Is it a priest long accustomed to theological study and mental prayer? It would be indeed difficult to recognize the soul of a girl behind these dissertations, at once simple and transparent and yet marked by truly virile logic, were it not for the incomparable sweetness shed over all Elizabeth's writings by the warmth and grace of her style, its delicacy and purity, its animation and even, at times, its playfulness. Like St. Teresa, the dear little sister loved above all else true, strong, beautiful doctrine." [*]

This " absolute conformity of views with the surest principles of mystical theology " is, indeed, the most characteristic feature of this essentially doctrinal spirituality. This was the dominant impression we constantly experienced when going over the documents left by Sister Elizabeth of the Trinity and it is what decided us to try to discover and explain their profound mean-

---

[*] *Souvenirs,* p. xvii.

ing. We wish, therefore, to define the nature of our undertaking thus: "*A theologian views a soul and a doctrine.*"

Although our main object is not to give an historical sketch, we have endeavored to be strictly objective in interpreting facts. There was no question of building up a mystical thesis *a priori* and then forcing evidence and documents to fit it. Rather, by means of the rules of the historical method, we have sought to discover the true meaning of the evidence and the documents, according to circumstances of time and place, the persons to whom the letters were addressed, and the religious and social atmosphere, in order that we might determine their full significance in the light of psychological conditions and the divine or human influences at work.

To make this survey thoroughly objective, we painstakingly went through a great many documents and did considerable research into sources. We collated all the writings with the originals, except a few letters which we were unable to see but of which we obtained certified copies. We used a great many writings which are published for the first time in this volume. Pen in hand, we interviewed as many witnesses as possible. In particular, we talked at length with Elizabeth Catez's own sister; we talked with her three most intimate friends before her entry into the convent; with the nuns who had been her contemporaries at Carmel, one of whom had been her close friend; with the confessor who had directed her between the ages of fifteen and twenty-one; with other acquaintances; with a priest who, being related to the family, had often seen and talked with her. Lastly, and above all, we interviewed the most authentic witness of her life, Mother Germaine of Jesus who, throughout Sister Elizabeth's life at Carmel, was both her Prioress and her Novice Mistress. Special mention must be made of this last exceptionally valuable witness. Now that, by a holy death, she is with God, we feel it a grateful duty to declare that the confidences we received from Mother Germaine of Jesus and our long hours of conversation with her concerning one who was truly " her child " were of the utmost value in the preparation of this study. We consulted her most scrupulously upon every-

INTRODUCTION

thing and repeatedly had the immeasurable satisfaction of receiving from her *full confirmation* of conclusions which we felt sprang from the documents. She was in perfect agreement with every essential point in this book.

When this critical sifting had been completed, the primary and fundamental task still remained to be done: to bring out in the light of the facts and confidences obtained, the *doctrinal sense* of the life and writings of Sister Elizabeth of the Trinity.

With our desire for objectivity, it seemed best to search out the living source of Sister Elizabeth's doctrine and thence to follow its development and progress. As to method, we found it necessary, in large part, to enter into explanation of the doctrine by way of the concrete psychology from which it grew. The mystical doctrine of Sister Elizabeth of the Trinity is not the abstract, didactic exposition of a professor of theology; it is above all the spontaneous outpouring of a contemplative soul. It is not the Carmelite's role to explain learnedly the ways of the spiritual life, but to live them in the silence of a soul wholly *hidden with Christ in God.*[5] It is for the Master to reveal the doctrinal wealth of such a life when, for the benefit of His Church, He sees fit to do so. Thus, the doctrinal message of St. Teresa of the Child Jesus was spread abroad; in quite another manner, unostentatiously but intensely, as befits the apostle of the hidden life, the doctrine of Sister Elizabeth of the Trinity has been revealed. *Divisiones gratiarum, idem Spiritus.*[6]

Hence the necessity of prefacing this doctrinal work with a long preliminary chapter which seeks to present the portrait of a soul whose upward progress is traced from the time of the first mystical intimations, when Elizabeth was nineteen, to the consummation of the transforming union on the Cross. This delineation explains the parallel evolution and progress of her mystical doctrine.

Only by thus studying her soul can we understand how, for her, the doctrine of silence did not assume a sense of general ascesis until after she had entered the solitude of Carmel and

[5] *Col.* III, 3.
[6] *I Cor.* XII, 4: "There are diversities of graces, but the same Spirit."

undergone the passive purifications of the novitiate; or how the mystery of the divine indwelling became increasingly the central point from which everything in her life radiated, and to which she referred her supreme vocation of "Praise of Glory of the Trinity," but within, "in the heaven of her soul."

After such a study, it was possible, while most carefully respecting the historical perspectives of the development of her thought on each point of doctrine, to analyze and accurately and surely to indicate *the principles of mystical theology to which the movements of this privileged soul were linked* and the dogmatic truths which had nourished most her inner life.[7]

Carried by grace into the cycle of the life of the Trinity, Sister Elizabeth of the Trinity lived her Baptism completely, under the special form of her Carmelite vocation. Among the human influences she received, that of St. John of the Cross was dominant. By assiduous study of the *Spiritual Canticle* and the *Living Flame of Love*, she had assimilated the loftiest principles of his mystical theology. As a young girl and as a novice, she had been passionately fond of Father Vallée's somewhat oratorical style but she soon passed beyond it, to rest in God in naked faith, above all human ways of thought. As with all great artists, we find in her a first phase of rather servile imitation of models; then a second, in which she is feeling her way and which lasts through the first three years of her novitiate. Then, suddenly, a magnificent creative period

[7] The same theological method, combining the historical and the doctrinal aspects, might be applied to the study of the lives of all the saints. It would seem that work in this vein would lead to a great enrichment and a valuable confirmation of mystical theology. In the light of the leading principles of mystical theology, it would be easy, by this same procedure, to bring out the great doctrinal lines of thought which animated, for instance, St. Teresa of Avila, St. Teresa of the Child Jesus, St. Bernadette, etc.

The great mystics would furnish the highest examples, St. Catherine of Siena perhaps, or St. Margaret Mary, or Mary of the Incarnation. An especially rich, but more complex example, would be St. John of the Cross: at once mystic and theologian.

There is a whole world waiting to be explored which would be immensely profitable in distinguishing the various streams of spirituality in the Church's life and building the history of mystical theology.

INTRODUCTION

opens up brilliantly with the composition, in one outburst and without alteration, of her sublime prayer to the Trinity. Henceforth, in her, the Holy Spirit has a perfect instrument at His disposal. She sings the divine indwelling and the praise of glory in an inimitable, etched style that establishes her as one of the spiritual masters of the French language. Meditation on the Epistles of St. Paul and the mystical works of St. John of the Cross and long hours of contemplative silence have worked this miracle. Above all, the *Word* has become the inner master of her life, as she herself said: " What He teaches me within me is ineffable." *The true source of her doctrine and her life is hidden in that statement.* That was the hour of the supreme triumph of grace in her soul, the full revelation in her of the Trinitarian riches of her baptismal vocation. Henceforth the quiet rhythm of this life " made perfect in one "[a] was limited to a few essential movements, always the same but very deep: the ascesis of silence; the indwelling of the Trinity and the sole preoccupation of working " unto the praise of Its glory "; identification with Christ and conformity to His death; imitation of the life of silent adoration of Our Lady of the Incarnation. Such were the great doctrinal thoughts which swiftly carried this simple but faithful life to the very highest summits of divine union. These are the most fundamental truths of Christianity, and it makes us happy to find a holy soul raising herself to God without miracles or extraordinary mortifications,[b] but simply by following the vocation Baptism itself marks out and by perfect obedience to the divine will, amid the ordinary happenings of daily life.

A Solesmes monk wrote to the most intimate friend of Sister Elizabeth of the Trinity: " I wish a theologian would comment on her writings." That is what this book, written for the glory of the Trinity, tries to do.

Fr. Marie-Michel Philipon, O.P.

St. Maximin, March 7, 1937
Feast of St. Thomas Aquinas.

---

[a] *John* XVII, 23.
[b] This detail was supplied by the Prioress of Dijon.

Chapter I

SPIRITUAL JOURNEY

> "*A Carmelite: in everything she bears the mark of this predestination.*"

Before we seek to sound analytically the depths of this soul, one general remark is called for: Elizabeth of the Trinity became a saint only after eleven years of struggle and constant retouching of details. Even after she had entered Carmel and had there spent several years of silently faithful religious life, it remained for her to undergo, at the hands of God, those purifications by which He brings heroic souls to the unchanging peace of the transforming union, above all joy and all suffering.

1.

Interior Life in the World

1. Childish failings. 2. Conversion. 3. Social life. 4. Good works. 5. Summer holidays. 6. *Agendo contra*. 7. The first mystical graces. 8. The meeting with Father Vallée, O.P.

1. As the daughter and granddaughter of soldiers, Elizabeth Catez bore in her veins the quickly roused blood of warriors. She inherited a fiery temperament. When not more than three or four years old, she once shut herself into a room of the family dwelling and stamped and raged behind the door, kicking that offending bulwark furiously all the while.

Until she was seven, these violent outbursts marked her childhood. It was impossible to control them. There was nothing to do but wait for the storm to subside of itself. Then her mother reasoned with her and taught her to overcome herself through love. "That child has a will of iron," her teacher would say. "She is determined to have what she wants."

She was but a child when her father died in her arms and left her with only her mother and her sister Marguerite. Marguerite was a gentle and retiring girl and Elizabeth shared every hour of her life with her until her entrance into Carmel.

Undisturbed by any other serious event, life flowed along in Dijon in happy, Christian fashion.

2. Her first confession wrought a change in Elizabeth's soul which she later called her *conversion*, a shock " which caused a complete awakening with respect to the things of God."[1] From that day forward she resolutely entered upon the struggle against her predominant faults: anger and oversensitiveness. This hard phase of spiritual warfare was to last until she was eighteen. The priest who prepared her for her first Communion and knew her well told an intimate friend of her mother: " With her temperament, Elizabeth Catez will be either a saint or a demon."

This first contact with Jesus, hidden in the Host, was decisive. " In the depths of her soul she heard His voice." The " Master took possession of her heart so completely that thenceforth her one desire was to give her life to Him."[2] To the astonishment of those around her, a sudden and profound change took place in Elizabeth and she began to make great strides toward that calm self-command which was soon to characterize her. One day, after Holy Communion, she seemed to hear the word " Carmel " spoken in her soul. She understood. She was only fourteen when, on another occasion, during her thanksgiving, she heard an interior call from the Master and she instantly made a vow of virginity in order to belong to Him alone. She was to die faithful to that vow and as pure as a lily.

Her poems, written between the ages of fourteen and nineteen, speak only the names of her beloved Jesus, her heavenly Mother, Mary, her angel guardian, the saints, and Joan of Arc, " the Maid whom none can dishonor."[3]

Carmel had a particularly irresistible fascination for her,

---
[1] *Souvenirs*, p. 6.
[2] *Poems*, " The Anniversary of my First Communion," April 19, 1898.
[3] *Poems*, " Joan of Arc," October 1895.

and her verses sing the praises of the externals of the Carmelite: the coarse serge habit, the white veil, the cheap wooden rosary, the hairshirt chastising the flesh and, lastly, the ring worn by the bride of Christ.[4] As she lived very near her dear Carmel, she often went onto the balcony of her room, " sadly dreaming," and gazed long and fixedly at the monastery.[5] Everything spoke to her heart: the chapel hiding the Master of her life, the ringing of the Angelus, the knell for the dead, the cells with their " tiny windows " and poor furniture, where the nuns rested after a long day of redemptive prayer. She was seventeen and longed for the realization of her dream, still so remote. She did try once to escape " this sad, seductive world " by having a priest friend speak to her mother, but Mme. Catez could not be moved. So, in prayer, Elizabeth confidently awaited God's hour.

3. After that attempt, she was claimed by a constant round of amusements and parties, in which Madame Catez quietly urged her to take part. Perhaps, without wishing to dissuade her daughter from her vocation, she secretly cherished the hope that God would not take her from her. Nor did Elizabeth need to be urged; it was enough for her that her mother wished it. She went everywhere and apparently always enjoyed herself. " She never seemed the least bit bored," is the constant refrain of those who knew her. No one could have guessed that Elizabeth was the future Carmelite whose intense interior life, wholly hidden within herself in Christ, was to bring to the Unchanging Trinity a most moving testimony of silence and recollection.

She made a beautiful figure, always simply but irreproachably dressed, and she received several offers of marriage. Typically, she bought new gloves for one of her last evening affairs, not wishing anyone to suspect her departure. She joyously took part in the social life of her circle, shunning nothing but sin.

4. Throughout the year, at Dijon, Elizabeth gave herself to good works in her parish. She helped with the choir, she taught catechism to the children and to older first communicants whom

[4] *Ibid.* " The Livery of the Carmelite," October 15, 1897.
[5] *Ibid.* " What I See from my Balcony," October 1897.

the little girls made fun of, and did whatever else she was asked. She also had charge of a club for " tough " children who worked in the tobacco industry. They were so passionately fond of her that she had to conceal her address from them to keep them from overrunning her home. As Sister Elizabeth of the Trinity, she later followed their lives and protected them with a Carmelite's silent prayer.

With exquisite tact, Elizabeth was at home with everyone, everywhere. She loved childhood because of its innocence and God granted her a wonderful gift of interesting youngsters. At parties for the family and friends, she sometimes had as many as forty children around her. She liked to get up tableaux, particularly of Jesus in the midst of the Doctors, and we find her dressing up her little company and teaching it how to act. She herself wrote both script and music for the plays and she was especially clever at arranging children's dances. Finally, when all the excitement of the play had died down, chairs would be set out in the garden and she would read to them while, all ears, they listened to " Patira." Sometimes they teased her to join in their games and she would smilingly give in. During the month of May, the little group she took to church used to make her stay in the back, as near the door as possible. And, " scarcely was the tabernacle closed than we would drag her off for a walk. Then she would make up wonderful stories to tell us. Elizabeth Catez always fitted into every mood." [6]

Let us remember this characteristic. In the cloister as in the world, Elizabeth of the Trinity tried not to seem different from others. With the rest, she appreciated the good tarts made by Francine, the best cook of Dijon, and laughed gaily at the heavy dinners typical of the south of France which filled them to the bursting point for three days after.

5. As the summer holidays came round, the family always left Dijon and went on long journeys. Thus Elizabeth visited Switzerland, the Alps, the Jura, the Vosges, the Pyrenees, and a considerable portion of France.

---

[6] From the evidence of a childhood friend.

Her letters show that she enjoyed herself; she was made much of in the whirling round of visits to relatives and friends and became strongly attached to a few chosen friends. More often, however, she seemed simply to mingle in the groups of girls of her own age, having, from motives both of charity and good breeding, a happy companionship with all.

"Our stay at Tarbes has been nothing but a long succession of pleasures: afternoon dances and musicales, country excursions, one after the other. The people at Tarbes are delightful. I have come to know a number of girls, each more charming than the rest. When X, who is a very good musician, and I were together, we never left the piano, and all the music shops in Tarbes could not keep us supplied with pieces to play at sight."[7]

"We are leaving today for Lourdes and it breaks my heart to leave my dear Yvonne. She is the prettiest girl and a wonderful character. As for Madame X . . . , not a trace of her illness remains; she is younger and more stunning than ever, and always so kind. The day before yesterday was my eighteenth birthday and she gave me a lovely set of turquoise blouse studs. Write to me soon. I must leave you to finish packing. I shall be thinking of you a great deal at Lourdes. From there we will tour the Pyrenees, going to Luchon, Cauterets, etc. I am wild over these mountains, which I am looking at while I write to you. I feel as though I could never live without them."[8]

She was especially charmed with Luchon. "It deserves its name of Queen of the Pyrenees. I was more excited about it than any place. The location is incomparable. We spent two days there and were able to make the trip through the Lys valley. We had gone out in a large landau, drawn by four horses, and were with cousins of R . . . , and S . . . , whom we had met again at Luchon. These ladies put us in the charge of someone we knew, who was also making the ascent as far as the Gouffre d'Enfer. We were 1801 meters above sea-level, hanging over that horrible abyss. Madeleine and I thought it so beauti-

---

[7] Letter to Mlle. A. C., July 21, 1898.
[8] *Ibid.*

ful that we almost wanted to whirl away in those waters but our guide, enthusiastic as he was, felt differently. He proved to be much more cautious than we, who galloped along the edge of the precipice without feeling the least bit giddy. Our friends gave a sigh of relief when we got back, for they had hardly felt easy about us during our escapade." [9]

Thus she hurried from one set of friends to another, enjoying the most delightful life, as she tells us herself. Lunéville was typical: " Lunching here, dining there, in addition to numerous tennis parties with the most charming girls." [10] In short, she had not a minute to herself. On the 14th of July, she was present at the review at the Champ de Mars because of her family's close friendships in military circles. As befits an officer's daughter, she was thrilled by the cavalry charge. " Just imagine all those helmets and cuirasses sparkling in the sun. . . . The dazzling performance ended in the evening, in the groves of the park, with fairylike illuminations rather resembling Venice. . . ."

Yet amid these worldly amusements, in her heart she was still homesick for Carmel. As soon as the guests had left, without the slightest effort Elizabeth was back again with the Lord she had never left. At Tarbes, in order to escape for a moment from the noisy gaiety, she took refuge in the Carmelite convent and the out-sister found her kneeling by the grille in the parlor. Gladly would she have kissed every wall in that house of God! Lourdes was close by and for three days she buried herself in recollection near Our Lady of the Rock. Holidays and social gaieties easily dropped from her mind. Rapt in prayer, she remained motionless for a long time before the Grotto, beseeching Mary Immaculate to keep her pure in her own image, and offering herself as a victim for sinners.[11]

Nothing could distract her from her Lord. Later on, from her Carmel at Dijon, she could write this postscript in a letter to her mother: " Do not forget to make your meditation on

---

[9] Letter to Mlle. D., August 1898.
[10] Letter to Mlle. A. C., July 9, 1897.
[11] *Poems*, " The Immaculate Conception," December 8, 1898.

Friday, when you are on the train; it is a very good opportunity, as I remember."[12] She spoke from experience. Likewise the earthly riches of the great cities she visited left her indifferent. For her, Marseilles meant Notre Dame de la Garde,[13] and Lyons, only Fourvières.[14] At Paris, to which she had gone with her mother and sister for the great Exhibition of 1900, only two things really interested her: Montmartre and Our Lady of Victories: "We went to the Exhibition twice. It is very fine, but I detest the noise and the crowd. Marguerite laughed at me and declared that I was like someone just returned from the Congo."[15]

6. During this period of her life, her generous watchword was " agendo contra." A note in her diary, made when she was nineteen, reads: " Today I had the joy of offering Jesus several sacrifices over my dominant fault, *but how much they cost me!* I recognize my weakness there. When I receive an unjust reproof, I feel as though the blood is boiling in my veins; *my whole being rises in revolt.* . . . But Jesus was with me. Deep down in my heart I heard His voice and then I was ready to bear anything for love of Him."[16] In order to find out whether she was really advancing in the way of perfection, she kept a little notebook in which, every evening, she marked down her victories and defeats.

Elizabeth tried to fast without her mother's knowledge, but the watchful Madame Catez discovered the fact in a few days and scolded her very severely. Once more Elizabeth obeyed. God did not will to lead her by the way of the great mortification of the saints. It was to be the same throughout her life at Carmel. The silent Trinity expected another kind of homage from her. " Since I can impose almost no sufferings on myself, I must accept the realization that this physical suffering is only a means—albeit an excellent one—of attaining to interior mortification and complete detachment from self. O Jesus! my Life, my Love, my Bridegroom, help me! It is absolutely necessary

---

[12] Letter to her mother," July 1906.
[13] Letter to M-L. M., October 6, 1898.
[14] Letter to A. C., Summer 1898.
[15] Letter to M-L. M., Summer 1900.
[16] *Diary*, January 30, 1899.

for me to reach that stage at which I may always, and in all things, *do the contrary of my own will!* "[17]

7. God could not wait long to reward Elizabeth's continual efforts to triumph over her nature by secret touches of His grace. The ascetic life leads to the mystical life and constitutes its necessary safeguard.

With her usual good sense, St. Teresa said: " Delicate living and prayer do not go together."[18] All this is quite normal. *The Living Flame of Love* presupposes the painful *Ascent of Mount Carmel*, with its *dark nights* and active and passive purifications such as to make the most resolute tremble. We are too prone also to forget the long contemplative ecstasies of the author of the *Spiritual Exercises* in his cell at Rome, where the enraptured Ignatius murmured over and over: " O beata Trinitas! " We need not deny absolutely diversities of tendencies and spiritual paths—*alius sic, alius sic ibat*—but the Scriptural truth includes all these shades, and saints of all schools meet at a point beyond them all. At the summit, they are all transformed into Christ, identified with the beatitude of the Crucified.

The " spiritual combat " against her faults and the triumph over her natural temperament led Elizabeth Catez to the first manifestations of those mystical graces which were to transform her life, at first slowly and by successive touches as though step by step; then, from the time of her religious profession, by a calm and continuous motion; finally, in the last phase, the six months spent in the infirmary, by giant strides lifting her to the loftiest heights of transforming union.

She did not become aware of these first divine touches (received during the course of a retreat in January 1899) until several months later, when she was reading the works of St. Teresa. Her diary's account of the matter is of the greatest importance in the history of her spiritual life. It marks her entrance into the mystical way after a hard spiritual struggle which had lasted more than eleven years; which, in fact, was never to end.

[17] *Ibid.*, February 24, 1899.   [18] *Way of Perfection*, c. iv.

"At present I am reading St. Teresa's *Way of Perfection*. I find it tremendously interesting and it is doing me a great deal of good. St. Teresa speaks so well about prayer and interior mortification, that mortification which, with God's help, I am determined to reach. Since I cannot for the present impose great sufferings upon myself, I can at least immolate my will at every moment of the day. Prayer—how I love the way St. Teresa handles this subject! When she speaks of contemplation, that degree of prayer wherein God does everything and we do nothing, wherein He unites our souls to Himself so intimately that it is no longer we who live but God living in us . . . oh, I recognized there *the moments of sublime rapture to which the Master deigned to raise me* so often during that retreat, as He has done since then too. What can I render to Him for such great benefits? After those ecstasies, those high raptures, during which the soul forgets everything and sees only its God, how hard and trying ordinary prayer seems! How painfully one must toil to unite all one's powers! How much it costs and how difficult it seems!" [19]

God was even then raising Elizabeth to the higher states of prayer, and this was obvious when she prayed. She would be seen coming slowly up the central aisle in the parish church; she would kneel down in her place and be immediately absorbed in deep recollection. For a long time she would remain motionless, as though wholly possessed by God. Her most intimate friend was always struck by the sudden change that would come over Elizabeth the moment she entered the church to pray. "She was no longer the same person."

For some time, she had been experiencing strange phenomena in the depths of her soul, which she could scarcely explain to herself. She felt as though she were dwelt in. "When I see my confessor," she said to herself, "I shall speak to him about it."

8. It was then that she met a Dominican Friar at Carmel,

[19] *Diary*, February 20, 1899.

the meeting with whom was to give a decisive orientation to her interior life.[20] Mother Germaine of Jesus, Sister Elizabeth's prioress and novice mistress and the author of the *Souvenirs*, justly remarked that " this providential meeting " recalls, by its effects of grace, that of which St. Teresa tells us in the Eighteenth Chapter of her *Life* and in the Fifth Mansion of her *Interior Castle* (First Chapter).[21] The Saint does indeed relate how " a great theologian of the Order of St. Dominic [Master Bañez, a celebrated professor at the University of Salamanca] by confirming from the doctrinal standpoint what she had experienced of the divine presence within her during prayer, brought her great consolation, in addition to the complete security which the truth gives."

When Elizabeth timidly questioned the distinguished religious as to the meaning of the movements of grace of which she had been aware for some time and which gave her the impression of being dwelt in, Father Vallée replied, in the forceful, thought-provoking language that characterized him: " But most certainly, my child; the Father is there, the Son is there, and the Holy Ghost is there." And, like the contemplative theologian he was, he proceeded to explain further how, by the grace of Baptism, the soul becomes that living temple

[20] Some account of this distinguished priest will be of interest to English and American readers: Iréné Vallée was born at Urville (Calvados) on June 28, 1841. In 1860, at the age of nineteen, he entered the Dominican Order at Flavigny, where he received the religious name of Gonzalvé and was the last novice to receive the habit from Lacordaire. Professed on September 5, 1861, he entered upon a long and fruitful apostolic career. Between 1881 and 1904 he preached constantly from some of the most famous pulpits in France, besides having close connections with several religious Orders. When, as a result of the Combes legislation, the French Dominicans were expelled in 1904, he saved the Province by founding the priory of Le Sauchoir, across the Belgian frontier in the diocese of Tournay, and there established the strict observance. In 1910, he returned to Paris, living in private and continuing his apostolic labors. After the Great War he was able to re-establish the Dominican simple novitiate at Amiens. He died at Paris on January 5, 1927, at the age of eighty-five. His own summing-up of Elizabeth of the Trinity was as follows: " Elizabeth de la Trinité avait le sens de la Redémption." (" Elizabeth of the Trinity knew the meaning of the Redemption.") (Translator.)

[21] *Souvenirs*, p. 66, note 1.

of which St. Paul speaks and how, together with the Holy Ghost, the whole Trinity is present with Its creative and sanctifying power, making Its dwelling in us, coming to abide in the most secret recesses of the soul, there to receive in an atmosphere of faith and charity the interior worship of praise and adoration that is Its due.

Elizabeth was delighted with this dogmatic explanation. Since it was grace that was urging her, she could, in perfect security, yield to her interior attraction and dwell in the innermost depths of her soul. During this interview she was overcome by an irresistible movement of recollection. The priest went on talking but he soon saw that Elizabeth Catez was no longer listening. " I was longing for him to be silent," she said later to the Prioress.

Sister Elizabeth of the Trinity is completely portrayed in this avowal: eager for silence under the influence of the grace received.

On his part, Father Vallée said of this decisive hour: " I saw her borne away as on a tidal wave."

Elizabeth was one of those souls who, having once seen the divine light, never turn aside. From that day on, everything was transformed and illumined; she had found her way. Henceforth, no matter what happened, the Trinity was to be her whole life.[22]

[22] After her mother had finally consented to her following her religious vocation (March 26, 1899), Elizabeth resumed the visits to Carmel which had been forbidden her for eight years. They were her support during the last two years she spent in the world. Mother Mary of Jesus was again Prioress. She it had been who, on the evening of Elizabeth's First Communion day, had given her a picture with these few lines, explaining the meaning of her name:
"Thy blessed name, O child, a mystery hides,
On this great day fulfilled.
God, Who is Love, within thy heart abides,
His temple here below ' ELIZABETH.' "
Elizabeth, then, means *House of God*.

Mother Mary of Jesus was a Trinitarian soul. Her ardent devotion to this mystery had developed suddenly, when she was but fourteen, as the result of a grace received one day during the Rogation procession. As the young girl responded to the Litany's first invocations to the Father, Son, and Holy Ghost, the mysterious

2.

The Carmelite

1. Elizabeth's Carmelite ideal. 2. Sensible graces of her postulancy. 3. The purifications of the novitiate. 4. Intense interior life.

When Elizabeth Catez was shown into her Carmelite cell she was heard to murmur: " The Trinity is there! "

At her very first community exercise in the refectory, when she had finished her frugal meal, Elizabeth was seen to fold her hands simply beneath her cape, then, her eyes closed, to fall into a profound mood of meditation. The nun who was serving, noticing her, said to herself: " It is too good to last." She was mistaken, the Carmel of Dijon possessed a saint.[23]

but most real presence of the Three Divine Persons in her soul was interiorly revealed to her. "After that," she said later, "I always tried to withdraw into that depth where They dwell." As foundress of the Carmel at Paray-le-Monial, she dedicated her beautiful monastery under the title of the Most Holy Trinity, which we enter by the Heart of Jesus. It was Mother Mary of Jesus who named Elizabeth Catez *Sister Elizabeth of the Trinity*, that name of grace which became the whole program of her religious life. Elizabeth went regularly to see the Mother Prioress, as did the little group of postulants *extra-muros* who frequented the grilles of the Carmel. Mother Mary of Jesus trained her in the Carmelite spirit and Sister Elizabeth, the future novice, gave her an account of her prayer. As she did not have much steady, continuous spiritual direction outside, she was very glad to go and ask of the Prioress the advice and suggestions she needed for her spiritual progress. She would consult her before making her resolutions in time of retreat. All the Mother's decisions seemed to her to come from God Himself and these visits to the Carmelite parlor helped her greatly.

[23] *Note on the Carmel of Dijon.* As is well known, the Venerable Mother Anne of Jesus, companion and fellow-worker with St. Teresa in the Carmelite Reform in Spain, came to France and there established the first monastery at Paris, in the Faubourg Saint-Jacques, on October 8, 1604.

Only one year later, in 1605, Mother Anne of Jesus founded the Carmel at Dijon, which had the honor of receiving the first nuns professed under the Reform in France. The spirit of St. Teresa reigned in the community in all its purity until the day the Carmelites were expelled from their house during the French Revolution. When, in 1854, it was restored by the Very Reverend Mother Mary of the Trinity, the spirit and traditions of the French Carmel returned with her and were faithfully maintained by the two prioresses who succeeded her: Mother Mary of

1. A week after her arrival at Carmel, Sister Elizabeth of the Trinity filled out a questionnaire, at recreation, which shows us her state of mind on the threshold of her religious life. The most characteristic features of her spiritual physiognomy are already clearly indicated there: her ideal of sanctity—to live by love in order to die of love; her ardent devotion to the Will of God; her love of silence; her devotion to the soul of Christ; the watchword of her whole religious life—to bury herself in the very depths of her soul in order to find God there. Nothing is forgotten, not even her dominant fault, oversensitiveness. The only things lacking are that stripping of self which will be the work of the passive purifications of the novitiate and the supreme grace which will transform her life by showing the meaning of her final vocation: to be a praise of glory to the Trinity.

> What is your ideal of sanctity?
> To live by love.
>
> What is the quickest way to reach it?
> To become very little, to give oneself wholly and irrevocably.

---

the Heart of Jesus and Mother Mary of Jesus, the future foundress of the Carmel at Paray-le-Monial.

Mother Germaine of Jesus, who succeeded the latter as Superior, remained Prioress from 1901 until 1906, that is, during the whole religious life of Sister Elizabeth of the Trinity. At regular intervals, over a period of twenty years, the Dijon Carmel had the grace of having her again as Prioress. Mother Germaine of Jesus was a great Carmelite: a prayerful, peaceful soul, very zealous for perfect observance, she was indeed the instrument of Providence who was to provide Sister Elizabeth of the Trinity with that setting of religious life in which her contemplative soul might freely develop in an atmosphere of silence and recollection. The servant of God, well aware of and very grateful for the motherly training given her, could in all truth write in a private note found after her death (and bearing on the envelope these significant words: Secrets for our Reverend Mother), "*I bear your mark.*" The new Prioress, in her first conference in chapter, in the presence of all the community, including Sister Elizabeth of the Trinity, thus outlined the spiritual program of her government: "To keep as perfectly as possible, in the wholly apostolic spirit of our Holy Mother, this Rule and these Constitutions which she has left us, after herself having observed them with such great perfection."

Such was the setting of perfect religious life in which Sister Elizabeth of the Trinity was able to realize her Carmelite ideal so quickly.

Who is your favorite saint?
The Beloved Disciple, who rested on the heart of his Master.

What point of the Rule do you like best?
Silence.

What is the dominant trait in your character?
Sensitiveness.

What is your favorite virtue?
Purity. "Blessed are the clean of heart, for they shall see God."

What fault of character do you most dislike?
Egoism in general.

Give a definition of prayer.
The union of her who is not, with Him Who Is.

What is your favorite book?
The Soul of Christ. In it I learn all the secrets of the Father Who is in heaven.

Have you a great longing for heaven?
I sometimes feel homesick for heaven but, except for the vision, I possess it in the depths of my soul.

In what disposition would you wish to die?
I would like to die in an act of love, and thus fall into the arms of Him Whom I love.

What form of martyrdom would you prefer?
I love all forms, but especially the martyrdom of love.

What name would you like to have in heaven?
"The Will of God."

What is your motto?
"God in me and I in Him."

In accordance with her special grace, it was in the very depths that she lived her Carmelite ideal. She went straight to the essentials: solitude, the life of continual prayer, the consummation in love.

"A Carmelite is *one who has beheld the Crucified*, who has seen Him offering Himself to His Father as a victim for souls and, meditating in the light of this great vision of Christ's charity, has understood the passion of love that filled His soul and has willed to give herself as He did. On the mountain of Carmel, in silence, in solitude, in a prayer that never ceases because it continues through all else, the Carmelite lives as though already in heaven, by God alone. The selfsame God Who will one day be the cause of her beatitude and will fully satisfy her in glory, is already giving Himself to her. He never leaves her; He dwells within her soul; more than that, *the two become but one.* And so *she hungers for silence* in order to be always listening, to penetrate ever more deeply into His infinite Being. She is identified with Him Whom she loves. She finds Him everywhere; she sees Him shining through everything." [24]

" There is the whole Carmelite life: to live in Him. Then all the sacrifices, all the immolations become divine. The soul sees Him Whom she loves through everything, and everything takes her to Him. It is a continual heart to heart union. Prayer is the essence of the life at Carmel." [25]

Her favorite point of the Rule was silence and, from the very first, she was delighted with the familiar motto of the early Carmelites: *Alone with the great Alone.*

2. As often happens, the first stage of the religious life of Sister Elizabeth of the Trinity was marked by a flood of sensible consolations. God leads souls to the heights slowly, taking them to Calvary by way of Thabor. Sister Elizabeth often went to her Prioress, declaring: " I cannot bear this weight of grace."

At that time, she would scarcely reach the choir and kneel down before being irresistibly enveloped in deep recollection. Her soul seemed to be immovably fixed in God. She passed through the cloister silent and absorbed, and nothing could distract her from her Christ. One day a nun saw her so seized upon by the divine presence while she was sweeping that the sister did not dare even speak to her. Outside of recreation hours, when Sister Elizabeth was joyous and charmingly spontaneous in manner, chatting with each of her sisters about what she knew would please her, her whole outward bearing showed a soul possessed by God. This recollection of her powers as though lost in God even caused some involuntary forgetfulness during the Divine Office of which she sincerely and humbly accused herself. She was visibly upheld by grace.

[24] Letter to G. de G., August 7, 1902.   [25] To the same, Sept. 14, 1902.

So passed the months of her postulancy. Her clothing took place on the 8th of December and Father Vallée came to preach the sermon. Completely given up to the joy of her total surrender to her Master, Sister Elizabeth that day lost consciousness of what was taking place around her, being wholly absorbed in that Christ Who had taken possession of her. In the evening, back once more in her little cell, alone with Him, her soul exulted. A song of thanksgiving rose to God from her heart. For a whole life of love she was at last alone with Him Who is Alone!

3. Thus far divine grace had been showered upon her. She had yet, through weary days, to experience her nothingness, to feel that she was a poor creature and capable of any failing and thus to become more understanding of her sisters' weaknesses.

For a long year God was to leave her to herself: to her helplessness, her weariness, her hesitation over her own future, even as to her vocation. On the very eve of her profession a priest would have to come and reassure her and declare what was God's will for her bewildered soul.

Facility in prayer disappeared. No more flying: she had to feel her soul dragging itself along. Her artist's nature lay dormant; her sensitiveness was dying. Many, many times did the young novice go to her Mistress and faithfully report her helplessness, her struggles, her temptations, the martyrdom suffered by her sensitive nature in passing through the terrible nights described by St. John of the Cross. To help in the accomplishment of the divine work, Mother Germaine of Jesus guided her kindly and firmly. At the time of Sister Elizabeth's entry into Carmel, she had realized how excessively sensitive she was. In the evening during the Great Silence, the young postulant loved to walk on the terrace; the sight of the sky helped to raise her soul to God. One evening Mother Germaine happened to pass by. It was the time of the Great Silence, so she said nothing, but the next day the young postulant heard these words addressed to her: " We do not come to Carmel to dream in the starlight! Go to God by faith."

Later on, in order to test her, Mother Germaine never lost an opportunity to reprimand her for the least shortcoming, the slightest oversight. Sister Elizabeth of the Trinity would then humbly kiss the ground and go on her way.

Mother Germaine of Jesus purposely disciplined an over-affectionate disposition which might easily have become dangerous. The brave child let her do so, for, from experience, she understood better than anyone else how necessary it was for her to watch over her heart at every instant. As a young girl, she had become extremely fond of a friend whom she met almost daily at Carmel and had had long, intimate conversations with her. She loved to write to her and to read and re-read her letters, especially the passages in which her friend declared that she loved her more than anyone else. This recalling of her girlhood's past in retrospect throws special light upon her religious psychology.

"Dear little sister, yes, let us be *only one*; let us never be separated. On Saturdays, if you are willing, we will receive Holy Communion for each other. This will be our contract and so shall we always be one. Henceforth, when God looks at Marguerite, He will see Elizabeth too. When He gives something to one, He will be giving to the other too, for there will be but one victim, but one soul in two bodies. Perhaps I am too sentimental, dear sister, *but I was so happy when you told me I was that sister whom you loved best. I love to re-read those lines.* You well know that you are indeed my little sister, beloved beyond all others; need I tell you so? When you were ill I felt that nothing, not even death, could separate us. Oh! sister dear, I do not know which of us two the good God will call first; our union will not cease then, but, on the contrary, will be perfected. How good it will be to talk to the Beloved of the sister one has left behind!

"Who knows? Perhaps He will ask our blood of both of us! Then what happiness to go to martyrdom together! I cannot think about it, it is too good. . . . Meantime, let us give Him our heart's blood, drop by drop." [26]

---

[26] Letter to M. G., 1901.

There is a certain sentimental emotionalism in these lines and, from the oral testimony of this same friend, we cannot but recognize that Elizabeth was excessively affectionate. Could anyone be astonished at weaknesses like these in the saints? Even St. Margaret Mary was momentarily held back by a too human affection for one of her sisters, for which the Sacred Heart reproached her. St. Thomas, who was both a great doctor and a great saint, teaches that no one on earth can completely divest himself of faults of weakness; not even the most perfect escape them.

A fine book—and a most consoling one for us!—could be written on the failings of the saints and the manner in which they corrected them, with God's grace aiding their own efforts.

As soon as Elizabeth Catez perceived that her heart was not free, she heroically detached herself, but gently and with exquisite tact. " Dearest Marguerite: I can safely confide something to you, though I do not want to hurt you. You see, in the chapel with you this morning I realized that being there together was even better than our nice talks; so, if you are willing, we shall spend with Him, side by side, the time we used to spend in the garden. Am I hurting you? Dear little sister, have you not felt as I do? It seems to me that you have. Tell me, quite simply. You know that you can say anything to your Elizabeth." [27]

After this generous act of detachment, this intimate friend told us, " I felt her move away."

Something similar, but very much deeper, took place during the phase of passive purification which Sister Elizabeth of the Trinity underwent during her novitiate. All her senses had to attain this complete detachment which alone can set the soul free.

No one around her, except her Prioress, ever suspected this stage of purgative suffering. At that time, everything which it would seem should have consoled her either left her indifferent or irritated her. Even a retreat preached by Father Vallée

[27] *Ibid.*

whose teaching, beautiful and profound as always, she truly appreciated, could not rescue her from this interior anguish. The priest himself no longer understood her and, over and over, sadly asked: " What have you done to my Elizabeth? You have changed her." The work he did not understand was God's doing and men could avail nothing.

From that hard year of trials, Sister Elizabeth gained a more robust faith and an experience of suffering that would enable her to understand and comfort other souls who were being tested by God. The essential result of this period of purgation was to render her more virile and to establish her definitely in a spiritual life based entirely on pure faith, which would henceforth go forward peacefully, under the eye of God, secure from any recurring assaults of oversensitiveness.

Physical health returned with the establishment of spiritual balance and the conventual Chapter admitted her to profession. She was informed of this fact on Christmas Day. As on all the most important occasions of her life Sister Elizabeth took refuge in the all-powerful prayer of Christ in the Mass. This time, however, she most particularly sought His help, begging for a whole novena of Masses from the venerable priest friend who had been the first person to whom she had confided her aspirations when, as a little girl, she had climbed upon his knee. Then Sister Elizabeth disappeared in retreat beneath her lowered veil. She passed like a shadow through the community halls, her face always veiled, and her Sisters enveloped her with their prayers. But soon the retreat, begun in such joyous anticipation of her profession, became so painful as even to raise doubts as to her future and her vocation. It was necessary to send for a religious of wide experience who reassured her. Sister Elizabeth believed the priest's word as the voice of God. It is customary in Carmel to prepare for profession by keeping a sacred vigil the night before. Sister Elizabeth was in choir, wholly united with her Lord, beseeching Him to take her life for His glory, when the Master visited her. " During the night preceding the great day, while I was in choir awaiting the Bridegroom, *I understood that my heaven was beginning on earth: the heaven of faith, with suffering and immolation for Him I love.*" [28]

A new stage of her spiritual life was beginning. No longer would there be sufferings from a sensitive nature not yet purified, or scruples and anxieties over mere nothings. Henceforth she would tread the road to her Calvary with the peaceful and unshakable confidence of a bride who knows she is loved: she would go forward amid the most heroic sufferings with the majesty of a queen.

4. Her profession once made, Sister Elizabeth of the Trinity set herself to the pursuit of religious perfection, without the least sentimental emotionalism but with a new enthusiasm and a calm, heroic strength which would lead her from sacrifice to sacrifice, up to the consummation of Calvary.

The whole program of her inner life was to realize her name, Sister *Elizabeth*, that is, the House of God, in which the Trinity dwells.

It is true that this seeking of the presence of God in all circumstances is the very essence of the Carmelite life and is in the established tradition of the Order. St. Teresa constantly recurs to it in her *Interior Castle.* " Intimacy with the Three Divine Persons " constitutes the central truth of her mystical doctrine.

By a special grace, Sister Elizabeth of the Trinity found the most characteristic inclination of her interior life in that doctrine. Her letters, her conversations in the parlor, her poems, her retreat resolutions, all converge on this indwelling which was, if we may trust her own testimony, " the beautiful sun lighting her life." [29] " The day I understood that, everything became clear to me." " My only practice is to enter into myself and lose myself in Those Who are there." [30]

As the years of her religious life passed, her soul buried itself more and more in this tranquil and peace-giving Trinity, Which at every moment imparted to her something of Its eternal life.

---

[28] Letter to Canon A., July 15, 1903.
[29] Letter to Madame de B., 1906.
[30] Letter to G. de G., end of September 1903.

At times, indeed, there were still some slight disturbances in her interior life, but more and more everything hushed to silence. " It is the greatest happiness to live in close union with God, to make one's life a heart to heart intimacy with Him, an exchange of love, to know that the Master is to be found in the depths of the soul. One is never alone then, but must have solitude in order to enjoy the presence of this adored Guest. . . . Everything is lighted up and it is so good to live." [31] " You ask me what I do in Carmel. I might answer that a Carmelite has only one thing to do: to love and pray." [32] " A Carmelite's life is a communing with God from morning till night and from night till morning. If He did not fill our cells and our cloisters, how empty they would be! But we see Him through all for we bear Him within us and our life is an anticipated Heaven." [33]

The tranquil rhythm of this spiritual life is simple, constantly coming back to certain unchanging, essential movements: to be silent and to believe in Love, Who is there, dwelling in the depths of the soul in order to save it. Many " nights " and weaknesses remain, it is true, but what do the involuntary waverings of a soul that lives in the presence of the Immutable matter? Gradually everything grows quiet and becomes divine.

And so the life of Sister Elizabeth of the Trinity flowed on. In that fervent Carmel, where so many other great souls were living by God and for His glory, it must not be imagined that she was an extraordinary figure, to be pointed out as " the Saint." It is the normal thing in monasteries to canonize religious only after they have been taken from the community! At Dijon, Sister Elizabeth of the Trinity was merely the ever faithful novice [34] who, like so many others and as a true Carmelite, was wholly " hid with Christ in God." [35]

[31] Letter to F. de S., April 28, 1903.
[32] Letter to Madame A., June 29, 1903.
[33] Letter to F. de S., 1904.
[34] Among the Carmelites, as in some other Orders, the young professed religious spend three years in the novitiate after they have made their vows. (Sister Elizabeth did not live to enter upon her full community life as a professed nun. Tr.)
[35] *Col.* III, 3.

3.

Toward Transforming Union

When, on November 21, 1904, under an impulse of grace and in a single spontaneous outburst, Sister Elizabeth of the Trinity had composed her sublime prayer to the Trinity, it still remained for her to climb the last summits of love.

It is not by chance that in the second sentence of the prayer, immediately after the first movement of adoration of the Trinity, Sister Elizabeth falls back upon herself: "Help me to become wholly forgetful of self." In three years of religious life, one object had remained stubbornly insurmountable: her own self. She had not yet attained that supreme deliverance of selfless souls whose only occupation is to love. That was to be the work of the last two years. At first, during eighteen months of secret fidelity, it was slow and laborious; then, with almost terrifying swiftness, beginning with that Palm Sunday evening when God descended upon her " as a prey," coming Himself to accomplish His work of destruction and consummation in her body and soul. Then was the transforming union wrought in her, not on Thabor but, according to her wish, in the image of the Crucified and in " being made conformable to His death."

This most sublime phase of her life remains for us to analyze.

For several months, Sister Elizabeth of the Trinity had suffered from such exhaustion that without the help of God she would have collapsed. Before she was removed from the office of portress, she had sometimes to make a real effort to ascend the first step of the stairs to answer a call: she was worn out. " In the morning, by the time we had said the Little Hours," she acknowledged subsequently to her Prioress, " I already felt at the end of my strength, and used to wonder how I could go on until evening. After Compline my *cowardice* was at its height, so that I was sometimes tempted to envy a nun who was excused from Matins. I spent the time of the Great Silence in real agony, which I used to unite with that of our Divine Master, keeping by His side close to the choir grille. It was an hour of pure suffering, but it gained me the strength for Matins. I found then a certain facility in applying myself to God. Afterwards my weakness returned and, without being noticed, I regained our cell as best I could, often leaning against the wall." [36]

At the beginning of Lent in 1906, after the mid-day recreation, Sister Elizabeth, according to her custom, opened her beloved St. Paul at random and came upon this text: " That I may know Him . . . and the fellowship of His sufferings, being made conformable to His death." [37]

This last expression struck her: *being made conformable to His death.* Did it not announce her forthcoming deliverance?

In the middle of Lent, the symptoms of a serious stomach disorder became obvious and, after the feast of St. Joseph, Sister Elizabeth of the Trinity was installed in the infirmary. " I was sure that St. Joseph would come for me this year," she said, quite delighted, " and here he is already."

A veritable crusade of prayers was begun, but in vain; the disease progressed steadily. Sister Elizabeth rejoiced. Disregarding all consideration of secondary causes, she called this mysterious illness, love's sickness. " It is God Who is working upon me and consuming me. I surrender myself completely, rejoicing in advance at everything He will do." On Palm Sunday, her condition was suddenly aggravated by a syncope and a priest was summoned that night. With her eyes shining and her folded hands clasping to her heart her beautiful profession crucifix, she repeated rapturously: " Oh, Love, Love, Love! "

" I have seen many sick persons," declared the priest who gave her the last Sacraments, " but I never saw a sight like this."

On Good Friday they thought she was dying, but the crisis passed and, on Holy Saturday morning, the infirmarians were astonished to find Sister Elizabeth kneeling on her bed.

The return to life was almost a disappointment to her. " On Palm Sunday evening I had a very serious attack and I thought that at last the time had come for me to take my flight to the

---

[36] *Souvenirs*, p. 175. [37] *Phil.* III, 10.

infinite realms, to behold unveiled that Trinity which had already been my dwelling place here below. In the peace and silence of the night I received Extreme Unction and my Master's visit. It seemed to me that He was waiting for that moment to break my bonds. What ineffable days I spent awaiting the great vision!" [38]

"To you, who have always been my confidant, I know that I can tell everything. The prospect of going to see Him I love, in His ineffable beauty, and of plunging myself into that Trinity which had already been my heaven here below filled my soul with immense joy. I cannot tell you how it hurt to come back to earth! It seemed so ugly when I came out of my beautiful dream. Only in God is all pure, beautiful and holy." [39]

This violent shock had driven her nearer to the invisible world. Accustomed as she was to live above secondary causes, Sister Elizabeth understood the providential meaning of her illness from the very first. She saw the divine hand in it, the "exceeding love" which now more than ever was pursuing her. She immediately adjusted herself to the divine plan. "If God has given me back a little life," she told herself, "it can only be for His glory." God willed to set her firmly on that last peak of Mount Carmel where, according to the celebrated sketch of St. John of the Cross, "there is no longer anything but the divine honor and glory."

Some months before her illness, during a "license day" in the summer of 1905, while talking with one of her Sisters, she had found in St. Paul the name which definitively expressed her particular grace: LAUDEM GLORIAE.[40] Thenceforth, all the efforts of her interior life were directed to that end. The task might have been long-drawn-out, but God hastened it. It often happens that God allows souls to advance in divine ways at their own pace and then suddenly intervenes and takes upon

[38] Letter to G. de G., May 1906.   [39] Letter to Canon A., May 1906.
[40] All readers of the biography (*Souvenirs*) of Sister Elizabeth will remember that the name which became so precious to her is always left in her imperfect Latin. The passage is from the *Epistle to the Ephesians* I, 11-12: "being predestinated . . . that we may be unto the praise of His glory." (Translator.)

Himself the direction of their lives down to the smallest details. Finally, under the impulse of an irresistible grace, He sweeps them unto Himself. He makes use of secondary causes: a great trial that shatters a life or an illness that seems to lead to death. In reality, it is the divine hour of Calvary wherein all things are consummated. Thus it was for Sister Elizabeth of the Trinity: the attack that struck her down on Palm Sunday evening and Good Friday was the signal for the supreme deliverance, the definitive entrance into the state of transforming union.

From that time on, Sister Elizabeth of the Trinity was completely detached from everything of earth, and lived here with a soul that dwelt in eternity.

The nuns who knew her most intimately declared that it was a revelation to them of what it meant to be a saint: " We felt her leaving us." " We could no longer follow her; she was already a being of the world beyond." They watched her go forward on the way of suffering " with a queenly dignity," to quote the expression of a witness who did not know that Sister Elizabeth had used the very same words.

It was clear enough what was happening. As her physical frame was gradually being destroyed, her soul, more and more blessed, soared aloft and forgot itself. Day and night she was obsessed by a single thought: to be the " praise of glory of the Trinity." She had only one desire now: to spend her life completely in the service of souls, and she dreamed of " dying transformed into Jesus crucified." " I am growing weaker daily and I feel that the Master will not delay much longer in coming for me. I am experiencing unknown joys: the joys of suffering. . . . It is my dream, before I die, to be transformed into Jesus crucified." [41]

Although this soul was essentially *Trinitarian*, her last months may be said to have been haunted by the thought of the Crucified, so true is it that, as St. Teresa remarks, the remembrance of the Sacred Humanity of Christ must never be effaced, not

[41] Letter to G. de G., late October 1906.

even in the highest mystical states. He Who as God is the term, as Man remains the Way: Calvary is the only way to the Trinity.

The constant yearning for the glory of the Trinity which is the very keynote of the whole interior life of Elizabeth's soul is, accordingly, closely mingled with the thought of Jesus crucified: "'*Configuratus morti ejus.*' That is what still haunts me, that gives strength to my soul in its sufferings. If you knew the sensation of destruction I feel in my whole being! The road to Calvary is opening before me and I am utterly joyful to walk it, as a bride beside my crucified Lord.

"On the 18th, I shall be twenty-six. I do not know whether this year will end for me in time or in eternity. I ask of you, as a child of its father, to be so good as to consecrate me in Holy Mass as a sacrifice of praise to the glory of God. Consecrate me so completely that I may no longer be *I* but *He*; so that the Father, looking upon me, may recognize Him; that I may be 'made conformable to His death,' and fill up in my flesh what is wanting to His Passion for the Church which is His Body; and then bathe me in the Blood of Christ that I may be strong with His strength." [42]

Thus Sister Elizabeth's spiritual life became increasingly reduced to the essential: transformation into Christ by love; an almost constant filial intimacy with Our Lady; the realization of her baptismal grace in its special relation to the Trinity. Borne away into the soul of Jesus crucified, the activity of her interior life soon became extremely simple: the glory of the Trinity. That is all.

Sister Elizabeth had reached that higher unity of the soul of those saints who have attained to the fulness of Christ. Everything else either entered into this unity or disappeared. The "palace of beatitude or of suffering" is all one for her. Longing for suffering does not exclude longing for heaven, which she feels more and more as she reads over those last chapters of the Apocalypse on the heavenly Jerusalem which are ever beside

[42] Letter to Canon A., July 1906.

her. She had never seemed at once so human and so divine. Her tender affection for her sisters in religion was especially evident.

"Never did the Heart of Christ so overflow as at the moment when He was about to leave His own. Nor have I, little sister, ever felt so keenly the need to protect you with my prayers. When my pain becomes sharpest, I feel so urged to offer it for you that I cannot do otherwise. Have you some particular need of it? Are you suffering? I give you all my sufferings; they are wholly at your disposal. If you knew how happy I am at the thought that my Master is coming for me! Death is indeed beautiful for those whom God has safeguarded, and who have not sought the things which are seen, because they pass away, but rather the things which are not seen and which are eternal.

"In heaven I shall be your ' angel '[43] more than ever. I know how much my little sister needs shielding in a city like Paris where her life is spent. St. Paul says that God chose us in Him before the foundation of the world, that we should be holy and unspotted in His sight. How fervently I shall ask Him that this great purpose of His will may be fulfilled in you! That it may be so, listen to the advice of the same Apostle: ' Walk in Christ; rooted and built up in Him.' When I am contemplating the Absolute Beauty, in all Its brightness, I shall ask Him to imprint It in your soul, so that even here on earth, where everything is soiled, you may be beautiful with His beauty, luminous with His light. Good-bye. Thank Him for me, for my happiness is immense. I shall meet you again in ' the heritage of the saints.' It is there that in the choir of Virgins, that generation pure as light, we shall sing the beautiful song of the Lamb and the eternal *Sanctus* in the radiant light of the Face of God. Then, says St. Paul, ' We shall be transformed into the same image, from glory unto glory.' I embrace you with all my heart's love and am your ' angel ' for all eternity."[44]

[43] To this correspondent, who had been a postulant at the Dijon Carmel, Elizabeth had been "angel," that is, the novice especially appointed to teach her the observance and help her in the early days.

[44] Letter to C. B., late Summer 1906.

The night of August 2, 1906, the anniversary of her entrance into Carmel, being unable to sleep, she settled herself near the window and remained there in prayer with her Master until almost midnight. She spent a sublime evening. " The sky was so blue, so still; the monastery was so deeply silent. . . . And as for me, I went over these five years, so filled with graces." [45]

Feeling that the end was near, Sister Elizabeth asked her Prioress to allow her to go into retreat the evening of August 15, that she might prepare for her passage to eternal life. In a note slipped into the hand of one of her Sisters, she says that she is going away with *Janua caeli* for these days of prayer and recollection. " This evening, *Laudem gloriae* is entering the novitiate of heaven, to prepare to receive the habit of glory, and feels urged to beg Sister A to think of her. ' For whom He foreknew,' St. Paul tells us, ' He also predestinated to be made conformable to the image of His Son.' That is what I am going to teach myself: conformity, identity with my adored Master Who was crucified for love! Then I shall be able to fulfill my office of Praise of Glory and even here below to sing the eternal *Sanctus*, while waiting to go and chant it in the heavenly courts of the Father's house." [46]

It was during these evenings and nights of silence with God, when she felt her Master leading her to her Calvary, that, at the request of her Mother Prioress, she composed *the last retreat of LAUDEM GLORIAE*, in order to explain how she conceived her office of " Praise of Glory."

Until the last week of her life, she used to drag herself to the evening Office and, all huddled up in a corner of the tribune, she would extract the last measure of strength from her exhausted body. As far as her extreme weakness permitted, she remained faithful to the end to the smallest observances of her Order. Frequently, during interminable sleepless nights, she endured a very martyrdom of body and soul. In a strong spirit of faith she then sought refuge with her Prioress, whom she called her " priest," appointed by God to consummate her sacrifice.

[45] Letter to her mother, August 3, 1906.
[46] Note to one of her Sisters in religion.

" 11 p. m. From the palace of suffering and beatitude. Mother dear, my dear Priest. Your little 'Praise of Glory' cannot sleep; she is suffering; but in her soul, though the anguish reaches there, all is so calm. It was your visit that brought her this heavenly peace. Help me to climb my Calvary; I feel so strongly the power of your priesthood over my soul, and I need you so much.

" Mother, I feel my *Three* so near to me. I am more overwhelmed with happiness than with suffering. My Master has reminded me that pain is my dwelling-place and that I must not choose my sufferiugs. So I am plunging myself with Him into the immensity of suffering with all its fear and anguish." (October 1906)

" My dearest Priest. Your little victim is suffering very, very much; it is a sort of physical agony. She feels cowardly, so cowardly that she could cry out. But He, the Being Who is the fulness of love, visits her, keeps her company, associates her with Himself, while He makes her understand that as long as He leaves her on earth He will give her suffering as her portion." (October 1906)

No matter how sharp the pain, no one ever caught her giving way in the slightest degree. Her lovely smile never left her lips. During those last weeks of real martyrdom, the gift of fortitude was made radiantly plain in her. One day she was asked whether she were suffering much; she made a gesture as though something were tearing her inside and her face was convulsed. Then she immediately resumed her tranquil serenity.

It was in this state of exhaustion that, on October 15, Father Vallée saw her for the last time. He was struck at the work of destruction which God was accomplishing in this soul and which was making it " so strangely, so divinely beautiful." He exhorted her to make a supreme effort to raise herself to the love which exceeds suffering. Much comforted by this last visit from the Father, she scaled the half-seen heights: those higher states of transforming union on Calvary, which have no resemblance to anything that takes place on earth.

On October 29, thanks to a slight respite, she was able to

go down to the parlor to see her family. They had brought her nieces, " those two lovely white lilies," and their mother made them kneel down by the grille. Raising her profession Crucifix, Sister Elizabeth blessed them.

When the moment came to say good-bye, she had the strength to whisper to her mother: " Mother, when the Out-Sister comes to let you know that I have finished with suffering, you will kneel down and say: ' Lord, Thou didst give her to me; Thou hast taken her away. Blessed be Thy Holy Name.' " [47]

By the following day, October 30, Sister Elizabeth of the Trinity could no longer leave the infirmary. In the evening she was shaken in her bed by a violent fit of shivering. During the night heaven again seemed almost ready to open to her. There was no time to delay; the grace of the last Sacraments was renewed very early the next morning. The Church was singing the First Vespers of All Saints. No longer able to write, Elizabeth dictated a last message: " I think the great day of my meeting with my adored Bridegroom, my one love, has come. I hope by this evening to be among that great multitude whom St. John saw before the throne of the Lamb, who serve Him day and night in His temple. Let us meet in that beautiful chapter of the Apocalypse and also in the last chapter, which sweeps the soul beyond this earth, into the vision wherein I am going to lose myself forever." [48]

At midnight, all the bells of the town rang out. " Oh! Mother," she cried, " those bells encourage me; they are ringing for the departure of *Laudem Gloriae*. They will make me die for joy, those bells! Let us go! " And she stretched her arms to heaven.

On All Saints' Day, about ten o'clock in the morning, the last hour seemed to have come. The community assembled in the

[47] When Mme. Catez, informed by the Out-Sister, came to the parlor where the body of her dead daughter was laid out, a cry of sorrow broke from her. Then a friend who was with her said: " Remember what Elizabeth told you." The brave mother remembered and, falling upon her knees, murmured: " My God, Thou didst give her to me; Thou hast taken her. Blessed be Thy Holy Name."

[48] Letter to Madame H., Oct. 31, 1906.

infirmary to recite the prayers for the dying. Sister Elizabeth roused herself, made sure that all her Sisters were present, and asked forgiveness of the community. Then, begged to speak, she uttered these words: " All passes away. . . . In the evening of life only love remains. . . . We must do everything for love. . . . We must constantly forget ourselves. . . . The Good God so loves us to be forgetful of ourselves. Oh, if I had always been so! "

Then began nine days of distressing agony. Stretched upon her bed as upon an altar, her eyes closed, all life concentrated in the depths of her soul, the saintly victim prayed constantly. When they tried to console her at being no longer able to receive the Blessed Sacrament, she said: " I am finding Him on the Cross; it is there that He is giving me life."

Violent headaches caused fears of cerebral congestion; the danger was averted by continual applications of ice, which melted immediately. Her brain seemed on fire. Her words, which were distinguished with difficulty, gave evidence of a divine union already accomplished. Her face, wasted and unrecognizable, at times took on a startling resemblance to the suffering features of the Holy Face, recalling Our Lord on the Cross. Three weeks previously, she had said to her Prioress: " If my master offered me the choice of dying in an ecstasy or in the abandonment of Calvary, I would choose the latter in order to be like Him." Her Master had granted her desire to the full. Within as without it was the crushing agony of Calvary. After a violent attack she was heard to cry: " Oh, Love, Love, Love, consume my whole substance for Thy glory; may it be spent drop by drop for Thy Church! "

Two days before her death, the doctor admitted to her that her pulse was extremely weak. She was delighted and found the strength to say: " In two days I shall be in the bosom of my ' Three.' Our Lady, who is all bright, will herself take me by the hand and lead me to heaven." The doctor, an unbeliever, was astonished at such joy. Sister Elizabeth spoke to him of the divine adoption, of the great mystery of Love leaning down to us. . . . These last efforts left her completely exhausted, but they could still hear her murmur in a sort of chant: " I am going to Light, to Love, to Life." Those were her last intelligible words.

On Friday, November 9th, at a quarter to six in the morning, she turned on her right side and put her head back. Her face shone; her beautiful eyes, which for a week had been closed and almost sightless, opened and fixed themselves with a wonderful expression a little above her Prioress, who was kneeling beside her bed. She lay in angelic beauty. Around her, her Sisters, who were reciting the prayers for the dying, could not take their eyes from her. Then, without having perceived her last sigh, they saw that Sister Elizabeth was no more.

It was the morning of the feast of the Dedication of the Lateran Basilica, one of her favorite festivals. While in choir, where lay her mortal remains, the Sisters were singing the praises of the House of God—*Beata pacis visio*—Sister Elizabeth, already in the unchanging vision of peace and the glories of the heavenly Jerusalem, the thought of which had dominated her last days, was mingling with the throng of the Blessed who, holding palms in their hands, rest not day or night saying: " Holy, holy, holy, Lord God Almighty, Who was, and Who is, and Who is to come." With them, falling down, adoring and casting down her crown, the reward of her martyrdom of love, she ceased not to repeat before the throne of the Lamb: *Dignus es, Domine*—Thou art worthy, O Lord, " to receive power, and divinity, and wisdom, and strength, and honor."[49]

Before the face of the Most Holy Trinity, Sister Elizabeth had become the PRAISE OF GLORY for all eternity.

---

[49] *Apoc.* V, 12.

Chapter II

THE ASCESIS OF SILENCE

> *"What is your favorite point of the Rule?"* . . . *"Silence."*

1. The saint of silence. 2. Exterior silence. 3. Interior silence. 4. Divine silence.

Two fundamental elements constitute the essence of all sanctity: self-abnegation and union with God. They appear in the lives of all the saints, but in infinitely various ways.

In the case of the Carmelite, the negative aspect takes the form of a complete separation. Carmel is the desert; God alone is there. Yet among Carmelites each one lives in her own manner the doctrine so dear to St. John of the Cross, the Mystical Doctor of Carmel: the doctrine, namely, that the creature is *nothing* and that God is *all*. One star differs from another not only by its size, but by its special light, its peculiar brilliance; God is multiform in His saints. It would be useless to try to force even two saints of the same religious family into an identical mould, for unalterable differences are concealed beneath certain common features. It is the task of a theologian who sets out to search the depths of a soul to know how to discern these differences. To distinguish is to see better.

There have been frequent attempts to compare or contrast St. Teresa of the Child Jesus and Sister Elizabeth of the Trinity. Their ways are essentially different. The Carmelite of Lisieux radiantly covers the whole Catholic world with rose petals scattered for love. She has taught the modern world how it can once more become " a child with the Good God." The Carmelite of Dijon fulfills her mission in interior souls. Sister Elizabeth of the Trinity was the saint of silence and recollection.

1. In her poems, when but fifteen, Elizabeth Catez expressed her dream of solitude with her Lord:

" To live alone with Thee." [1]

Later, when she was nineteen, she wrote in her diary: " Soon I shall be all Thine; I shall dwell in solitude, alone with Thee, concerned only with Thee, living only with Thee, talking only with Thee." [2] And when in the country during the summer, she loved to slip away to lonely woods.[3] From the day she entered religion she was enchanted with the Carmelite solitude. *Alone with the Alone!* There we have the whole life of Carmel.

The Carmelite is essentially a contemplative hermit, whose native land is the desert of Carith and whose refuge is the cleft in the rock. Not that she forgets souls in peril—St. Teresa was led to found her Reform by the sight of the ruin wrought by Luther's heresy—but the witness she is called to bear to God is that of a solitary whose gaze remains fixed on Him alone, eager to forget all else; a silent but most moving attestation that the divine Beauty alone is worthy of the attention of a soul raised by grace to share in the life of the Trinity. God alone suffices.

Her apostolic action is that of prayer, which obtains everything. One single soul raised to the state of transforming union is more useful to the Church and to the world than a multitude of others engaged in constant activity. Sister Elizabeth of the Trinity was the type of silent contemplative whose overflowing apostolic action extends to the entire universe.

From the very first, she was seen to enter completely into this spirit of silence and death which is the condition of all divine life in Carmel. She had a special devotion to the prophet Elias, who was the first to lead the eremetical life and whom God had commanded to flee from the dwellings of men and to hide himself, far from the multitude, in the desert: *Get thee hence . . . and hide thyself by the torrent of Carith.*[4] He it was who taught the hermits of the holy mountain of Carmel to detach

---

[1] *Poems*, August 1896.
[2] *Diary*, March 27, 1899.
[3] Letter to Madame A., September 29, 1902.
[4] *III Kings* XVII, 3.

themselves from all that is not God, to live alone in the presence of the living God, forgetting all others.

To lead the life of a hermit, like the holy solitary Elias; to live in little cells, like the monks of Mount Carmel in the caves by the Prophet's spring: such was the dearest wish of St. Teresa's heart. " The kind of life which we aspire to lead," she writes in the Thirteenth Chapter of the *Way of Perfection,* " is not only that of religious; more than that, it is the life of hermits." " Let us call to mind our holy Fathers, those hermits of other days, whose life we seek to copy. What sufferings did they not have to bear, and in what loneliness! "

Following the example of the courageous Reformer, her first daughters buried themselves in the desert of Carmel. " Their solitude was their delight," St. Teresa tells us. " They assured me they were never tired of being alone. A visit, even from their brothers and sisters, was a torment to them. She held herself happiest who had most time to spend alone in a hermitage."

SILENCE and SOLITUDE: there you have the purest spirit of Carmel.

" You may have foundations in deserts . . . each one shall have a separate cell . . . each one shall remain in his cell or near it, meditating day and night on the Law of the Lord, and watching in prayer." (The Holy Rule)

" Whenever the Nuns are not engaged at Community acts nor in the offices of the house, each Sister shall remain in her cell or in the hermitage assigned to her by the Prioress . . . and in this way she will observe what the Rule ordains, that each one shall live in solitude . . .

" There shall be ground enough to build some hermitages, that the Religious, after the example of the Holy Fathers, may retire to them for prayer . . .

" That occasion for breaking silence by being together may be avoided, there shall never be a common workroom . . ." (Constitutions)

Sister Elizabeth of the Trinity possessed in an exceptional degree this attraction for silence, which flees all created things in order to remain in faith in the presence of the living God. Her whole ascesis may be reduced to silence, in the widest sense of the word. In her eyes, silence constitutes the most fundamental requirement for the soul that desires to be raised to the divine union.

While we do not wish to confine her thoughts within too rigid limits, for that would be incompatible with the free inspirations to which under the guidance of the Holy Ghost Sister Elizabeth of the Trinity surrendered herself, we may yet distinguish three kinds of silence in her line of thought: exterior and interior silence and, finally, a wholly divine silence, in which the soul is completely passive and which is one of the highest effects of the gifts of the Holy Ghost. For want of a better name and drawing on an expression of her own, we may call it " sacred silence," or " God's silence." It is analogous to the *Divinum Silentium* of the drawing made by St. John of the Cross.[5]

2. Exterior silence is not the most necessary; in certain circumstances it is even impossible. Then the soul's resource is to take refuge within itself, in that interior solitude which alone is necessary for union with God. But outward silence must be sought as much as possible, because it helps interior silence and normally leads to it; the love of silence leads to the silence of love.

Sister Elizabeth loved the enclosure. Useless visits to the parlor were a torment to her. On several occasions she gently but firmly reminded her relatives of this point of the Rule. She faithfully abstained from correspondence during Advent and Lent, unless obedience made it a duty to write. When we take account of all the circumstances, it is only by what seems an obviously providential permission that she was able to leave so many letters behind her, notwithstanding her longing to remain in silence behind the grilles of her Carmel.

The same silence governed her contacts with her Sisters within the monastery. She accepted " silence challenges " more

---

[5] Cf. *The Complete Works of St. John of the Cross*, Vol. I, Frontispiece. London: Burns Oates & Washbourne, 1934.

than once and the very few failures in keeping silence of which she accused herself were always from motives of charity. She was faithful to this spirit of silence to the very last day of her life. " Once," relates a nun, " I had obtained permission to take something to her in the infirmary and stay with her until the end of recreation. Sister Elizabeth received me joyfully. The bell rang; gently and with a sweet smile, she resumed her silence. I felt that I must not prolong the conversation. There was nothing stiff about her, but fidelity to the Rule came before all else."

She was always coming back to silence. The young Sisters knew so well that it was her special program that, on the eve of novenas or retreats, they would whisper mischievously: " Silence! You will spend it in silence, won't you? " And she would smile and nod.

During her illness, as the Prioress insisted that she should go out in the fresh air, Sister Elizabeth chose the most solitary spot in the garden. " Instead of working in our little cell, I have settled myself like a hermit in the loneliest spot in our large garden, and spend delightful hours there. All nature seems to me so full of God; the wind sighing in the tall trees, the little birds singing, the lovely blue sky—all these things speak to me of Him." [6]

Above all, she loved the silence of her cell, which she called her " little paradise " and in which she delighted to take refuge. " A straw bed, a little chair, a wooden table; there you have the furniture. But it is full of God and I spend such happy hours there, alone with the Bridegroom. I keep silence; I listen to Him; it is so good to hear everything from Him . . . and then, I love Him! " [7]

She was especially fond of the time of the Great or Night Silence. She so loved her silent Carmel. " Carmel is a corner of heaven; in silence and solitude we live there alone with God Who is Alone." [8]

Two or three times a year, more or less according to the

[6] Letter to her mother, August 1906.
[7] Letter to Madame A., June 29, 1903. [8] Letter to M-L. M., Oct. 26, 1902.

custom of different houses, the nuns have "license days," that is, days when they may visit one another in their cells, as did formerly the hermits of the desert. Sister Elizabeth lent herself with good grace to this custom, of which St. Teresa approved in order that the Sisters might mutually encourage one another in the love of their Beloved. In fact, it was during one of these days that she received one of the greatest graces of her life: her name, "Praise of Glory." But it is obvious, that given human weakness, these visits, which should cause the spirit to flame with zeal, may degenerate into trivial chatter and be a sheer loss so far as union with God is concerned, which is the only object of a Carmelite's life. Sister Elizabeth joyfully returned to the silence she loved beyond everything else. She once wrote to her sister: "We had a license on election day, that is, we could pay one another little visits during the day. But, you know, *a Carmelite's life is silence*." [9]

3. The Carmelite's true silence is the silence of the soul, in which she finds God.

As a faithful disciple of St. Teresa and St. John of the Cross, Elizabeth strove to impose silence on the powers of her soul and to withdraw herself from all created things. With pitiless zeal she immolated everything: her sight, her thought, her heart. " It is in Carmel as it is in heaven; we must be separated from everything in order to possess Him Who is All." [10]

Even as a girl, this idea of complete separation from creatures had a powerful attraction for her. " Let us empty ourselves; detach ourselves from everything. Let Him be the only one, Him Alone. Let us leave earth, all creatures, everything perceived by the senses." [11]

In the midst of social gatherings and gay parties, her soul fled from the tumult and raised itself to God. " It seems to me that one can never be drawn away from Him when one acts only for Him and is ever in His holy presence, under that divine gaze that penetrates into the innermost recesses of the soul.

[9] Letter to her sister, October 1901.
[10] Letter to her mother, August 1903.   [11] Letter to M. G., 1901.

Even in the world we can listen to Him in the silence of a heart that wills to belong to none but Him." [12]

Sister Elizabeth had a special devotion to St. Catherine of Siena on account of the great Dominican mystic's teaching on the *interior cell*, wherein she had found her constant refuge in the midst of the bustling activity of men and her prodigious apostolic work in behalf of the papal policy.

This interior silence, so precious to Sister Elizabeth, was soon to assume for her the form of a general ascesis and take a foremost place in her mystical life. This is teaching straight from the Gospels: whoever desires to be lifted up to God in prayer must reduce to silence in himself both the empty tumult without and the din within, and retire into the depths of his soul and there in secret, " having shut the door," [13] recollect himself in his Father's presence.

Thus did Christ pray during those silent nights in Palestine, when, at evening, He went forth alone into the mountain, to spend the time until morning " in the prayer of God." [14]

The lives of the anchorites and Desert Fathers in the first centuries of the Church, in their withdrawal from all useless intercourse, clearly show us this purifying function of silence in the primitive conception of Christian ascesis. The desert led to the silence of the soul in which God had His dwelling.

In accordance with her particular grace, Sister Elizabeth of the Trinity understood this Gospel teaching in a completely Carmelite sense: silence of all the powers of the soul, which are kept for God alone. No more tumult in the outward senses, in the imagination and sensitive self, in the memory, the understanding, the will; to see nothing, hear nothing, take pleasure in nothing; to stop at nothing that may distract the heart or retard the soul on its way to God!

First of all, the sense of sight must be watched. Did not the Master say: " If thy eye scandalize thee, pluck it out. . . . If thy eye be single, thy whole body shall be lightsome." [15] Impurity and a host of imperfections are caused by this want of

[12] Letter to Canon A., December 1, 1900.
[13] *Matt.* VI, 6.   [14] *Luke* VI, 12.   [15] *Matt.* VI, 22.

watchfulness over the eyes. David, who could speak from sad experience, besought God: "Turn away my eyes that they may not behold vanity,"[16] that vanity of the earth which had caused his soul to fall. The virgin soul does not allow itself to cast a single look away from Christ.

Silence of the imagination and other faculties of the soul is no less necessary. We carry a whole interior world of sensations and impressions about with us, and it threatens to take possession of us at every moment. There also we must practice the asceticism of silence. A soul which continues to entertain itself with its memories, "which indulges in any desire"[17] apart from God, is not a silent soul as Sister Elizabeth of the Trinity understands the term. It still has "discords"[18] and clamorous sensibilities which prevent the harmonious chorus which should never cease to rise to God from all the powers of the soul.

The understanding, in turn, must hush all human commotion within itself. The "least useless thought"[19] would be a false note which must be silenced at any price. An overly keen intellectualism, which allows too much play to the understanding for its own sake, is a subtle obstacle to the true silence of soul where God is found in pure faith. Like her master, St. John of the Cross, Sister Elizabeth of the Trinity was ruthless in this respect. "We must extinguish every other light,"[20] and attain to God by nakedness of spirit, and not by building a learned structure of beautiful thoughts.

Above all, there must be silence in the will. The whole drama of our sanctification takes place there; the will is the faculty of love. Rightly does St. John of the Cross assign to the will the final purifications that prepare the way for transforming union. *Nothing, nothing, nothing, nothing, nothing,* on the way; and on the Mountain, *nothing*.[21] Sister Elizabeth resolved to follow her spiritual guide to the uttermost point on the "narrow way" that leads to the summit of Carmel. She strongly urges the soul

---

[16] *Ps.* CXVIII, 37.
[17] *Last Retreat*, 2nd day.
[18] *Ibid.*
[19] *Ibid.*
[20] *Ibid.*, 4th day.
[21] Drawing by St. John of the Cross of the *Ascent of Mt. Carmel.*

that would reach divine union to rise above even its most spiritual personal tastes to the complete abnegation of all self-will. " To know nothing "; to make no distinction between feeling and not feeling, enjoying and not enjoying; [22] to be resolute in passing everything by in order that, in complete self-forgetfulness and abnegation, the soul may be united to God alone. Thus far did Sister Elizabeth carry her ideal of silence and absolute solitude, far from all created things. We know that the last hours of her life were the living realization of this ideal.

Consequently, with her we must understand this ascesis of silence in its deepest sense. It is not a material separation from external things, but a solitude of spirit, a detachment from all that is not God. Silent in the face of all happenings, whether within itself or outside, the soul " ceases to distinguish between them, but breaks through them and passes them by to rest in the Master Himself above all else." [23]

This is the night of St. John of the Cross, the dying to all natural activity. " The soul that aspires to dwell with God in the impregnable fortress of holy recollection, must, at least in spirit, be separated, detached and withdrawn from the thought of all else." [24] This is absolute silence in the presence of God alone.

Sister Elizabeth of the Trinity devoted a whole chapter of her last retreat to singing the praises of this blessed state of the soul completely set free by interior silence: "' I will keep my strength to Thee' is another of Christ's songs in which I desire to join incessantly. My Rule tells me: 'In silence shall be your strength.' To keep our strength for the Lord is to keep our whole being in unity by interior silence; to collect all our powers, to occupy them in the one work of love, to have the ' single eye ' which allows the light of God to enlighten us." [25]

This silence embraces everything. " A soul which listens to

[22] Cf. *Last Retreat*, 4th day.
[23] *Heaven on Earth*, 4th prayer.   [24] *Ibid.*, 5th prayer.
[25] *Last Retreat*, 2nd day. (References to the quotations contained in this *Last Retreat* and *Heaven on Earth* will be found in the Appendices, where both are given in full.)

self, which is preoccupied with its sensibilities, which indulges in useless thoughts or desires, scatters its forces. It is not completely under God's sway. Its lyre is not in tune, so that when the Divine Master strikes it, He cannot draw forth celestial harmonies; it is too human and discordant.

"The soul which reserves anything for self in its interior kingdom, whose powers are not all ' enclosed ' in God, cannot be a perfect ' praise of glory '; it is unfit to sing continually the *canticum magnum* of which St. Paul speaks, because it is not in unity. So that, instead of persevering in praise in simplicity whatever may happen, it must be continually tuning the strings of its instrument which are all a little off key." [26]

4. There is another silence, which the soul is unable to produce by its own activity, but which God Himself causes within it, if it remains continually faithful, and which constitutes one of the highest fruits of the Holy Ghost: the *divinum silentium* of the drawing of St. John of the Cross. The spiritual powers are no longer dispersed in a search for things; henceforth the soul knows only God. Unity has been established.

"How necessary is this blessed unity for the soul that craves to live here below the life of the blessed—that is, of simple beings, of spirits! Did not the Divine Master mean to teach this to St. Mary Magdalen when He spoke of the *unum necessarium?* How well that great saint realized it! She had recognized her God by the light of faith under the veil of His humanity and in the silence, and unity of her powers, she ' heard His word,' and could sing: 'My soul is continually in my hands,' and also, the little word: ' *Nescivi!* '

"Yes, she knew nothing but Him. Whatever noise and bustle there was around her: ' Nescivi! ' She might be blamed: ' Nescivi! ' Neither care for honor nor exterior things could draw her from her sacred silence.

"Thus it is with a soul dwelling in the fortress of holy recollection. By the light of faith, it sees its God present, dwelling within it, while, in turn, the soul is so present to Him in its

[26] *Ibid.*

beautiful simplicity that He guards it with jealous care. Then, whatever turmoil there may be outside or whatever tempests within, however its honor may be assailed: 'Nescivi!' God may hide Himself, withdraw His sensible grace: 'Nescivi!' 'For His sake I have suffered the loss of all things,' it exclaims with St. Paul. Henceforth the Master has full liberty—liberty to infuse Himself into the soul, to give Himself 'according to the measure of the giving of Christ,' and the soul, thus simplified and unified, becomes the throne of Him Who changes not, because unity is the throne of the Blessed Trinity." [27]

In a celebrated passage, St. John of the Cross alludes to the silence of the Trinity: "One word spake the Father, which Word was His Son, and this word He speaks ever in eternal silence . . ." [28] Sister Elizabeth found, in this silence of the Trinity, the model of her own: "Let a deep silence reign in the soul, the echo of that Word which is sung in the Trinity." [29]

By the transforming union, the soul enters into this silence of God. Everything in it is stilled; nothing of earth remains, there is no light but the light of the Word, no love but Eternal Love. The soul is clothed in divinity. Its life rises to a plane far above all the restlessness of created things and dominates them; it enters into communion with Immutable Life and becomes, in Sister Elizabeth's own words, "as calm and changeless as though it were already in eternity."

By a special, most secret touch of the Holy Ghost, the life of the soul is borne away into the unchanging and silent Trinity. The soul still lives by faith here below; yet by one of the highest effects of the gift of wisdom, it lives by God, after the manner of God, wholly absorbed in God. Henceforth it hears only the Eternal Utterance: the generation of the Word and the spiration of Love. The whole universe is for it as if it were not. At this stage, face to face with the mystery of God, silence is the soul's great refuge—" a profound and deep silence, that silence of which David spoke when he cried: 'Silence is Thy praise.'

[27] *Ibid.*
[28] *Complete Works of St. John of the Cross*, Vol. III, p. 251.
[29] Note to her sister.

Yes! that is the most perfect praise, for it is sung eternally in the bosom of the tranquil Trinity." [30]

The divine way of life sets the pattern for the virtues of the soul which has reached such heights. Forgetful of self and stripped of everything earthly, Sister Elizabeth of the Trinity was raised to that height in the last days of her life, there to seek her ideal of silence and solitude in the bosom of God. " Be you therefore perfect, as also your heavenly Father is perfect." As she writes: " ' God,' says St. Denis, ' is the great Solitary.' My Master bids me imitate this perfection, to render Him homage by living in strict solitude. The Divinity dwells in eternal and profound solitude. He cares for the needs of His creatures, without in any way leaving it, for He never goes out from Himself, and this solitude is nothing but His Divinity." [31]

" I must guard against being withdrawn from this holy interior silence by keeping myself always in the same state, the same isolation, the same retirement, the same detachment. If my desires, my fears, my joys or my sorrows, if all the impulses coming from these four passions, are not completely ordered to God, I shall not be solitary; there will be turmoil within me. Therefore, calm, the slumber of the powers, the unity of the whole being are needed. 'Hearken, O daughter . . . incline thy ear; forget thy people and thy father's house. And the King shall greatly desire thy beauty.' This injunction is, I feel, a call to silence. 'Hearken . . . incline thy ear.' But in order to listen, we must forget our ' father's house,' that is, whatever pertains to the natural life, of which the Apostle says: ' If you live according to the flesh you will die.' To forget our people is more difficult, for this ' people ' is that world which is, as it were, a part of ourselves. It includes our feelings, memories, impressions, etc. In a word, it is *self*. We must forget it, give it up. Then when the soul has broken with it and is wholly delivered from all it means, ' the King shall greatly desire ' its beauty, for beauty—at least God's beauty—is unity." [32]

" The Creator, seeing the beautiful silence that reigns within

---

[30] *Last Retreat*, 8th day.   [31] *Ibid.*, 10th day.   [32] *Ibid.*

His creature, who is deeply recollected in her interior solitude, greatly desires her beauty. He leads her into that immense and infinite solitude, into that 'large place' of which the Psalmist sings, which is His very Self." [33]

This supreme solitude establishes the soul in the very silence of the Trinity.

In the sublime aspiration with which she ends her prayer, Sister Elizabeth takes her refuge in that solitude, there to lose herself, even here below, in the tranquil and unchangeable Trinity. " O my God, Trinity whom I adore, help me to become wholly forgetful of self, that I may be immovably fixed in Thee, as changeless and calm as though my soul were already in Eternity. May nothing disturb my peace or draw me out of Thee, O my immutable Lord, but may I at every moment penetrate more deeply into the depths of Thy mystery. . . .

" . . . O my 'Three,' my All, my Beatitude, *Infinite Solitude*, Immensity wherein I lose myself, I yield myself to Thee as Thy prey. Bury Thyself in me that I may be buried in Thee until I depart to contemplate in Thy Light the abyss of Thy greatness."

---

[33] *Ibid.*, 11th day.

Chapter III

THE INDWELLING OF THE BLESSED TRINITY

"My only practice is to enter 'within,' and to lose myself in Those Who are there."

1. The saint of the Divine Indwelling. 2. Her doctrine of the Divine Indwelling. 3. The place of this presence: the inmost center of the soul. 4. Its essential acts: the activity of faith, the exercise of love. 5. In pure faith. 6. The primacy of love. 7. Practice of acts of recollection. 8. Short catechism of the presence of God. 9. Progress in the presence of God. 10. The two chief effects of this presence: forgetfulness of self and transforming union. 11. "Oh! if only I could tell every soul . . ."

Silence is only a condition of true life. With the mystery of the abiding presence of the Trinity, we reach the central point of the doctrine and life of Sister Elizabeth of the Trinity, truly the saint of the Divine Indwelling. In that again, she was a Carmelite.

If there is one truth which is dear to the mystical teaching of Carmel, it is this very mystery and this certitude, that God is present in us and that in order to find Him we must enter "within," into this interior kingdom. All spiritual life may be summed up in that. In her *Way of Perfection*, when commenting on the *Pater Noster*, St. Teresa significantly remarks that God is not only in heaven, "but in the inmost center of our soul," and that we must know how to recollect ourselves to seek and find Him there. In the *Interior Castle*, this presence of the Trinity marks the culminating point of her mysticism: souls who have reached transforming union live habitually in the company of the Divine Persons, and find in the fellowship of the Trinity the most blessed joys to be found on earth. St. John of the Cross also makes it the point of convergence of his whole mystical theology, especially in the highest states. Devotion often led him to say the Votive Mass of the Blessed Trinity, and as he was offering the Holy Sacrifice, his soul would be so irresistibly drawn toward this mystery that he had literally to fight against ecstasy. The Carmelite tradition has remained faithful to the teaching of these two great spiritual masters. It is not rare to meet souls in Teresian convents whose silent life is completely orientated toward the mystery of the Trinity. Did not St. Teresa of the Child Jesus offer herself as a victim on the feast of the Trinity? Her offering to Merciful Love is part of an essentially Trinitarian prayer: " O my God! Blessed Trinity, in order to live in an act of perfect love, I offer myself as a victim of holocaust to Thy Merciful Love. . . ." [1] Nevertheless, we must recognize that Sister Elizabeth of the Trinity received a very special grace to live by this mystery. God, Who predestined her to the mission of drawing souls within themselves in order to make them conscious of the divine riches of their Baptism, made of her in very truth the saint of the Indwelling of the Trinity.

1. On the first page of the notebook of her girlhood days, she had copied as a watchword this thought from St. Teresa: " You must seek Me in thyself." [2] About the age of nineteen, she felt " as though Someone dwelt in her." Often Elizabeth repeated to a friend: " It seems to me as though He were there," and she would make a gesture as though holding Him in her arms, and pressing Him to her heart. " When I see my confessor," she said to herself, " I shall ask him what is happening in me."

We have seen how Providence arranged that she should meet Father Vallée, and how the latter, as a contemplative theologian, enlightened her on the Christian dogma of the Divine Indwelling. For Elizabeth Catez, this was a dazzling light which gave the decisive orientation to her life. Reassured as

---

[1] *Autobiography of St. Teresa of the Child Jesus.*
[2] Poem sent by St. Teresa to Monsignor Alvaro de Mendoza.

to the truth of this mystery of faith, from that day forward she buried herself in the depths of her soul with a feeling of complete security, there to seek her " Three." The evidence given with respect to this period leaves no doubt on the subject; even before she entered the cloister, Elizabeth was " possessed " to an exceptional degree by the mystery of the Divine Indwelling. She spoke of it repeatedly to her intimate friends: " The Trinity was everything to her." [3]

From the time of this sudden revelation, which lighted her whole life, she never flagged. Within a few months she almost ceased speaking of it, but she seemed " seized upon " by the Trinity. This expression, used by a witness, well stresses the *passivity* of her soul under the action of the Holy Ghost from the time of the first mystical graces granted in the retreat in 1899.

" Let us lose ourselves in this Holy Trinity, in this God Who is all love and let Him carry us away into those regions where there is no longer anyone but Himself, Himself alone." [4] " ' God in me, I in Him,' let that be our motto. Oh! how good is this presence of God within us, in the inner sanctuary of our souls. There we always find Him even though we may have no sensible feeling of His presence. But He is there, all the same. It is there that I love to seek Him. Let us try never to leave Him alone. Let our lives be a continual prayer. Who can take Him from us? Who can even distract us from Him Who has taken full possession of us, Who has made us all His? " [5]

Sister Elizabeth had already discovered the watchword of her life. A week after her entrance into the convent, she had but to copy it on the questionnaire which she was asked to answer: " What is your motto? " " God in me, I in Him."

In Carmel, this life in the presence of God is considered as a sacred heritage which is traced back to the days of the Patriarch Elias: " As the Lord liveth the God of Israel, in Whose sight I stand." [6] It is the very essence of Carmel. All the sacrifices, the

[3] Evidence of a friend.
[4] Letter to M. G., 1901
[5] *Ibid.*
[6] *III Kings* XVII, 1.

silence, the purifications have but one object: to keep the soul free to apply its powers to this continual presence of God.

Consequently, on this point, Sister Elizabeth found in Carmel a whole spiritual doctrine which had become familiar to her in the setting of her previous life. As to her interior life, her entrance marked the beginning of its complete development. Hitherto, Elizabeth had shown herself to be a very innocent, very devout girl, to whom, in recompense for her heroic fidelity, God had granted some mystical *touches*, but she still stood in need of instruction and of spiritual training. The meeting with Father Vallée had securely settled her soul in the half-perceived light; assiduous reading of St. John of the Cross supplied her with the doctrine; the surroundings of religious life did the rest.

She herself carefully marked the passages of her new spiritual master in which he treats of the nature and effects of this mysterious but very real and substantial presence of the Holy Trinity in the soul. By a unique grace, Sister Elizabeth of the Trinity was able to find in this presence of the Three Divine Persons in the depths of her soul her "heaven on earth," the secret of her heroic sanctity.

From the very first, she was enchanted with her Trinitarian name: "Have I ever told you my name at Carmel—Mary Elizabeth of the Trinity? It seems to me that this name indicates a particular vocation. Isn't it beautiful? I so love this mystery of the Most Holy Trinity! It is an abyss in which I lose myself."[7] "I am Elizabeth of the Trinity, that is to say, Elizabeth disappearing, losing herself, letting herself be completely possessed by the 'Three.'"[8]

That was the watchword of her life as a Carmelite: "My only devotional practice is to enter 'within,' and lose myself in Those Who are there. I feel God so alive in my soul that I have only to recollect myself in order to find Him within me. That is the secret of all my happiness."[9]

"Let us live with God as with a Friend. Let us make our faith a living thing, so as to remain in communion with Him

[7] Letter to Canon A., June 14, 1901.
[8] Letter to G. de G., Aug. 20, 1903. [9] Letter to Canon A., July 15, 1903.

through everything. That is how saints are made. We carry our heaven within us, since He Who completely satisfies every longing of the glorified souls, in the light of the Beatific Vision, is giving Himself to us in faith and mystery. It is the same thing. IT SEEMS TO ME THAT I HAVE FOUND MY HEAVEN ON EARTH, SINCE HEAVEN IS GOD AND GOD IS IN MY SOUL. THE DAY I UNDERSTOOD THAT, EVERYTHING BECAME CLEAR TO ME AND I WISH I COULD WHISPER THIS SECRET TO THOSE I LOVE in order that they also might cling closely to God through everything, and that Christ's prayer might be fulfilled: 'Father . . . that they may be made perfect in one.' " [10]

By a phenomenon of appropriation, familiar to souls that are dominated by one idea, she refers everything to that. Liturgical feasts which seem to have no connection with the mystery of the Trinity hidden in her soul are brought back to it by a transposition that is quite natural to her. Christmas provides us with a characteristic example: " Christmas in Carmel is something unique. In the evening, I settled myself in choir, and there I spent my whole vigil with our Lady, waiting for the Divine Babe Who, this time, was to be born no longer in a stable, but *in my soul*, in our souls, for He is Emmanuel, ' God with us.' " [11]

Her poetic inspiration finds its fundamental theme in this Indwelling of the Divine in the depths of the soul:

O BEATA TRINITAS! [12]

May His Grace, as a stream in flood, overflow thee,
As a river of peace fill thy soul;
Beneath its calm billows may it hide thee secure
That nought from without may touch thee.

In this abyss, this calm, this mystery,
Thou wilt be visited by the Divinity;
It is there, in silence, that I keep thy feast, Mother,
While with thee I adore the Blessed Trinity.
—*Laudem Gloriae.* June 1906.

---

[10] Letter to Madame de S., 1902.
[11] Letter to her aunts R., December 30, 1903.
[12] To a Sister in the Carmel of Dijon.

On the occasion of the Lay Sisters' feast, she writes: " On the feast of St. Martha, we kept the feast of our good Sisters of the white veil. In honor of their holy Patroness, they have a holiday from their duties, so that they may spend their time with Magdalen in the sweet rest of contemplation. The novices take their place and do the cooking. I am still in the Novitiate, for we remain there for three years after profession, so I spent a good day at the kitchen range. While holding the handle of the frying pan, I did not go into ecstasy like my Mother, St. Teresa, but I *believed in the Divine Presence of the Master*, Who was in the midst of us, and at the very center of my soul adored Him Whom Magdalen had been able to recognize beneath the veil of humanity." [13]

Her correspondence is full of advice concerning the presence of God: " May your soul be His sanctuary, a resting place for Him on this earth where He is so grievously offended." [14] " May He make of your soul a little heaven, where He may happily rest. Take away from it everything that might offend His divine eye. Live alone with Him. Wherever you are, whatever you may be doing, He never leaves you. Therefore, stay always with Him. Enter into the depths of your soul; you will always find Him there, longing to do you good. I say a prayer for you that St. Paul used to say for his converts: he asked that Christ might dwell in their hearts by faith, that they might be rooted in charity.[15] This expression is so deep, so mysterious. Yes, may God Who is all love be your unchanging dwelling place, your cell and your cloister in the midst of the world. Remember that He abides in the inmost center of your soul, as in a sanctuary and He wills to be loved there even to adoration." [16]

Adapted to persons and circumstances, the same fundamental thought recurs again and again: the true life is in the depths of the soul with God. There it is that Sister Elizabeth found those who were dear to her; it is also the secret of the happiness which made her life an anticipated heaven.

[13] Letter to her aunts R., Summer 1905.
[14] Letter to Madame de B., August 17, 1905.
[15] Cf. *Eph*. III, 17.   [16] Letter to Madame de B., Summer 1905.

Sister Elizabeth of the Trinity was truly a soul of one idea. When at Prime on Sunday, the Church put upon her lips the Athanasian Creed, like her Mother, St. Teresa, she was carried away by this mystery of mysteries, in which her soul dwelt always. She consecrated every Sunday to the Holy Trinity, and when Trinity Sunday came round, she was overwhelmed by an irresistible grace. For several days the earth simply did not exist for her. " This feast of the ' Three ' is truly my feast. For me, there is no other like it; never have I so well understood the mystery, and all the meaning of the vocation expressed by my name. I give you tryst in this great mystery in order that it may be our center . . . our home. I leave you with this thought from Father Vallée, to be the subject of your prayer: ' May the Holy Spirit bear you away to the Word, and the Word lead you to the Father, that you may be perfect in the One, as are Christ and our Saints.' " [17]

Thus the years and the graces of the religious life daily buried her more deeply in her soul with Him Whose touch at each moment imparted to it eternal life. The smallest events served to reveal how completely this soul was possessed by the Trinity.

She is informed of the arrival of a little niece, and immediately her soul rises to the Trinity: " We gave a real ovation to little Sabeth. This morning at recreation, our good Mother was pleased to show us her photograph, and you may guess how fast Aunt Elizabeth's heart beat. Oh! my Guite, I think I love her, the little angel, almost as much as her little mother does, and that is saying a lot! And then, you see, I feel so penetrated with respect before this temple of the Most Holy Trinity. To me, her soul seems like a crystal that radiates the good God. If I were near her, I should go down on my knees to adore Him Who dwells within her. Please kiss her for her Carmelite aunt, then take my soul with your own to recollect yourself beside your little Sabeth. If I were still with you, how I should love to pet her, to sing her to sleep—what should I not do for her? But the good God has called me to the mountain that I may be her

[17] Letter to her sister, June 1902.

angel and wrap her in my prayers. All the rest, I joyously sacrifice for her sake." [18]

In her visits to the parlor and in her letters, as in all contacts with her mother, her sister, her friends, and indeed, all who came near her, she unobtrusively but persistently carried on her apostolate of this Divine Presence within the soul. " Think of the fact that you are in Him, that He makes Himself your abode here below. And then that He is in you, that you possess Him in the very depths of your being, that at every hour of the day and night, in every joy or sorrow, you may find Him there, quite near, within you. That is the secret of happiness, the secret of the saints. They knew so well that they were the temples of God; that when we unite ourselves to this God, we become ' *one spirit with Him*,' [19] as St. Paul says. Illumined by that light they faced everything." [20]

And so, we might quote all her writings. To anyone who looks closely, it is evident that more and more the mystery of the Trinity became the predominating truth of her life, while all else faded and disappeared.

On the 21st of November, the feast of the Presentation, the whole community renewed their religious profession. While Sister Elizabeth of the Trinity was pronouncing the formula of her vows with her companions, she felt an irresistible movement of grace raise her up to the Holy Trinity. When she returned to her cell, she took up her pen, and on a common sheet of paper from a notebook, without hesitation and without a single correction, in one stroke, she wrote her celebrated prayer, that burst like a cry from her heart: [21]

" O my God, Trinity Whom I adore! Help me to become utterly forgetful of self, that I may bury myself in Thee, as changeless and as calm as though my soul were already in eternity. May nothing disturb my peace or draw me out of Thee, O my immutable Lord! but may I at every moment penetrate more deeply into the depths of Thy mystery!

---

[18] Letter to her sister, March 1904.
[19] *1 Cor.* VI, 17.   [20] Letter to M-L. M., Aug. 24, 1903.
[21] This prayer was found among Elizabeth's papers without any title.

" Give peace to my soul; make it Thy heaven, Thy cherished dwelling place, Thy home of rest. Let me never leave Thee there alone, but keep me there, all absorbed in Thee, in living faith, adoring Thee and wholly yielded up to Thy creative action!

" O my Christ, Whom I love, crucified by love, fain would I be the bride of Thy Heart; fain would I cover Thee with glory and love Thee . . . until I die of very love! Yet I realize my weakness and beseech Thee to clothe me with Thyself, to identify my soul with all the movements of Thine Own. Immerse me in Thyself; possess me wholly; substitute Thyself for me, that my life may be but a radiance of Thine own. Enter my soul as Adorer, as Restorer, as Savior!

" O Eternal Word, Utterance of my God! I long to pass my life in listening to Thee, to become docile, that I may learn all from Thee. Through all darkness, all privations, all helplessness, I crave to keep Thee ever with me and to dwell beneath Thy lustrous beams. O my beloved Star! so hold me that I cannot wander from Thy light!

" O Consuming Fire! Spirit of Love! descend within me and reproduce in me, as it were, an incarnation of the Word; that I may be to Him another humanity wherein He renews His Mystery!

"And Thou, O Father, bend down toward thy poor little creature and overshadow her, beholding in her none other than Thy Beloved Son in Whom Thou hast set all Thy pleasure.

" O my 'Three,' my All, my Beatitude, Infinite Solitude, Immensity wherein I lose myself! I yield myself to Thee as Thy prey. Bury Thyself in me that I may be buried in Thee, until I depart to contemplate in Thy Light the abyss of Thy greatness! "

November 21, 1904.

In order to compose such a prayer, one of the most beautiful in Christian literature, a whole life of sanctity was required, together with a special charisma causing it to well up from her heart.

Devout souls live on it for months and years without ever growing weary, and while they murmur it in silence, Sister Elizabeth, faithful to her mission, draws them to recollection, helps them to go out from themselves by a simple, loving movement, and carries them peacefully into the Trinity.

After 1904, the year in which she composed the prayer to the Trinity, when God came to visit her through suffering, it was still in this Divine Presence that Sister Elizabeth found strength for her smiling heroism. At the very last hour of her life, she turned with redoubled tenderness to her friends and relatives to leave them as a legacy, her cherished devotion to the "Three." . . . "I leave you my faith in the abiding presence in our souls of the God Who is all love. I commit it to you. It is this intimate contact with Him ' within ' which has been the beautiful sun shining through my life, making of it an anticipated heaven. It is what supports me today in my suffering. I am not afraid of my weakness, for within me is the Strong One, and His Power is Almighty. As the Apostle says: ' It works above all that we can hope.' " [22]

In still more moving words, she leaves the same heritage to her sister: " Little sister, I am glad to go up above to be your angel; how jealous I shall be for the beauty of your soul, already so loved on earth! I leave you my devotion to the ' Three.' Live within with Them in the heaven of your soul. The Father will overshadow you and place a cloud between you and the things of earth, in order to keep you all His. He will impart His Power to you, that you may love Him with a love stronger than death. The Word will imprint upon your soul, as in a crystal, the image of His own beauty, so that you may be pure with His purity, lightsome with His light. The Holy Ghost will transform you into His mystic lyre which, in silence, beneath His divine touch will give forth a glorious hymn to Love. Then you will be the ' praise of His glory,' which it has been my dream to be on earth. You will take my place. I shall be *Laudem Gloriae* before the throne of the Lamb, and you will be *Laudem Gloriae* in the center of your soul." [23]

[22] Letter to Madame G. de B., 1906.   [23] Letter to her sister, 1906.

For Sister Elizabeth of the Trinity, the abiding presence of God in the depths of her soul was the secret of her rapidly attained sanctity. We may trust her own testimony written only a few hours before her death: " Above, in the home of love, I shall be actively thinking of you. I shall ask—and it will be the sign that I have entered heaven—that you may have a special grace of union, of intimate communion with the Master. I confide to you the secret which has made my life an anticipated heaven: THE BELIEF THAT A BEING WHOSE NAME IS LOVE IS DWELLING WITHIN US AT EVERY MOMENT OF THE DAY AND NIGHT, AND THAT HE ASKS US TO LIVE IN HIS COMPANY." [24]

2. It would be vain to ask of Sister Elizabeth of the Trinity a strictly systematized doctrine, with all the material arranged in order. As a contemplative, she lived the highest mysteries of the Faith and, in particular, the dogma of the Divine Indwelling, without in any way trying to do the work of a doctor or a theologian, without even suspecting that God had reserved a universal significance for her writings.

In her private notes she recurs to passages from St. John of the Cross which had particularly struck her, especially those from the *Spiritual Canticle*, in which the holy Doctor treats of the nature and effects of the mysterious Divine Presence. There we find the classic doctrine of Catholic theology in a lofty, contemplative light: God is substantially present in all beings by His contact with them as their Creator; to this presence, which is common to all, is added a special presence in the souls of the just and in the blessed, as the object of their knowledge and love in the supernatural order.

Sister Elizabeth had meditated upon these texts at length and had drawn from St. John of the Cross the elements of a mystical teaching on this Divine Presence in the souls of the just which constitutes one of the most traditional and most consoling truths of Christianity.

In the thought of the Church, its origin has always been recognized as found in the plain teaching of Jesus: " If anyone

[24] Letter to Madame G. de B., 1906.

love Me, he will keep My word, and My Father will love him, and We will come to him and make our abode with him." [25] The text is clear. The Son and the Father dwell together within the faithful soul as does the Holy Spirit Who makes but One with Them. The whole mystery of the generation of the Word and the spiration of Love is silently wrought in the most intimate depths of the soul; our spiritual life becomes an unceasing union with the Life of the Trinity within us. Divinized by the grace of adoption, the soul is raised to the Divine Friendship, and introduced into the family of the Trinity, there to live as the Father, the Word, and Love, and with Them, by the same light and by the same love, " made perfect in One." [26]

In His high-priestly prayer, our Lord has left us the description of this deiform life of perfect souls admitted to the *consortium* of the life of the Trinity: " Holy Father, keep them in Thy name whom Thou hast given Me: that they may be one, as We also are. . . . That they all may be one, as Thou, Father in Me and I in Thee; that they also may be one in Us. . . . That they may be one as We also are One: I in them and Thou in Me, that they may be made perfect in one. . . . That the love wherewith Thou hast loved Me may be in them and I in them." [27]

After the Master has spoken so explicitly, what more do we need? There is no unity of nature between the Holy Trinity and us—that would be pantheism—but unity of grace by which, as adopted children, we are associated with the very life of our Father Who is in heaven, with the image of His Son and in the same Spirit of Love.

Without the Trinity, the soul is deserted. It is inhabited when, possessing within it the Divine Persons, it enters by faith and charity into intimate " fellowship " [28] with the Father, the Son, and the Holy Ghost. The Three Divine Persons are substantially present in the soul of a baptized infant who has become, in St. Paul's words, " the temple of the Holy Ghost." [29] Our whole spiritual life, from Baptism to the Beatific Vision,

---

[25] *John* XIV, 23.
[26] *John* XVII, 23.
[27] *John* XVII, 11-26.
[28] *I John* I, 3.
[29] *I Cor.* VI, 19.

develops as a rapidly increasing progressive ascension toward the Trinity. The Beatific Vision and, *a fortiori*, all the intermediate mystical states, even the highest, are in germ in Baptism. We do not consider sufficiently the primordial importance of this baptismal grace to which we owe our entrance, as adopted children, into the family of the Trinity.

This magnificent theology of the Divine Indwelling underlies the spiritual teaching and the mystical life of Sister Elizabeth. It enables us to follow her into the deepest recesses of her soul. There was no need of long dissertations on how the mystery is possible for her to understand it. Through infused wisdom and in all simplicity, but with rare depth of thought, Sister Elizabeth had penetrated into the meaning of her baptismal vocation and understood that, even on earth, she was called to live, according to the expression of St. John which was so dear to her, in the " fellowship " [30] of the Trinity.

As a sort of legacy she even composed a whole retreat for her sister to explain to her how to "find her heaven on earth." Together with the retreat of *Laudem Gloriae*, these pages, written in the last weeks of her life and sent to her sister after her death, may be said to constitute a little summa of her spiritual doctrine at its most completely developed stage.

In the very first prayer of this retreat, Sister Elizabeth considers our supernatural destiny in the high contemplative light of the prayer of Christ the Priest, according to the Master's own words in which He calls souls to grace to be " made perfect in one," [31] in the unity of the Trinity.

" ' Father, I will that where I am, they also whom Thou hast given Me may be with Me; that they may see My glory which Thou hast given Me, because Thou hast loved Me before the creation of the world.' Such was Christ's last desire, His supreme prayer before returning to the Father. He wills that where He is, we too may be, not only through all eternity but even in time, which is eternity begun and ever in progress. Where, then, are we to be with Him that His divine ideal may

[30] *I John* I, 3.   [31] *John* XVII, 23.

be realized? The hiding-place of the Son of God is in the bosom of the Father or the Divine Essence, transcending all mortal vision, and hidden from all human understanding, as Isaias said: 'Verily Thou art a hidden God.' Yet it is His will that we should abide permanently in Him, that we should dwell where He dwells in the unity of love and that we should be, so to speak, the shadow of Himself. By Baptism, says St. Paul, 'we are buried in Christ,' and again: 'God hath made us sit together in the heavenly places, through Jesus Christ: that He might show in the ages to come the abundant riches of His grace.' He adds: 'Now, therefore, you are no more strangers and foreigners, but you are fellow citizens with the saints and domestics of God.' The Blessed Trinity, then, is our dwelling place, our Father's house which we ought never leave." [32]

3. The place of this meeting of the soul with its God is within itself, in the very depths of its being. The mystics call this place the seat of God's most secret operations, which He alone enters and where He alone can act: the *mens*, or the summit of the soul. Sister Elizabeth of the Trinity preferred to keep to the terminology of St. Teresa and St. John of the Cross, and to term it "the center of the soul," its deepest center.

"This heaven, our Father's house, is in the center of our soul. When we are deep within ourselves, we are in God." [33] We need not go outside ourselves to find Him; the kingdom of God is "within you." [34] St. John of the Cross says that it is in the substance of the soul, which is inaccessible to the devil and the world, that God gives Himself to it. Then all the movements of the soul become divine and though of God still are the soul's, because our Lord effects them in it and with it. The same saint also states that God is the center of the soul. When the soul loves, comprehends, and enjoys Him with all its strength, it has attained to its deepest and ultimate center in God. When, however, the soul has not attained to this state, though it be in God, Who is the center of it, still it is not in its deepest center, because there is still room for it to advance.

[32] *Heaven on earth*, 1st prayer.
[33] Letter to her sister, August 1905.   [34] *Luke* XVII, 21.

Love unites the soul to God and the greater its love, the deeper does it enter God and the more is it centered in Him. Thus, a soul which has but one degree of love is already in God Who is its center, but when its love has attained the highest degree, it will have penetrated to its inmost depth or center, and will be transformed until it becomes most like God. Such a soul, recollected in itself, may be addressed with the words of Father Lacordaire to St. Mary Magdalen, 'Ask no more after the Master of anyone on earth or in heaven, for He is your soul and your soul is He.' "[35]

4. This mysterious and real Divine Presence remains inaccessible to the senses. God is a Spirit, and they that approach Him must do so " in spirit and in truth." [36]

Sister Elizabeth is particularly careful to insist upon this, to emphasize the fact that the feelings have no place here. The stumbling-block of beginners in the spiritual life is the desire to feel God, and even souls advanced in perfection find it difficult at times to rid themselves of this desire, which continues to exist under the most subtle pretexts. Personal experience had taught Sister Elizabeth of the Trinity to distrust feelings, and the remembrance of the hard purifications of her novitiate kept her soul alert to seek only the " peace of God which surpasseth all understanding." [37]

After the first sensible, even intoxicating, joys of the Divine Presence concerning the actuality of which Father Vallée had reassured her, Elizabeth Catez was very soon obliged to cling to pure faith in order to find God present within her. " It is no longer a veil but a thick wall which hides Him from me. I find it hard after having felt Him so near, but I am ready to remain in this state as long as it pleases my Beloved to leave me in it, for faith tells me that He is there all the same. Of what use are consolations and sensible sweetness? All that is not God; and it is God alone we seek. So let us go to Him in pure faith." [38]

---

[35] *Heaven on earth*, 3rd prayer.
[36] *John* IV, 24.
[37] *Phil.* IV, 7.
[38] Letter to M. G., 1901.

5. In order to advance safely on this " magnificent way of the Presence of God," [39] faith is the essential act, the only one that gives us access to Him Who is the living but the hidden God." '*He that cometh to God must believe that He is.*' It is St. Paul who speaks thus. He also says: 'Faith is the substance of things to be hoped for, the evidence of things that appear not.' That is to say, faith makes future blessings so certain and present to us that they are evolved in our soul and subsist there before we actually enjoy them. St. John of the Cross says that faith serves as feet to take us to God, and is possession itself in an obscure manner. Faith alone can enlighten us concerning Him Whom we love, and should be chosen by our soul as the means by which to attain divine union. It fills us with spiritual gifts.

" Christ, when speaking to the Samaritan woman, alluded to faith when He promised to give those who should believe in Him ' a fountain of water springing up into life everlasting.' Faith gives us God even in this life; behind the veil, yet still God Himself. ' When that which is perfect is come,'—that is, the clear vision—' that which is imperfect '—or the knowledge given by faith—' shall be done away.'

"' We have known and have believed the charity which God hath to us.' This is our great act of faith, the means of rendering love for love to our God. It is ' the mystery, which hath been hidden ' in the heart of the Father, of which St. Paul speaks, which at last we fathom, and which thrills our soul. When it has become able to believe in this ' exceeding love ' overshadowing it, we may say of it as was said of Moses that it ' endured, as seeing Him that is invisible.' The soul no longer stops at tastes or feelings. Thenceforth it cares little whether it feels God or not, whether He sends it joy or suffering; it believes in His Love. The more it is tried, the stronger is its faith, for it overleaps, as it were, all obstacles and finds its rest in the bosom of Infinite Love, which can do naught but works of love.

[39] *Last Retreat*, 9th day.

"So to this soul, vivified by faith, the Master can whisper in secret the words He once spoke to Mary Magdalen: 'Go in peace, thy faith hath saved thee.' "[40]

To the end, Sister Elizabeth remained faithful in going to God by pure faith: "A Carmelite is a soul of faith."[41] Even after the exceptional grace of the last feast of the Ascension that she spent on earth, by which the Three Divine Persons had been made irresistibly manifest to her as present in the center of her soul holding "Their Almighty Council" day and night,[42]—even after that, Sister Elizabeth of the Trinity, a recluse in the solitude of the infirmary, would still have to seek her Master by faith. It is the absolute condition of all divine life on earth.

"I am the good God's little recluse, and when I return to my dear cell to continue the intercourse we have begun, a divine joy takes possession of me. I greatly love solitude alone with Him, and I lead a little hermit life which is really delightful. It is far from being exempt from weaknesses; I also need to seek my Master, Who hides Himself well. But then I rouse up my faith, and I am happier not to taste the joy of His presence in order to give Him the joy of my love."[43]

Her religious life was the realization of the words she heard in choir the night before her profession: "Heaven in faith, with suffering and immolation for Him Whom I love."[44]

6. It is even more necessary to practice charity than faith. These two great theological virtues are the two wings by which we ascend to God; it is not enough to believe, we must love ... above all, we must love! Like all saints, Sister Elizabeth of the Trinity emphasized this primacy of love upon which the Master Himself so insisted, reducing the Law, the Prophets, and all the Commandments of God to this first principle: "Hear, O Israel . . . thou shalt love the Lord thy God with thy whole heart and with thy whole soul, and with thy whole strength."[45]

---

[40] *Heaven on earth*, 8th prayer.
[41] Letter to Madame de S., 1906.
[42] Thus she expressed to her Prioress the grace granted her on Ascension Thursday, 1906.
[43] Letter to her sister, July 15, 1906.
[44] Letter to Canon A., July 1903.
[45] *Mark* XII, 29-30; *Deut.* VI, 4.

We are here at the peak of Christian doctrine, and it is fitting to pause. There is no more moving spectacle than the faithfulness with which the Apostles, the Fathers of the Church, and the saints recur to this saying of the Master, which the Church repeats again and again, in different words, to succeeding centuries.

Leaning on the breast of his Lord, St. John sounded the depths of this divine precept which, in his eyes, summed up all Christ's teaching. Even as an old man, he had it constantly on his lips, and when those around him sometimes seemed astonished, he gave them a reply worthy of the Beloved Disciple: "It is the Master's precept, and it is enough." [46] St. Paul taught the same doctrine when he wrote: "Walk in love." [47] "Love is the fulfilling of the law." [48] St. Augustine's celebrated saying is well known: "*Ama et fac quod vis*"—"Love and do what you will." [49] After him, St. Bernard repeats that "the measure of loving God is to love Him without measure." [50] St. Dominic, patriarch of a great intellectual family, acknowledged: "I have studied in the book of charity more than in any other." [51] And St. Thomas briefly declares: "Love is the life of the soul." [52]

Need we go on? All the literature of the saints is but a paraphrase of the commandment of love. St. Teresa remarked with regard to souls who have reached the summit of perfection: "Their whole occupation consists in loving." [53] St. John of the Cross, the Doctor of Love far more than the Doctor of the Nights, wrote: "In the evening of life, we shall be judged on

---

[46] St. Jerome, *Epis. ad Gal.* III, ch. 6, *P. L.* XXVI, col. 433.
[47] *Eph.* V, 2.
[48] *Rom.* XIII, 10.
[49] The usual form, which is a good translation of the text: "Dilige, et quod vis fac" in St. Augustine's *Joan.* VII, 8.
[50] *De diligendo Deo.*
[51] *Vitae Fratrum*, lib. II, ch. 25.
[52] *Summa Theologica*, II-II, q. 23, a. 2 ad 2.
[53] Cf. also St. John of the Cross, *Spiritual Canticle*, Stanza XXVIII, where we have the same teaching as in the *Interior Castle*, cc. VI and VII.

love."[54] Echoing, after twenty centuries, the great *Diliges*[55]—thou shalt live by love—of her Master, St. Teresa of the Child Jesus left the modern world her beautiful poem: "To Live by Love." The fact is that we here reach the quintessence of Christianity. At the beginning of his masterly *Treatise on the Love of God*, St. Francis de Sales declared: "Everything in Holy Church is with love, in love, for love and by love."[56]

The reason for this is very simple. Charity establishes us in a state of friendship with God. All the riches of the Trinity become ours by grace and glory; we truly enter into the "fellowship" with the Father, the Son, and the Holy Ghost; we are enabled to rejoice[57] in the Divine Persons. This spiritual intercourse between God and the soul develops according to the purest laws of friendship. God gives Himself and brings us His own beatitude; man in return loves God as a friend, loves Him infinitely more than himself, and has his happiness in that of his God.

Sister Elizabeth of the Trinity had made her own the teaching of her Master. She loved to recur to St. John's words: "We have believed the charity which God hath to us."[58] We may even say without fear of exaggeration that she had established her whole spiritual life in the light of "the exceeding charity,"[59] of which St. Paul speaks. "I feel so much love upon my soul; it is like an ocean into which I plunge and lose myself. It is my vision on earth, while I await the vision face to face in the Light. He is in me and I am in Him. I have only to love Him, to let myself be loved, at all times, in all circumstances. To awake in love, to move in love, to sleep in love, my soul in His Soul, my heart in His Heart, that I may be purified and delivered from my miseries by contact with Him. . . ."[60]

"Night and day in the heaven of her soul, she would sing of

[54] Maxims of St. John of the Cross, IV, Charity.
[55] Cf. *Matt.* XXII, 37.
[56] Preface to the Treatise.
[57] Cf. *Summa Theologica*, I, q. 43, a. 3 ad 1.
[58] *I John* IV, 16.
[59] *Eph.* II, 4.
[60] Letter to Canon A., August 1903.

the love of her Lord." [61] "I no longer desire anything but to love Him; *to love Him all the time*, and, like a true spouse, to be zealous for His honor; to make Him happy, by making Him a home and a shelter in my soul, that there in my love, He may forget all the abominations of the wicked."[62]

"The Son of God loved me and delivered Himself for me.[63] There we have love's terms: to give itself . . . to flow entirely into the one loved. Love causes the lover to go out of himself, to be carried in ineffable ecstasy into the bosom of the beloved. Is this not a beautiful thought? May it be as a luminous motto for our souls; may they let themselves be borne away by the Spirit of Love and, in the light of faith, go even now to sing with the blessed the hymn of love which is sung eternally before the throne of the Lamb. Yes, let us begin our heaven in love. God Himself is this love. St. John tells us so: 'God is charity.'[64] Let us abide in His Love and may His Love abide in us." [65]

Like St. Teresa of the Child Jesus, and perhaps under her influence,[66] she found her vocation in love. "I want to be a saint in order to make Him happy; ask Him to let me live only by love; it is my vocation."[67] "I believe—and St. John of the Cross expressly says so—that it is love which shortens our stay here on earth. There is a wonderful chapter in which he describes the death of souls who are victims of love: there are the last assaults of love, then all the rivers of the soul which are already so immense as to stem like seas, lose themselves in the ocean of Divine Love. St. Paul says that Our Lord is a '*consuming fire.*'[68] If by a simple, loving gaze of faith we remain ever united to Him and if, like our beloved Master, we can say, when each evening comes, because I love my Father, 'I do always the things that please Him;[69] He will be able to consume

---

[61] To the same, June 1906.
[62] Letter to Madame A., Feb. 15, 1903.
[63] *Gal.* II, 20.
[64] *I John* IV, 8.
[65] Letter to Madame A., Feb. 15, 1904.
[66] She had made notes on *The Autobiography* of the Saint.
[67] Letter to G. de G., Aug. 20, 1903.
[68] *Heb.* XII, 29.   [69] *John* VIII, 29.

us, and we shall be lost in the immense *fire*, to burn there at our ease for all eternity." [70]

At the moment when all is dying in her, this primacy of love shines out more brilliantly than ever. She receives the priest who comes to administer Extreme Unction with the cry: " Oh Love . . . Love . . . Love . . . Love." [71]

Before taking flight to God, she writes to a friend: " The hour is approaching when I shall pass from this world to my Father, and before I go I want to send you a few words from my heart, a last testament from my soul. Never did the Master's Heart so overflow with love as at that last moment when He was about to leave His own. It seems to me that something like that is taking place in His little bride in the evening of her life, and I feel as though a wave were welling up from my heart into yours. . . . In the light of eternity, the soul sees all things as they are. How empty is everything that has not been done for God and with God! I beg of you to set the seal of love on everything that you do. That alone is lasting." [72]

This too is the last thought she leaves her Sisters reciting the prayers for the dying around her: " In the evening of life, everything passes away; only love remains. We must do everything for love." [73]

So it is that, for Sister Elizabeth, the whole practical teaching of the Divine Indwelling resolves itself into a continual exchange of love: " There is a Being, Whose Name is Love, and Who wills that we should live in His Company." [74]

7. The practice of the presence of God is not reserved for contemplative souls only. The grace of Baptism places the whole Trinity in every soul: " This ' better part ' [75] which seems to be my privilege in my beloved Carmelite solitude is offered by God to every baptized soul." [76]

It is enough to cling to God by faith, charity, and the practice of the Christian virtues. Some people think that to live in the

[70] To C. B., 1906.
[71] *Souvenirs*, p. 180.
[72] Letter to Madame de B., 1906.
[73] *Souvenirs*, p. 254.
[74] Letter to her mother, Oct. 20, 1906.
[75] *Luke* X, 42.
[76] Letter to Madame de S., July 25, 1902.

presence of God means we must assume a stiff attitude and keep our eyes closed. Nothing is more ridiculous. While the spiritual life and, consequently, the kingdom of God within us ' does not consist of meat and drink,' [77] to quote the Apostle's words, the same St. Paul tells us that God may yet receive a great service of praise by means of all this.

Don Bosco rolled in the dust with his children and, during recreations, Sister Elizabeth of the Trinity good-naturedly played the part of a martyr; they did not thereby lose the presence of God. The essential lies in the intention which, so far as possible, we must keep actually directed to God.

This is where the difference between the saints and ourselves begins. In their actions the saints seek the glory of God, " whether they eat or drink," [78] while many Christians no longer know how to find God even in prayer, because they imagine that the spiritual life is something inaccessible, reserved for a very small number of privileged souls called "mystics," and thus they complicate the whole matter. The true mysticism is that of our Baptism. It means living our life with the Trinity ever before us, under the seal of the Crucified, that is, in the daily crucifixions of our ordinary lives.

Sister Elizabeth of the Trinity insisted on this point when dealing with the souls who came to her, and whom God was keeping in the world: " You want to be all His, although living in the world; it is so simple. He is always with you; be with Him always yourself. Through all your actions, in all your sufferings, when your body is exhausted, remain in His sight. See Him *living* in your soul." [79]

Nothing can hinder us from being united to Him by love; neither the joys nor the sorrows of earth, neither health nor sickness, neither the flattery nor the malice of men; nothing, not even " our faults," [80] adds Sister Elizabeth, repeating St. Augustine's daring statement in his commentary on St. Paul's words to the Romans: " To them that love God all things work together for good "; " EVEN SIN—*etiam peccata* " because of the

---

[77] *Rom.* XIV, 17.
[78] *I Cor.* X, 31.
[79] Letter to Madame A., Sept. 29, 1902.
[80] *Last Retreat*, 7th Day.

pardon that glorifies the Divine Mercy, and the humility that remains in the soul, which now better knows its weakness.

Sister Elizabeth does not complicate matters. In order to live by this great mystery of God's Indwelling within us, she gives but one practical instruction: "Make acts of recollection in His presence."

"Mother dear, take advantage of your solitude to be recollected with the good God. While your body is resting, think how He is rest to your soul, and how, just as a child loves to be in its mother's arms, so you also may find your repose in the arms of this God Who is all around you. We cannot depart from Him, but alas! at times we forget His holy presence, and leave Him all alone, while we concern ourselves with things apart from Him. It is so easy, this intimacy with God; it is restful rather than tiring, like a child resting under its mother's eye. Offer Him all your sufferings; that is a good way of uniting yourself to Him, and it is a prayer that is pleasing to Him." [81]

"You see there is a saying of St. Paul's which is like a summing up of my life, and might be written of every moment in it: 'For His exceeding charity.' [82] Yes, all this flood of graces is 'because He has loved me exceedingly.' Mother dearest, let us love Him; let us live with Him as with a loved one from Whom we cannot be separated. You must tell me if you are making progress in the way of recollection in the presence of God. You know I am the 'little mother' of your soul; therefore I am very concerned about it. Remember those words of the Gospel: 'The kingdom of God is within you.' [83] Enter into this little kingdom, to adore the Sovereign Who dwells there as in His own palace." [84]

Sister Elizabeth had made her mother a little contrivance for marking these acts of recollection, and in one letter asks whether the latter is using it faithfully. "You must tell me if the little beads are faithfully moved." [85]

---

[81] Letter to her mother, July 30, 1906.
[82] *Eph.* II, 4.
[83] *Luke* XVII, 21.
[84] Letter to her mother, June 1906.
[85] *Ibid.*

8. Two letters are particularly revealing with respect to the means employed by the servant of God herself, and her own psychology in the presence of this mystery of the Divine Indwelling which was everything to her.

The first is addressed to a child who had a very gifted nature, but also a capricious temperament which was a trial to those around her. With really motherly tenderness, Sister Elizabeth writes to her: " Yes, I am praying for you, and I keep you in my soul, quite near the good God, in that little private sanctuary where I find Him at every hour of the day and night. I am never alone. Our Lord is always there praying in me, and I pray with Him. You make me sad, darling, I know that you are unhappy, and I assure you that the fault is your own. Be tranquil. I do not think you are unbalanced, but nervous and overexcited, and when you are like that, you make others suffer also. Oh! if only I could teach you the secret of happiness as God has taught it to me! You say that I have no worries or sufferings. It is true that I am very happy, but you do not understand that even though a person is tried, she can be happy at the same time. We must always keep our eyes on God. At first, it is necessary to make an effort when we are boiling inside; but quite gently, with patience and with God's help, we end by overcoming ourselves. You must do as I do; build a little cell within your soul. Think how the good God is there and enter it from time to time. When you feel nervous, when you are unhappy, take refuge there quickly and tell the Master all about it. If you knew Him a little, prayer would not bore you; to me it seems a rest, a relaxation. We simply come to Him we love, to keep near to Him like a little child in its mother's arms, and let our heart speak. You used to be so fond of sitting beside me and telling me secrets. You must go to Him just like that. If you knew how well He understands! You would no longer suffer if you understood that. It is the secret of Carmel. It is the life of a Carmelite to commune with God from morning to night, and from night to morning. If He did not fill our cells and our cloisters, how empty they would be! But we see Him through all for we bear Him within us, and our life is an anticipated heaven." [86]

The second letter is addressed to her mother. Sister Elizabeth of the Trinity was not wont to hurry either persons or events. Without being neglectful, she knew how to await God's hour. It required a crisis in her illness which nearly caused her death before she could enter fully into her mother's soul, that she might in turn train her. During a visit to the parlor which seemed likely to be the last, the hearts of mother and daughter communed at length and understood each other in the intimate manner of those who love and feel that the end is near. Sister Elizabeth took advantage of this to initiate her much loved mother into the secret of her interior life. It was for them the beginning of a new kind of friendship which was wholly spiritual and lived under the eye of God. On the following day Elizabeth wrote her a letter which is really a little catechism of the presence of God.

" ' If anyone love Me, he will keep My word, and My Father will love him, and We will come to him and make Our abode with him.' [87] My darling little Mother, I am beginning my letter with a statement. You see, I loved you so much, but since our last meeting, I love you twice as much again. It is so good to pour one's heart into that of one's mother and to feel that the two beat in unison. It seems to me that my love for you is not only that of a child for the best of mothers, but also that of a mother for her child. You are quite willing that I should be the mother of your soul, are you not? We are in retreat for Pentecost; I still more so than the others, separated from everything in my little cenacle. I am asking the Holy Spirit to reveal to you that presence of God of which I spoke to you. I looked over some books for you which deal with the subject, but I think it better to see you again before giving them to you. YOU MAY TRUST MY DOCTRINE FOR IT IS NOT MINE. If you read the Gospel according to St. John, you will see that

---

[86] Letter to F. de S., 1904.   [87] *John* XIV, 23.

our Lord constantly stresses this commandment: 'Abide in Me and I in you.'[88] And again, you have that beautiful thought which I put at the beginning of my letter, in which He speaks of *making His abode in us*.[89] In his Epistles, St. John desires that we should have *fellowship* with the Most Holy Trinity. This expression is so sweet and so simple. It is enough—St. Paul says so—to believe that God is a Spirit[90] and that we go to Him by faith. Think of the fact that your soul is 'the temple of God.'[91] Again it is St. Paul who tells you so. At every moment of the day and night, the Three Divine Persons are dwelling within you. You possess the Sacred Humanity only when you receive Holy Communion, but the Divinity, that Essence which the blessed adore in heaven, is in your soul. Then, when one knows that, it is a question of a wholly adorable friendship; one is no longer ever alone. If you prefer to think of the Good God as being close to you rather than within you, follow your attraction, provided that you live with Him. Do not forget to use my little chaplet; I made it specially for you, with so much love. I hope too that you are making those three prayers, of five minutes each, in my little sanctuary. Think of how you are with Him and act as one does with someone one loves. It is so simple; there is no need of beautiful thoughts, only an outpouring of the heart."[92]

9. We do not sufficiently consider the fact that this divine presence which is bestowed upon the soul of the Christian in Baptism is "ever in progress."[93] Every new degree of sanctifying grace brings with it a new presence of the Trinity.[94] Not that God changes; it is the soul becoming more and more divine which enters into more intimate contact with the Persons of the Holy Trinity.

The Father is more present in the measure in which the grace of adoption imparts to the soul a greater resemblance to the Divine Nature.

---

[88] *John* XV, 4.
[89] *John* XIV, 23.
[90] *John* IV, 24.
[91] *II Cor.* VI, 16.
[92] Letter to her mother, June 1906.
[93] *Heaven on earth*, 1st prayer.
[94] Cf. *Summa Theologica*, I, q. 43, a. 6 ad 2.

The Word is more present in the measure in which the soul, enlightened by His gifts, can no longer see divine and human things save in Him Who is Uncreated Wisdom, the Substantial Light, the Eternal Thought wherein God expresses all that He sees: the Trinity and the universe.

The Spirit of Love is more present in the measure in which the soul, stripped of self and of all affection for creatures, no longer permits itself to be led except by the action of this Spirit, Who completes in God the life-cycle of the life of the Trinity.

The teaching of theology is unhesitating on this point. The presence of the Trinity in a soul increases in proportion with the graces it receives, particularly at certain times when God visits it by the effects of exceptional graces: graces of religious profession and of the priesthood, graces of passive purifications, or mystical graces that raise souls step by step to transforming union.

Sister Elizabeth does not emphasize this most important doctrine which governs the whole progress of our spiritual life in this world, but in her own way she reaches it by another road and lays great stress upon it. " He wills that where He is we also may be, not only through all eternity but even in time, which is eternity begun and *ever in progress.*" [95]

10. The effect of this divine presence in the soul are many. Every baptized Christian is free to enjoy the Divine Persons as he will. This friendship of the baptized soul with the Father, the Son, and the Holy Ghost is the very essence of our spiritual life. It ought to be cried from the housetops.

" On the day when I understood that," said Sister Elizabeth, " everything became clear to me." [96]

The first effect of the presence of the Trinity in the soul by grace is that the soul is permitted to enjoy God; its beatitude begins on earth since, though it has not the vision, it already possesses by hope and love Him Who constitutes that vision.

It is infinite Love which envelops the soul, and wills, even here, to associate it with all its blessings. The soul knows ex-

---

[95] *Heaven on Earth*, 1st prayer.   [96] Letter to Madame de S., 1902.

perimentally that the Trinity is living within it, the Trinity it will behold in heaven.[97]

" When this soul realizes what riches it possesses, the natural or supernatural joys which might come to it from creatures or even from God only induce it to enter within itself to enjoy the substantial Good it owns, which is nothing else but God Himself. So that St. John of the Cross declares it has a certain resemblance to the Divinity." [98]

If we wished to mention in detail all the effects of the presence of the Trinity in our souls, we should be obliged to enumerate even the smallest details of all God's benefits in the natural and supernatural orders. Sister Elizabeth was in the habit of ceaselessly burying herself " within," where her faith found the real and substantial, although invisible, presence of Him Who is the source of grace. " He dwells within us in order to save us, to purify us and to transform us into Himself." [99]

She begged two things in particular of God present and living within her: to love Him to the point of complete forgetfulness of self and to be transformed into Him. " May His reign of love be then fully established in your interior kingdom, and may the weight of this love draw you to complete forgetfulness of self. . . . Happy the soul who has attained this complete detachment." [100]

" Yes, I believe that the secret of peace and happiness is to forget oneself, to cease to be concerned with oneself. That does not mean ceasing to feel physical or spiritual sufferings; the saints themselves have endured these crucifying states; only they did not stop there, but constantly put these things behind them. When they felt themselves affected by them, they were not surprised, for they knew ' that we are dust,' [101] as the Psalmist sings, but that with God's help, ' I shall be spotless and shall keep myself from my iniquity.' [102] Since you allow me to speak to you as to a loved sister, it seems to me that God is asking of you an abandonment and an unlimited confidence in

[97] Letter to G. de G., August 20, 1903.
[98] *Last Retreat*, 11th day.
[99] Letter to G. de G., February 1905.
[100] Letter to Madame A., 1906.
[101] Ps. CII, 14.
[102] Ps. XVII, 24.

those sorrowful hours when you feel these terrible voids. Think how He is then creating in your soul a greater capacity to receive Him, that is to say, in making it in a way as infinite as Himself. Try then, so far as your will is concerned, to remain quite joyous beneath the hand that is crucifying you. I will even say—look upon every suffering, every trial as a proof of love [103] coming to you directly from the good God to unite you to Him.

"To forget yourself as regards your health does not mean neglecting to take care of yourself—for that is your duty and the best of penances—but do it with the most perfect detachment, saying 'Thank you' to God whatever happens. When the burden of the body makes itself felt and wearies your soul, do not be discouraged but go by faith and love to Him Who said: 'Come to Me . . . and I will refresh you.' [104] As regards spiritual sufferings, never let yourself be cast down at the thought of your miseries. The great St. Paul says: 'Where sin abounded, grace did more abound.'" [105] To me it seems that the weakest soul, even if it is the most guilty, is just the one which has the best grounds for hope, and this act by which it forgets itself to throw itself into the arms of God glorifies Him more and gives Him more joy than all the falling back upon self, and all the self-examination which makes it live in its wretchedness, while in its center it possesses a Savior Who comes at every moment to cleanse it.

"Do you remember that beautiful passage where Jesus says to His Father that He has 'given Him power over all flesh, that He may give eternal life'? [106] That is what He wishes to do in you. He wishes you to be constantly going out of yourself, to put aside all anxiety, in order to retire into that solitude which He desires for Himself in the depth of your heart. He is always there, although you do not feel Him. He is waiting for you and desires to establish with you that *admirabile commercium*,[107] of which we sing in the beautiful liturgy; an intimacy like that

[103] Cf. *Heb.* XII, 6.   [105] *Rom.* V, 20.
[104] *Matt.* XI, 28.   [106] *John* XVII, 2.
[107] *Antiphon*, 1st Vesp., *Feast of the Circumcision*.

between spouse and bride. Your weaknesses, your sins, all that is troubling you is what He wishes to deliver you from by this continual contact. Has He not said that He comes not to judge but to save? [108] *Nothing* should hinder you from going to Him. Do not attach much importance to whether you are fervent or discouraged; it is the law of our exile to pass from one state to the other; but have faith that He never changes—that in His loving kindness He is ever bending over you, to carry you away and establish you in Him. If, despite everything, emptiness and sadness overwhelm you, unite this agony to His in the Garden of Gethsemane, when He prayed to His Father: 'If it be possible, let this chalice pass from Me.' [109] It may seem difficult to forget yourself: do not worry about it. If you only knew how simple it is! I am going to tell you my secret. Think about this God Who dwells within you, Whose temple you are.[110] It is St. Paul who says that, so we may believe it. Little by little, the soul becomes accustomed to live in His sweet company. It realizes that it bears within itself a little heaven in which the God of love has established His abode. Then it is as though the soul breathed a divine air. I would even say that only the body remains on earth, and that the soul dwells, beyond clouds and veils, in Him Who is the Unchangeable.

"Do not say that that is not for you, that you are too wretched; on the contrary, that is a reason the more for going to Him Who saves. It is not by looking at our miseries that we shall be cleansed, but by gazing upon Him Who is all purity and sanctity. St. Paul says that 'He predestinated us to be made conformable to the image of His Son.' [111] When you are suffering most, think that in order to make His work more beautiful, the Divine Artist is using the chisel, and remain in peace beneath the hand that is working upon you. That great Apostle of whom I speak, after having been rapt to the third heaven, felt his weakness and cried to God Who answered: 'My grace

---

[108] *John* XII, 47.
[109] *Matt.* XXVI, 39.
[110] *I Cor.* III, 17.
[111] *Rom.* VIII, 29.

is sufficient for Thee, for power is made perfect in infirmity.'[112] Is that not very comforting? Courage then, Madame and dear sister, I am commending you very specially to a little Carmelite who died at twenty-four years of age, in the odor of sanctity, named Teresa of the Child Jesus. Before she died, she said she would spend her heaven in doing good upon earth, and her grace is to enlarge souls, to speed them forth on waves of love, confidence, abandonment. She said that she found happiness when she began to forget self. Will you invoke her every day with me, that she may obtain for you that knowledge which makes saints, and gives so much peace and happiness to the soul? "[113]

Sister Elizabeth here told her deepest secret. For several years, the last obstacle to the development of the fulness of holiness in her was this want of perfect forgetfulness of self. She long implored the Blessed Trinity in prayer, " Help me to become wholly forgetful of self," until the day came when the Trinity delivered her, leaving all her powers free to spend themselves solely in loving. As we have said, that marked the final development of her spiritual life and of the triumph of love; the supreme grace of an essentially contemplative spirituality, which draws souls to interior recollection to make them go out of themselves and think only of glorifying God.

The correlative effect of this self-forgetfulness is the consummation of transforming union. At the end of her life particularly, Sister Elizabeth loved to dwell on this. In proportion as God wrought in her His work of destruction, it was felt that this blessed transforming union became more and more her constant preoccupation, the longed-for term to which the saintly invalid looked in order the better to realize her desire " to be made conformable to the Crucified," and her dream of being a " praise of glory." She would glorify God in the measure in which she was transformed into Him.

That was the end she sought, always employing the same means: making use of the Divine Presence and allowing herself

---

[112] *II Cor.* XII, 9.   [113] Letter to Madame A., Nov. 24, 1905.

to be purified and saved by continual contact with God. " He so loves to forgive us, to raise us up, and then to carry us away in Him, in His purity, in His divine sanctity. That is how He will purify us by continual contact with Him, by His divine touches. He wants us to be so pure. He Himself will be our purity. We must allow ourselves to be transformed into a single image with Him." [114] " He thirsts to associate us with all that He is, to transform us into Himself." [115]

While she was composing her last retreat of " The Praise of Glory," Sister Elizabeth loved to dip into the sublime pages of *The Spiritual Canticle* and *The Living Flame of Love*, in which St. John of the Cross describes this transformation of the soul into the Trinity, which is, indeed, the highest point of his mystical theology. She delighted in these passages and with unswerving fidelity set herself to obtain from God this final grace.

" ' *Deus noster ignis consumens.*' ' Our God,' wrote St. Paul, ' is a consuming fire,' that is, a fire of love which destroys, which transforms into itself whatever it touches. The mystic death of which St. Paul speaks becomes very simple and sweet to souls who yield themselves up to the action of its flames within the depths of their being. They think far less of the work of destruction and detachment left to them to accomplish than of plunging into the furnace of love burning within them which is the Holy Ghost Himself—the same Love which in the Blessed Trinity is the bond between the Father and His Word. Such souls enter into Him by a living faith; there, in simplicity and peace, they are raised by Him above all created things, and above all sensible devotion, into the ' sacred darkness ' and transformed into the divine image. As St. John expresses it, they live ' in fellowship ' with the three adorable Persons, whose life they share; that is the contemplative life." [116]

" Thus the great means of attaining this perfect resemblance to the Heavenly Father which the Master requires is again

[114] Letter to G. de G., Aug. 20, 1903.
[115] To the same, Sept. 14, 1903.   [116] *Heaven on Earth*, 6th prayer.

and always the presence of God, according to that watchword which God Himself gave to Abraham: 'Walk before Me and be perfect.' On this magnificent way of the presence of God, the soul unerringly travels 'alone with One Who is the Alone,' led by the help of His right hand, overshadowed with His shoulders, trusting under His wings, . . . not afraid of the terror of the night, of the arrow that flieth in the day, of the business that walketh about in the dark; of invasion or of the noonday devil.' "[117] The time of transforming union has come, and the soul no longer desires anything but the Beatific Vision.

"'As the hart panteth after the fountain of water, so my soul panteth after Thee, O God. My soul hath thirsted after the strong living God. When shall I come and appear before the face of God?' Yet as 'the sparrow hath found herself a house, and the turtle a nest for herself, where she may lay her young' so, while waiting to be taken to the holy city of Jerusalem—'*Beata pacis visio*'—the soul arrived at these heights has found her retreat, her beatitude, heaven beforehand where she already begins her life of eternity."[118] She knows that the Trinity dwells within her and that suffices for her happiness.

"This is the mystery to which my lyre is tuned today. My divine Master has said to me, as to Zaccheus: 'Make haste and come down for . . . I must abide in thy house.' Make haste and come down, but where? Into the innermost depths of my being, after having left self, separated from self, stripped myself of self; in a word, WITHOUT SELF. 'I must abide in thy house.' It is my Master Who says this, my Master Who desires to abide in me, with the Father and His Spirit of Love, so that, in the words of the Beloved Disciple, I may have 'fellowship' with them. 'Now, therefore, you are no more strangers and foreigners but you are already domestics of God,' says St. Paul. I think that to be a domestic of God is to abide in the bosom of the tranquil Trinity, in the innermost depths of myself, in the invincible fortress of holy recollection described by St. John of the Cross.

[117] *Last Retreat*, 9th day.   [118] *Ibid.*, 16th day.

"David sang: 'My soul longeth and fainteth for the courts of the Lord.' Such, I think, should be the feeling of every soul when it enters its inner 'courts,' to contemplate its God and keep in closest contact with Him. It faints in a divine swoon before this all-powerful love, this infinite Majesty which dwells within it. It is not that life forsakes it, but the soul itself disdains this natural life and withdraws from it. Feeling such life to be unworthy of a spirit raised to such dignity, it dies to this life and flows into God.

"How beautiful is the creature, thus stripped and freed of self! It is then 'disposed to ascend by steps through the valley of tears,' to pass from all that is less than God, 'to the place which He hath set,' that 'large place' sung by the Psalmist which, so it seems to me, is the unfathomable Trinity: 'Immensus Pater: Immensus Filius: Immensus Spiritus Sanctus.'

"It rises, ascending above the senses, above nature, above self. It passes beyond all joy and all sorrow, never to rest until it has penetrated *within* Him Whom it loves, Who will Himself give it the 'repose of the abyss.' And all this will be done without leaving the holy fortress. The Divine Master has said to it: 'Make haste and come down.' Nor will the soul leave it when at last it lives, like the inimitable Trinity, in an 'eternal present,' adoring God eternally for His own sake and becoming, by a gaze that ever grows more simple, more unifying, 'the brightness of His glory'; or, in other words: the ceaseless 'praise of glory' of His adorable perfections." [119]

11. It is in order that we may attain to this abyss of glory, remarks St. John of the Cross, that God has created us to His image and likeness. . . .

"Oh souls, created for these marvels, and called to see them realized in you, what are you doing? On what wretched trifles do you waste your time? Your ambitions are but for base things; your pretended goods but misery. How can you fail to understand that in seeking after the glories of earth, you remain buried in poverty and ignominy? You are unaware of these

[119] *Ibid.*

incalculable treasures reserved for you, and know only how to render yourselves unworthy of them." [120]

Elizabeth of the Trinity was moved by a similar feeling of divine sadness when on August 2, 1906, the fifth anniversary of her entrance into Carmel, after reviewing all the graces she had gained from this continual living in the presence of God—graces lost by so many souls who might have lived by them—she wrote:

"Oh, would that I could tell all souls what a source of strength, of peace and of happiness they would find if they would consent to live in this intimacy. Only they do not know how to wait. If God does not bestow Himself in a manner that they can feel, they leave His Holy Presence; and when He comes to them with all His gifts, He finds no one there; the soul has gone out to exterior things. They do not dwell in the depths of themselves." [121]

---

[120] *Spiritual Canticle*, Stanza XXXIX.
[121] Letter to her mother, Aug. 3, 1906.

Chapter IV

THE PRAISE OF GLORY

> *"In the heaven of my soul: the glory of the Eternal . . . nothing but the glory of the Eternal."*

1. The new name. 2. A Praise of Glory is a silent soul. 3. The praise of all His gifts. 4. Eternal life begun. 5. The praise of the crucified soul. 6. The soul is a heaven that sings of God. 7. The office of a Praise of Glory.

Owing to an anthropomorphism which it is almost impossible to overcome, the majority of souls judge of all things, and even of God, in relation to themselves, whereas they ought to consider everything, and themselves, in relation to God. Thus to many, sanctity seems to be an end in itself. In reality, sanctity itself is subordinated to a higher end, which is absolutely the last end: the glory of the Trinity. God created all things and sent His Son into the world only for His glory. If He had acted for any other than Himself, He would no longer be God.

This most elementary truth for those who have a sense of the divine transcendence appears as the dominant factor in the lives of the saints only at the later stages, after perfect unity has been achieved in their souls. When they have become a single spirit with Him, their thoughts are identified with the divine wisdom and their wills with the divine will. Only our Lord and His Mother from the first moment of their existence perfectly carried out this program of divine glorification which is the means by which all holiness is achieved on earth.

There is, in fact, a double movement in our love of God: He is loved for our sake, and He is loved for His own sake.

To love God for our sake is perfectly legitimate. It is to seek in Him the satisfying term of all our powers. In this sense, the

Psalmist sings: "It is good for me to adhere to my God."[1] And Sister Elizabeth never tired of repeating: "I have found my heaven on earth, since heaven is God, and God is in my soul. The God whom we possess by faith, and the blessed by vision is one and the same."[2]

St. Augustine points out another manner of loving God and seeking after divine union: "To live by God for God's sake"; and St. Thomas: "To live not for ourselves but for God."[3] This is the summit and the highest definition of the spiritual life. Not that the love is a disinterested Pure Love that excludes the desire of eternal beatitude which is so sanctifying, but one which loves God for God's sake first, as is right. In everything, but above all in love, "God must be served first."

The saints become thoroughly penetrated with this truth only after they have been completely set free from themselves by means of the cares and crosses of this life. Then there begins for them that deiform life by which they "put on" God's way of living. Their calm and luminous faith makes them see all things in the light of the Word. In hope, they feel themselves to be already established in the unfailing possession of the riches of the Trinity. Their love seems to be identified with that blessed rest in which God finds ineffable happiness in Himself. Their justice is an unconquerable will to render honor and glory to God in everything. Their prudence reveals to them the sovereign Providence which directs the smallest details of the government of the universe. They are pure with that inaccessible purity which isolates the divine Essence from all created contact. Their strength by which they triumphantly overcome all human unrest is akin to God's unchangeableness. This beauteous eventide of the life of a saint is like an anticipated and peace-giving vision of the manner of life in eternity. The soul lives there in the deiform state, in the unity of the Trinity.

[1] *Ps.* LXXII, 28.
[2] Letter to Madame de S., 1902.
[3] *Summa Theologica*, II-II, q. XVII, a. 6 ad 3: *Caritas facit tendere in Deum uniendo affectum hominis Deo: ut silicet homo non sibi vivat, sed Deo.*

It is the final phase of the transforming union which is habitual in the case of the blessed but which is attained on earth only by a very few perfect souls.

1. Something analogous took place in the evening of the life of Sister Elizabeth of the Trinity which drew in so early. For some time she had felt imprisoned within herself, unable to get free. God delivered her by personally intervening, after having prepared her for this final grace by revealing to her her new name, that name which was to give to her spiritual life its definitive meaning. God did this on a license day.

Sister Elizabeth had gone to visit an older nun in her cell,[4] and was listening to her like a pupil. Both were simply discussing their spiritual graces and mutually encouraging each other in the love of their God, as the wicked plot together to do evil. All at once, Elizabeth's companion said to her: " I have found a splendid passage in St. Paul: ' God has created us for the praise of His glory.' " The younger religious was rapturously impressed. When she returned to her cell, wishing to refer to the Latin text, she took up the Epistles and began to search for the passage that had struck her so forcefully. Not finding it, she went back to the Sister. " I cannot find the place. Will you be kind enough to show it to me again? " The nun added, when relating the incident: " After that, she never mentioned it again to me. It was only later on, after she was in the infirmary, that I noticed that our Mother and other Sisters were calling her ' *Laudem Gloriae.*' I had not attached any importance to the passage of St. Paul's. I had not had the same grace as Sister Elizabeth, who had been led to take from it her name of ' the praise of glory.' " The divine grace had indeed made use of that phrase from her favorite St. Paul to raise this soul to the heights.

This grace was given her in the course of the summer of 1905. At first, it developed slowly, although giving a definitely new orientation to her interior life. On the 1st of January she wrote: " I am going to tell you a secret: my dream is to be the

---

[4] This is the account as given by the nun concerned.

'praise of His Glory.' I read that in St. Paul, and my Bridegroom has made me understand that this is my vocation here in exile, while waiting to go and sing the eternal *Sanctus* in the city of the saints. But this calls for great fidelity since, in order to be a 'praise of glory,' I must be dead to everything that is not He, so that I may be moved only by His touch, and poor Elizabeth still does foolish things where her Master is concerned. But, like a tender Father, He forgives her; His divine look purifies her. Like St. Paul, she tries to forget those things that are behind and stretch forth to those that are before." [5]

Henceforth, whenever Sister Elizabeth was able to speak privately to a priest correspondent, she asked him, at Mass, to consecrate her as a " victim of praise," or as a " praise of glory."

When, on Palm Sunday evening, her Master swooped down upon her, as upon a prey, in a sudden seizure, she thought that all was over. Joyfully, she awaited death. When she was surprised by a slight return of health, He made her understand that the tasks of earth were no longer for her and that, thenceforth, He wished her to be wholly occupied with His glory alone. Then it was that Sister Elizabeth realized better the import of her name, that new name which was to be hers on earth and in eternity. " To be a praise of glory of the Trinity " —that was what her Lord required of her, on this bed of pain that had become " the altar of her continual immolation with Him." [6]

Her interior life became simplified: " To let herself be crucified in order to be the 'Praise of Glory,' " that was all. First slowly, then rapidly, she began to be utterly forgetful of herself. Through all, she unceasingly sought His praise. Everything else seemed vain to her. Even her name of Elizabeth of the Trinity did not now fully express her vocation, and with her intimate friends, she no longer signed herself " Elizabeth " but " *Laudem Gloriae*." Sister Elizabeth had meant the soul hidden deep within itself, there to enjoy the presence of God; *Laudem*

---

[5] Letter to Canon A., January 1906. [6] To the same, July 1906.

Gloriae marked another and an incomparably higher stage: the soul whose one thought was His glory.

It was the swan song of her fading life. Henceforth, only divine harmonies evoked by the Holy Spirit came from the soul of this great artist. There were no more violent efforts to unite the powers of her soul; she possessed them all in unity. The *Canticum Novum*, the song of the new name of the unceasing " Praise of Glory," rose ceaselessly from that soul. Useless thoughts or vain desires had disappeared. In her soul, at peace and crucified, there reigned that unity which is wrought by the triumph of love. All the strings of her lyre were ready to vibrate at the least breathing of the Spirit. The solemn notes of her painful Calvary mingled with the thrilling accents of the divine exultation which she felt at the near approach of the joys of the blessed. All was in harmony and rose to God as a hymn of glory which the Word sang in this soul wholly transformed into Him.

There is something divine in this beautiful evening of the life of Sister Elizabeth of the Trinity. At the news of her death and recalling her last weeks, Father Vallée wrote to Madame Catez that the last hours were " strangely beautiful and divine." On the Cross, God completed His work of making her conformable to His Son. She herself dreamed of nothing else but becoming identified by love with " Him who was the perfect ' Praise of Glory,' "[7] Christ Crucified, " to show Him forth in the sight of the Father."[8] " I live in the heaven of faith, in the center of my soul, and I try to give joy to my Master by being, even here on earth, the ' praise of glory.' "[9]

That was the term she used quite naturally with those with whom she was intimate. With her Mother Prioress, there was no question of anything else. Especially after her illness, this child no longer had any secrets from her Prioress. She was the " priest " who was to offer the little " praise of glory " to the Holy Trinity. Private conversations and special feasts in-

---

[7] *Last Retreat*, 1st day.
[8] *Ibid.*, 14th day.   [9] Letter to Canon A., May 1906.

variably brought her back to the same thought. For the feast of St. Germaine, knowing it would be the last time she would spend it on earth, Sister Elizabeth asked a friend to draw her a design representing the Most Holy Trinity, and three souls holding a harp on which to sing Its praises. "One of these souls must be more beautiful than the others, for it must represent our Mother. The other is a little spiritual sister in this Carmel, and the third myself." She wished her friend to write on this picture: "Deus predestinavit nos ut essemus *Laudem Gloriae ejus*.—God has predestined us to be the praise of His glory." [10] It was a question, in short, of representing symbolically her definitive vocation of Praise of Glory.

In the infirmary she was thus able for the last time to keep the feast of her Mother Prioress, whom she loved so dearly and with such daughterly affection. "In the evening, Mother's little private feast took place in our little cell, just between our Mother and her two 'Benjamins.' My dear little sister, who is a real seraph, will repay you before our Lord for the joy you gave her. On a little table, decorated with flowers, she had arranged quite an exhibition. Your beautiful gift was in the place of honor, with the picture of the Holy Trinity, for which I owe you all my thanks. Ribbons floated on either side; the medal from Mama and a little present from Guite were there also, then little pieces of needlework, and finally the spiritual bouquets with your Mass their loveliest flower." [11]

With those of her sisters in religion who were in her confidence with respect to her "secret" of grace, she no longer called herself anything but *Laudem Gloriae*. In a postscript to her farewell letter written to her sister Marguerite, she added: "This will be my name in heaven." [12]

This new name is of the greatest importance to the psychologist or the theologian, who would understand the final development of her baptismal grace in the case of Sister Elizabeth of the Trinity. That "personal name" whereby the

[10] Letter to Madame H., June 3, 1906.
[11] To the same, July 1906.   [12] Summer 1906.

Shepherd differentiates and calls each of His sheep, enables us to fix upon the term of the predestination of a soul. It is our conviction that that name is the most characteristic feature of the mission of Sister Elizabeth of the Trinity.

The great obstacle for the Carmelite, as for every contemplative soul, is to live with an eye on self instead of living in herself with God. The special grace of Elizabeth of the Trinity, who became *Laudem Gloriae,* is to withdraw souls into the depths of themselves, but *in order to make them go out of themselves,* by means of love and the praise of glory.

We should know scarcely anything of her spiritual life once it had reached to these heights had not Mother Germaine, who already considered her a little saint, been providentially inspired to request her to write down her secret. " . . . When, for the last time here, she entered into retreat, from the 15th to the 31st of August, I ordered her to note down her simple thoughts as to the way in which she understood or envisaged her vocation of ' Praise of Glory.' She understood and smilingly assented." [13]

She took a small notebook and then, between eleven o'clock and midnight, when she was sure that her Prioress would not come, during her very trying sleepless nights, she set to work to write. When the book was full from cover to cover, she returned it to the Prioress and thought no more about it. These pages, which were manifestly dictated by the Holy Ghost to a soul utterly plunged in pain and happiness, are a veritable spiritual masterpiece and rank Sister Elizabeth of the Trinity among the greatest mystical writers. It is impossible to explain these sublime aspirations, written without a change and without an erasure, except by a real charisma for composition, and instinctively we think of the rapid way in which St. Catherine of Siena, urged by the same Spirit, dictated her wonderful *Dialogue.* These are feats that are beyond human art, in which we clearly recognize the supra-technical touches of the Spirit of Love who is both divine Art and supreme Beauty.

[13] I owe this detail to Mother Germaine herself.

Those who would sound the depths of the mind of Elizabeth of the Trinity must turn to her last retreat. The *Last Retreat of " Laudem Gloriae "* is, so to speak, her little mystical summa, the quintessence of her spiritual teaching at the highest point of her mystical experience. It is a real treatise on transforming union, as she conceived it along the lines of her vocation of a " Praise of Glory," and as she interiorly lived it. In it she leaves a plan of life to all " Praises of Glory," who would thereafter follow in her steps along the road of a sanctity which is wholly forgetful of self and wholly devoted to the purest glory of the Trinity.

As we study her conception of her office of " Praise of Glory," we find once more the most fundamental lines of her spirituality: silence, absolute detachment, love of the Trinity, worship of the will of God and increasingly earnest identification with the soul of Christ crucified. We find them, however, in another light, one which changes everything: in the pure light of the glory of the Trinity. It is a whole new spiritual world which bursts upon our sight, as though the touch of a magic wand had made it possible for us to see friends whom we had felt near us in the dark.

The soul no longer knows anything but Jesus Christ, crucified for love, while its dream is to die transformed into Him; the Trinity, whose unceasing " praise of glory " it would be; and our Lady, that Mother of Grace whose mission is to form in the soul the living and faithful image of the First Born, the Son of the Eternal, of Him who was the perfect " Praise of Glory " of His Father.

These were Elizabeth's deepest thoughts as she entered upon the days of recollection of her last retreat on earth, on the evening of August 15th, beseeching *Janua Caeli* to prepare her for her journey to eternity. Here again as always, her concrete psychology explains her doctrine.

2. A " Praise of Glory " is first and foremost a silent soul. Thus, we again find the fundamental ascesis of the servant of

God: "I knew not." This is the whole program of the "Praise of Glory," to be stripped of everything and of itself; to be free to respond to the merest breath of the Spirit.

"'*Nescivi.*' 'I knew not.' So sings the bride of the Canticles, after she had been brought into the inner cellar. That, it seems to me, should also be the song of a 'Praise of Glory,' on the first day of her retreat, when the Master makes her sound the depths of the abyss, that she may learn to fulfill the office which will be hers in eternity and which she also ought to perform now in time, which is eternity begun.

"I know nothing, I desire to know nothing, but 'Him . . . and the fellowship of His sufferings, being made conformable to His death!'"[14]

"How necessary is this blessed unity for the soul that craves to live here below the life of the blessed—that is, of simple beings, of spirits!

"Then whatever turmoil there may be outside or whatever tempests within, however its honor may be assailed: *Nescivi*! God may hide Himself, withdraw His sensible grace; *Nescivi*.[15] Withdrawn into the depths of itself, in silence and in the unity of its powers, the soul is completely given up to the praise of His glory."

Sister Elizabeth of the Trinity thus repeats the doctrine of "knowing nothing," which is the basis of the mystical theology of her great spiritual Master, St. John of the Cross.

3. This negative aspect of absolute detachment, so characteristic of the spiritual teaching of Sister Elizabeth of the Trinity and of the great mystics, is but the preliminary phase. This "Nothingness" which is sought after by the soul, is the preparatory condition for possessing the "All," in which our spiritual life positively consists. The spirit of the Gospel is most particularly manifested as an essentially positive religion. God is glorified in the measure of His gifts. Our Lord and His Mother rendered Him the greatest glory because they received the most. This is a fundamental doctrine of right

---

[14] *Last Retreat*, 1st day.   [15] *Ibid.*, 2nd day.

spirituality. We commonly hear it said: "Oh, if only I enter heaven, even in the lowest place . . ." Such a thought shows a lack of understanding of real love of God and concern for His glory. This is a capital point in the doctrine of Sister Elizabeth of the Trinity and in the Christian conception of the world.

What is the glory of God? The radiant manifestation of what He is, the revelation of His infinite perfections.

There are two kinds of glory in God: His personal glory within Himself, and His external glory in the universe He has created. There is no question here of His essential glory, that glory which God finds in Himself, in His Word, in the unique eternal Thought which adequately expresses all that He is in the indivisible Unity of His Essence and the Trinity of the Persons. The Word expresses everything: the inexhaustible fecundity of the bosom of the Father, the beauty of the Son, the Love that perfects Them in Unity, the universe which has come into being by their creative might and which remains in the hands of God like a plaything. Thus the Father manifests His own glory to the Son. The Father shines out in the Word, the image and splendor of His glory; the Word manifests to the Father all that He is in Himself. In Him, the Father and the Son know the Eternal Love that unites Them. Such is the essential glory of God, that personal intra-Trinitarian glory which is the Word.

The universe adds nothing to this infinite glory, and before the Holy Trinity even the very soul of Christ must acknowledge its nothingness. In the three-fold society of the divine Persons and the indivisible unity of their Essence, God is sufficient to Himself. All that can come to Him from without, even from Christ, is only accidental. And yet, notwithstanding, God claims it absolutely, because the hierarchy of values and the order of creation so requires. To the Creator belong honor, wisdom, power, and glory.

By a wonderful balance between the divine wisdom and the other divine attributes, God finds this accidental glory only in our happiness, *and even in proportion to that happiness.* "In this is my Father glorified, that you bring forth very much fruit,"[16] the Master taught. The holiest soul gives Him the most glory. In this sense, the Incarnate Word, on account of the incomprehensible riches bestowed upon His Sacred Humanity, is the most perfect "Praise of Glory" of all God's gifts. After Him, at an infinite distance, comes the soul of Our Lady, the creature who received the most after Christ, and then the saints. To be content with a mediocre sanctity is, therefore, to have a false conception of the divine glory.

With a depth of understanding astonishing in a mere girl, Sister Elizabeth of the Trinity, moved by grace, rose effortlessly into this lofty sphere of wisdom, the most God-like vantage point from which a created mind can judge of the universe in the light of God. She understood perfectly that she was bound to become a saint in the first place for God; and to become as great a saint as possible because His glory was closely linked with her sanctity.

In her diary, she wrote: " I will be a saint "; then there is an erasure and an addition: " a saint for Thy sake." The end of her life was a magnificent realization of the desire she expressed at the age of nineteen.

She understood that the higher a soul is raised on the summits of transforming union, the better it will fulfill its office of " Praise of Glory." God is glorified in the measure in which " the beauty " of His perfections is reflected in souls. The glorified souls, those who contemplate God in the simplicity of His Essence, have attained to this supreme transformation. "' Then I shall know even as I am known,' says St. Paul, meaning by intuitive vision. . . . That is why . . . they are ' transformed into the same image from glory to glory, by the Spirit of the Lord.' Then they are a ceaseless praise of glory to the divine Being Who contemplates His own splendor in them . . . ' God created man to His own image.' Such was the plan of the Creator, that He might view Himself in His creature, and might see His own perfections and beauty re-

[16] *John* XV, 8.

flected through him as through a pure and flawless crystal. Is that not a kind of extension of His own glory? The soul . . . that allows the Divinity to reflect Himself in it . . . such a soul is truly the 'Praise of Glory' of all His gifts. Whatever happens, and during the most commonplace employments, it sings the *canticum magnum*, the *canticum novum*, and this canticle thrills God to His very depths." [17]

To give witness to God with all her powers, by directing them to Him alone; that is what she understood by the praise of glory of all His gifts. For Elizabeth, a true " Praise of Glory " is eager to receive the maximum from God. Such a soul remains under His hand like a lyre, and all His gifts are like a string that vibrates day and night to sing the praise of His glory.[18]

We are far from the cramping vision of all those narrow conceptions which, instead of setting souls free to cast themselves eagerly on God, withdraw them into themselves, depress them, and paralyze the development of perfect love.

4. Ever attracted to the peaks, Sister Elizabeth of the Trinity sought her model for the " Praise of Glory " among the blessed who in prayer and adoration stand day and night before the throne of the Lamb.

Influenced by the SPIRITUAL CANTICLE and the LIVING FLAME OF LOVE, the dominant thought of her last days became that of the Beatific Vision, and this communicated, as it were, a rhythm of eternity to all her soul's outpourings. The closing chapters of the Apocalypse, particularly the last, became her usual spiritual nourishment. Thence she drew that sense of eternity which animated nearly every page of her Last Retreat. To those around her, she would repeat: " My Master speaks to me now only of eternity."

With a faultless sense of doctrine, she there touched upon another truth familiar in Catholic theology: our divine life on earth is " eternal life begun." " I believe," she says, " that we should give immense joy to the heart of God by imitating, in the heaven of our soul, this occupation of the blessed." [19]

[17] *Last Retreat*, 3rd day.   [18] *Ibid.*, 2nd day.   [19] *Ibid.*, 3rd day.

"Yesterday, St. Paul raised the veil a little way so that I could catch a glimpse of the lot 'of the saints in light,' and ascertain how they employ themselves, so that I might try, as far as possible, to *conform my life to theirs* and fulfill my vocation of *Laudem Gloriae*. Today it is St. John the Disciple whom Jesus loved, who will partly open the 'eternal gates' for me, that my soul may rest in Jerusalem the holy, sweet 'vision of peace.' He tells me to begin with that 'the city hath no need of the sun, nor of the moon, to shine in it.' For the glory of God hath enlightened it, and the Lamb is the lamp thereof. If I wish my interior city to agree with, to resemble in some measure, that of the immortal 'King of ages,' and shine with the great illumination given by God, I must first extinguish every other light, so that in the holy city the Lamb may be the lamp." [20]

The life of the blessed is a life of light and love. On this double movement Sister Elizabeth traced the program of the "Praise of Glory" who desires to imitate their occupation in the heaven of her soul. The virtue of faith supplies for the Beatific Vision, which is impossible on earth.

"Here faith, the fair light of faith, appears to me. That and no other ought to enlighten me to go to meet the Bridegroom. The Psalmist sings that 'He made darkness His cover'; but seems to contradict himself by saying elsewhere that 'He is clothed with light as with a garment!' This apparent contradiction appears to me to mean that I ought to plunge into the sacred darkness, keeping all my powers in night and emptiness. Then I shall meet my Master, and the light which clothes Him as a garment will enwrap me too with His light alone, 'having the glory of God.' It is said of Moses that he endured as seeing Him that is invisible. Such should be the attitude of a "Praise of Glory" who desires to persevere in her hymn of thanksgiving whatever happens; to be enduring in her faith as if she saw Him that is invisible; enduring in her faith in His 'exceeding charity.' 'We have known and have believed the charity which God hath to us.'

[20] *Ibid.*

"'Faith is the substance of things to be hoped for, the evidence of things that appear not.' What does it matter to the soul that retires within itself, enlightened by this word, whether it feels or does not feel, whether it is in light or darkness, enjoys or does not enjoy? It is struck by a kind of shame at making any distinction between such things . . . To this soul, this enduring believer in the God of love, may be applied the words of the Prince of the Apostles: "In Whom . . . believing, you shall rejoice with joy unspeakable and be glorified.'"[21]

There is a second feeling which should animate the "Praise of Glory" who would imitate the occupation of the blessed: the adoring activity of love. The whole psychology of the "Praise of Glory" ought to be modelled on that of the souls in glory. "'They rested not day and night saying: Holy, holy, holy Lord God Almighty, Who was, and Who is and Who is to come . . . They fell down before Him . . . and adored Him . . . and cast their crowns before the throne, saying: Thou art worthy, O Lord our God, to receive glory, and honor and power!' How can I imitate within the heaven of my soul, the ceaseless occupation of the blessed in the heaven of glory?

"'They fall down . . . and adore . . . and cast down their crowns.' First of all the soul should 'fall down,' should plunge into the abyss of its own nothingness, so sinking into it that, according to the beautiful expression of a mystical writer, 'it finds the true peace, invincible and perfect, that naught can trouble, for it has cast itself so low that none will descend to follow it.'

"Then it can *adore*. Adoration! Ah, that word comes from heaven! It seems to me that it can be defined as the ecstasy of love; love crushed by the beauty, the strength, the vast grandeur of Him it loves . . . 'Exalt ye . . . for the Lord our God is holy,' as the psalm says. And again: 'They shall adore Him always for His own sake.'"[22]

Thus does this psychology of the blessed in eternity become for her the living exemplar of holiness on earth. "A soul which

---

[21] *Ibid.*, 4th day.   [22] *Ibid.*, 8th day.

meditates upon these thoughts, which understands their meaning with the 'mind of the Lord' as St. Paul says, lives in an anticipated heaven above all that passes, above itself. It knows that He Whom it adores possesses in Himself all happiness, all glory, and 'casting its crown' before Him, *as do the blessed*, it despises itself, loses sight of self, and finds its beatitude in the beatitude of Him Whom it adores, whatever its sufferings or grief, for it has gone out from self and passed into Another. The soul, in this attitude of adoration, resembles the wells spoken of by St. John of the Cross, which receive the waters flowing from Lebanon, so that those who look on it may exclaim: 'The stream of the river maketh glad the city of God.'" [23]

5. Nevertheless, to the end of her spiritual life, Sister Elizabeth of the Trinity, a Trinitarian soul if ever there was one, remained *more and more* centered in Jesus Christ. The dream of *Laudem Gloriae*, during her weary, sleepless nights, was to die " not only pure as an angel " but " transformed into Jesus Crucified." [24]

She had this divine Model ever in view. Her ideal was to contemplate Him in order to reproduce Him; she yearned to show Him forth in the sight of the Father. But she knew that supreme conformity to the likeness of Christ leads to " being made conformable to His death."

During the days of her last retreat, this thought was never absent from her for a moment. While she was composing her retreats on the Divine Indwelling of the Trinity and on the Praise of Glory, she would often murmur to her Mother Prioress in an invalid's weak voice: " I feel that He is leading me to Calvary." It is there that all sanctity is perfected.

A " Praise of Glory " is essentially a crucified soul. It has gazed upon the great multitude in heaven " which no man could number "; it knows that " ' these are they are are come out of great tribulation, and have washed their robes, and have made them white in the blood of the Lamb. Therefore they are before the throne of God, and they serve Him day and night in His

---

[23] *Ibid.*   [24] Letter to G. de G., October 1906.

temple: and He that sitteth on the throne shall dwell over them. They shall no more hunger nor thirst, neither shall the sun fall on them, nor any heat. For the Lamb which is in the midst of the throne shall rule them and shall lead them to the fountains of the waters of life, and God shall wipe away all tears from their eyes.'

"All these elect souls, palm in hand, bathed in the light of God, must needs have first passed through the 'great tribulation' and known the sorrow, 'great as the sea,' sung by the prophet. Before 'beholding the glory of the Lord with open faces,' they have shared the abjection of His Christ, before being 'transformed into the same image from glory to glory' they have been conformed to the image of the Word Incarnate, crucified by love.

"The soul that longs to serve God day and night in His temple (by which I understand that inner sanctuary of which St. Paul speaks when he says: 'The temple of God is holy, which you are') must be resolved to take a real share in the Passion of its Master. It is a redeemed soul, and, in its turn, must redeem other souls. Therefore it will sing upon its lyre: 'God forbid that I should glory, save in the cross of Our Lord Jesus Christ.' 'With Christ, I am nailed to the Cross.' And again: 'I fill up those things that are wanting of the sufferings of Christ in my flesh for His Body which is the Church.'

"'The queen stood on thy right hand.' Such is the attitude of this soul. It walks the road to Calvary, at the right hand of the crucified, crushed and humble King, Who, strong, calm, and full of majesty goes to His Passion to show forth 'the glory of His grace,' according to St. Paul's strong expression. He desires His bride to join in His work of redemption and the way of sorrow which she treads seems to her the way of beatitude, not only because it leads there, but also because her holy Teacher makes her understand that she must pass beyond the bitterness of suffering to find her rest in it as He did.

"Then she can 'serve God day and night in His temple.' Neither interior nor exterior trials can make her leave the holy fortress in which He has enclosed her. She no longer thirsts or hungers, for in spite of her overwhelming longing for heaven, she is satisfied with the food that was her Master's—the will of the Father. She no longer feels the 'sun fall upon her,' that is, she does not suffer from suffering, and the 'Lamb . . . can lead' her 'to the fountains of the water of life,' where He will, as He will, for she looks not at the paths whereon she walks, but only at the Shepherd who guides her.

" God, bending down towards this soul, His adopted daughter, who so closely resembles His Son, the First Born of every creature, recognizes it as one whom He has predestinated, called, justified; and His Fatherly heart thrills at the thought of perfecting His work, that is, of glorifying the soul by transferring it to His Kingdom, there to sing through endless ages 'the praise of His glory.'" [25]

6. Faithful to the ruling thought of these last days—to begin to accomplish in this life, her eternal vocation of *Laudem Gloriae*—Sister Elizabeth sought to fulfill " in the heaven of her soul " the activity of the blessed " in the heaven of glory." This state of soul is the supreme development of her interior vocation of *House of God*. Her fundamental grace was to live in recollection, with her interior Guest in the depths of her soul. There she had found her heaven on earth. By a normal process of evolution, she was likewise to live her final vocation of " Praise of Glory " within herself. " Since my soul is a heaven wherein I dwell while awaiting the heavenly Jerusalem, this heaven, too, must sing the glory of the Eternal, nothing but the glory of the Eternal." [26]

In this inner heaven, all interior activities, the whole exercise of love and the practice of the virtues, is a " Praise of Glory " to the God Who dwells therein, as the external works of God proclaim the glory of the Eternal. This divine glorification in the silence of the soul is the creature's highest praise of God.

"' *Cacli ennarant gloriam Dei.*' This is what the heavens show forth: ' the glory of God.' ' Day to day uttereth speech.' All the light, the communications from God to my soul, are this ' day ' which ' uttereth speech ' of His glory to the next.

[25] *Last Retreat*, 5th day.   [26] *Ibid.*, 7th day.

' The commandment of the Lord is lightsome,' says the Psalmist,' enlightening the eyes.' Consequently, my fidelity to all His commandments and interior promptings causes me to live in the light; it is also the ' speech ' which ' uttereth ' His glory.

"But what a sweet mystery! ' Lord, He Who looks upon Thee doth shine,' cries the prophet. The soul which, by its far-seeing inner gaze, contemplates God through all with a simplicity that separates it from all else, ' shines '; it is a day that ' uttereth speech ' of His glory ' today.' " [27]

In the interior heaven, everything sings the glory of the Eternal; spiritual joys and consolations, as well as all spiritual crucifixions. " ' Night to night showeth knowledge.' How consoling this is! My helplessness, my repugnances, my ignorance, *my very faults* themselves declare the glory of the Eternal! And sufferings of body and soul ' show forth the glory of God! '

" David sang: ' What shall I render to the Lord, for all the things that He hath rendered to me? I will take the chalice of salvation.' If I take this chalice crimsoned with the Blood of My Master, and in joyous thanksgiving mingle my own blood with that of the sacred Victim, Who gives it a share of His own infinity, it may bring wonderful glory to the Father. Then my suffering is a ' speech ' which transmits the glory of the Eternal.

" There (in the souls which ' show forth His glory '), ' He hath set His tabernacle in the sun.' The ' sun ' is the Word—the Bridegroom. If He finds my soul empty of all that is not included in the two words—His love, His glory—He chooses it, for His ' bridal chamber.' He enters it impetuously ' rejoicing as a giant to run the way ' so that I cannot hide myself from His heat. This is the ' consuming fire ' which will work that blessed transformation spoken of by St. John of the Cross, when he said: ' Each of them seems to be the other, and they are both but one '—a ' Praise of Glory ' to the Father." [28]

7. By a very curious change of perspective, which is easily explained by the concrete unity of Sister Elizabeth's religious psychology during the last days of her life, although the last retreat of *Laudem Gloriae* ends by a movement of her soul

---

[27] *Ibid.* [28] *Ibid.*

referring to the indwelling of the Trinity, her short treatise composed for her sister's use in order to show the latter how to find her " heaven on earth " ends, on the contrary, with one that sums up the whole vocation of a " Praise of Glory."

This passage, which is less well known than her prayer, is highly deserving of our attention. Moved by an irresistible grace, at the end of her life Sister Elizabeth reveals to us her supreme ideal of sanctity. Returning to the text of St. Paul to the Ephesians, which had so strongly impressed her and which is, indeed, the classic passage of theology on the final meaning of our predestination in Christ, her artist's soul chants its last office here below with a strongly accented rhythm. Nothing can be added to this compact, doctrinal passage, which is, as it were, her heart's last testament, not only to her sister but to all souls that, following her example, desire to realize the vocation of a " Praise of Glory."

" We have been ' predestinated according to the purpose of Him Who worketh all things according to the counsel of His will, that we may be unto the praise of His glory.' It is St. Paul who speaks thus—St. Paul, inspired by God Himself. How can we fulfill this great dream of the heart of our God, this immutable desire regarding our souls—in a word, how can we respond to our vocation and become perfect ' Praises of glory ' of the Most Blessed Trinity? In heaven, every soul is a praise of the glory of the Father, the Word and the Holy Ghost, because each soul is established in pure love and lives no longer its own life but the life of God. Then, St. Paul says, it knows Him as it is known by Him." [29]

In other words: " A ' Praise of Glory ' is a soul that dwells in God, that loves Him with the disinterested love, which does not seek self in the sweetness of this love; a soul that loves Him above all His gifts, which would have loved Him as much had it received nothing from Him and which desires good for the object of its love. Now how can we actually wish and will good to God, except by accomplishing His will, since this Will ordains all things for His greater glory? Such a soul should surrender

---

[29] *Heaven on Earth*, 13th prayer.

itself fully, blindly to this will, so that it cannot possibly will anything but what God wills.

"A 'Praise of Glory' is a silent soul, a lyre beneath the touch of the Holy Ghost, from which He can draw divine harmonies. Knowing that suffering is a string which produces still more exquisite tones, this soul rejoices at having it on its instrument that it may thus more sweetly move the heart of its God.

"A 'Praise of Glory' is a soul that contemplates God in faith and in simplicity; it reflects all that He is and is a fathomless abyss into which He can flow and outpour Himself. It is a crystal through which He can shine and view His own perfections and splendor. A soul which thus permits the Divine Being to satisfy within it His craving, to communicate all He is and has, is truly the 'Praise of Glory' of all His gifts.

"Finally, a 'Praise of Glory' is one who is always giving thanks; whose acts, movements, thoughts, aspirations, while more deeply establishing her in love, are like an echo of the eternal *Sanctus*.

"In the heaven of glory, the blessed rest not day or night saying 'Holy, Holy, Holy, Lord God Almighty . . . and falling down adore Him that liveth forever and ever.'

"In the heaven of her soul, the 'Praise of Glory' begins now the task which will be hers for all eternity. Her chant is uninterrupted, for she is under the influence of the Holy Ghost, Who effects all her actions and, although fixed on God without distractions, she sings and adores perpetually and has, so to speak, become absorbed in praise and love, in her passion for the glory of her God.

"Let us, in the heaven of our soul, be a 'Praise of Glory' to the Holy Trinity and a praise of love of our Immaculate Mother. One day the veil will be withdrawn and we shall be brought into the eternal courts; there we shall sing in the bosom of Infinite Love, and God will give us 'the new name' promised to him that overcometh. What will that name be? *Laudem Gloriae*." [30]

---

[30] *Ibid.*

Chapter V

CONFORMITY TO CHRIST

'May I be another humanity added to His own.'

1. Our predestination in Christ. 2. The intimate presence of Jesus. 3. Devotion to the Soul of Christ. 4. To be identified with every movement of the soul of Christ. 5. To express Christ in the sight of the Father. 6. To be 'another humanity' to Him. 7. Conformity to His Death.

There is one trait which forms a common bond between the saints of all ages: their conformity to Christ. St. Paul tells us that they "whom God foreknew He also predestinated to be made conformable to the image of His Son."[1] According to the traditional expression, the Christian is another Christ: *Christianus alter Christus*.

This grace of being made like unto Christ is by its essence multiform. There are people who strikingly reproduce some particular feature of the life of Jesus: His silence at Nazareth or the power of His word over the multitudes and His dominion over souls; others, like Jeremias, portray the suffering Messias or, like Job, the ignominy of His Passion and His abandonment by "His own"; still others exhibit His humility, His patience, His contempt of riches, His life of adoration and reparation, His love of His Father, the light of His teaching, His prudence as Supreme Head of the Church, or the strength of His martyrdom on the Cross. The best-beloved imitate their Master's absolute detachment: "They are virgins; these follow the Lamb whithersoever He goeth."[2] The sanctity of Christ is, in a sense, infinite. In Himself, Jesus offers us a model of all the virtues, and God could multiply saints on earth indefinitely without

---

[1] *Rom.* VIII, 29.   [2] *Apoc.* XIV, 4.

101

ever exhausting the "incomprehensible riches"[3] of the supreme grace of Christ, the model of our own.

Hence, it is not surprising to find in Sister Elizabeth this living resemblance to her Master. "'I live, now not I, but Christ liveth in me!' That is the dream of my Carmelite soul."[4]

This transformation into Christ, which began at Baptism, continued ceaselessly during every stage of her life. As she wrote in her diary: "I want to make Him loved by the whole world. . . ."[5] "I love till I could die of love . . ."[6] The most worldly gatherings could not draw her away from the invisible presence of her Lord. When she became a Carmelite, she passionately pressed to her heart her profession crucifix, on which was engraven the motto: *Jam non ego, vivit vero in me Christus.* Christ is the center of her sublime prayer to the Trinity, in which the whole impulse of her spiritual life is expressed in one loving outburst: "O my Christ, Whom I adore, fain would I be the bride of Thy Heart . . . fain would I love Thee . . . until I die of very love! On her sickbed she had but one desire: "To die transformed into Jesus Crucified."

Her devotion to Christ holds the central place in her doctrine as in her life. From what sources did she draw it?

During a conventual retreat, given in October 1902, Father Vallée had explained with vigor and in the spirit of lofty contemplation, the great principles of Thomist Christology. He had particularly stressed the actual nature of the Incarnate Word, and His essential character of Savior; the grace which belongs to Christ as our Head; His knowledge, His love, His prayer, etc. Although she received little interior consolation from it, this retreat opened to Sister Elizabeth immense horizons on the mystery of Christ, and her life immediately showed the effect. "We have had such a beautiful retreat, a profound and divine retreat. Father Vallée spoke the whole time about our Lord. I wish you could have been beside me so that your soul might have been borne away with mine. Through every-

---

[3] *Eph.* III, 8.
[4] Letter to the Abbé Ch., November 23, 1904.
[5] *Diary*, January 30, 1899.　　[6] *Diary*, March 1899.

thing, let us always remain in communion with this Incarnate Word, this Jesus Who dwells within us and desires to tell us all His mystery. On the eve of His Passion, speaking of ' His Own,' He said to His Father: ' The words which Thou gavest Me, I have given to them . . . and the glory which Thou hast given Me, I have given to them.' [7] He is ever living in our souls and ever at work there. Let us allow ourselves to be built up by Him. May He be the soul of our soul, the life of our life, so that we may be able to say with St. Paul: ' For to me to live is Christ.' [8] He does not want us to be sad at the sight of whatever we have not done wholly for Him. ' He is our Savior; it is His mission to forgive.' And Father told us in retreat: ' In Christ's Heart there is but one action; to blot out our sins and to lead our soul to God.' " [9]

Particularly in St. Paul's Epistles did Sister Elizabeth find light for her soul. She went to them " to drink of Christ," as St. Ambrose says. Elizabeth could not have gone to a better school. The Doctor of the Gentiles had received from God the mission of showing the world the riches of Christ, and the treasures of knowledge and divine wisdom hidden in Christ. ' *Cor Pauli, Cor Christi.*' [10] Paul had the Heart of Christ. The formulae of faith which he gave to the first Christians are an epitome of the whole teaching of the Church on the mystery of Christ.

Sister Elizabeth of the Trinity, whose artistic temperament was extremely free in its inspiration, was averse to everything savoring of a rigid method, yet she arranged a regular system for studying her dear St. Paul. Her well-analyzed notes with precise citations refer chiefly to one of the aspects of the mystery of Christ. She frequently had recourse to the Apostle's writings in order to find the basis for the action of her contemplative soul, and she often quoted long passages from St. Paul in their entirety, in her letters or in her two retreats, so closely

[7] *John* XVII, 8, 22.
[8] *Phil.* I, 21.
[9] Letter to Madame A., November 9, 1902.
[10] St. John Chrysostom, *Hom. XXXII in Epis. ad Romanos.* P. L. IX, col. 680.

had her thought become identified with his. Our predestination in Christ and the restoration of everything in the universe through Him; our incorporation in the Son of God, Head of the Mystical Body composed of all the redeemed; the necessity of being identified with every movement of His divine Soul, of expressing Him in the sight of the Father, and of being to Him, as it were, another humanity, in which He may renew His whole mystery of Adorer and Savior—through contact with St. Paul all these great horizons of the theology of the Redemption became familiar to Sister Elizabeth's contemplative thought and gave it that doctrinal breadth which imparts riches and strength to her spiritual writings.

To enumerate all the texts which she used would involve innumerable quotations. We shall simply indicate the broad lines of the mystical doctrine with which they inspired her.

1. Contact with St. Paul gave her doctrine a strongly marked Christocentric character.

Sister Elizabeth took careful note of the fundamental text in the Epistle to the Romans, in which St. Paul developed the whole meaning of our predestination in Christ: "'For whom He foreknew, He also predestinated to be made conformable to the image of His Son . . . and whom He predestinated, them He also called. And whom He called, them He also justified. And whom He justified, them He also glorified.'

"Such is the mystery of predestination, of divine election as the Apostle saw it.

"Those 'whom He foreknew.' Were we not of the number? May not God say to our souls what of old He said by the voice of His prophet: 'And I passed by thee and saw thee; and behold thy time was the time of lovers; and I spread my garment over thee . . . and I swore to thee and I entered into a covenant with thee. And thou becamest mine!' Yes, we have become His by Baptism. That is what St. Paul means by the words: 'Them He *called*.' We are called to receive the seal of the Blessed Trinity. At the same time when, in St. Peter's words, we were 'made partakers of the Divine Nature,' we received " the beginning of His substance.' Then He has *justified* us by His Sacraments, and by direct contact when the soul has been recollected in its innermost depths; ' justified us also by faith ' and according to the measure of our faith in the redemption which Jesus Christ has acquired for us.

" Finally, He wills to *glorify* us and therefore, says St. Paul, ' hath made us worthy to be partakers of the lot of the saints in light.' But we shall be glorified in the measure in which we have been made conformable to the image of His Divine Son.

" Let us contemplate this adored image: let us stay unceasingly within His radiance, that it may sink into us. Then, let us go to everything with the attitude of soul with which our Master approached all things. Then we shall realize the great desire of God Who ' purposed in Him to re-establish all things in Christ.' " [11]

Instead of dwelling upon the providential economy of our redemption in Christ as a speculative theologian would do, Sister Elizabeth of the Trinity leaves aside all purely theoretical exposition and immediately applies the doctrine to her soul, seeking to find in it a " rule of life."

" ' *Instaurare omnia in Christo*.' Again it is St. Paul who teaches me. He, who has just been immersed in the divine counsels, tells me that God ' hath purposed . . . to re-establish all things in Christ.' The Apostle comes to my aid again to help me individually to realize this divine plan and give me a rule of life: ' Walk in Jesus Christ the Lord, rooted and built up in Him and confirmed in the faith . . . abounding in Him in thanksgiving.' " [12]

Each point of this programme furnishes matter for a mystical paraphrase of a practical order. We must not demand an objective exegesis following the rigorous laws of the historical method. Sister Elizabeth of the Trinity read St. Paul as a contemplative seeking in Holy Scripture the ' light of life,' [13] for her soul. When apparently commenting on St. Paul's

[11] *Heaven on Earth*, 9th prayer.
[12] *Last Retreat*, 13th day.
[13] *John* VIII, 12.

expressions, she actually reveals to us the inner core of her own spiritual insight.

Like a true Carmelite, she first insists—and most strongly—upon the complete detachment which must precede divine union.

"'*To walk in Jesus Christ*' appears to me to mean to go out from self, to lose sight of, to forsake self, that we may enter more deeply into Him every moment—enter so profoundly to be *rooted* in Him, that we may boldly challenge all events with the defiant cry: ' Who then shall separate us from the love of Christ? ' When the soul is so deeply fixed in Him as to be *rooted* in Him, the divine sap flows freely through it and destroys whatever in its life was trivial, imperfect, unspiritual. Then, in the Apostle's words, ' that which is mortal ' will be ' swallowed up by life.'

"Thus stripped of self and clothed with Jesus Christ, the spirit has nothing to fear either from external contacts or interior difficulties; all such things, far from being an impediment, only root it more firmly in its love for its Master. Whatever happens, the soul is ready to adore Him for His own sake, being free, liberated from self and all else. It can sing with the Psalmist: ' If armies in camp should stand together against me, my heart shall not fear. If a battle should rise up against me in this will I be confident . . . for He hath hidden me in His tabernacle,' that is, in Himself.

"I think this is the meaning of St. Paul's words, to be ' rooted ' in Jesus Christ.

"Now, what is it to be ' built up ' in Him? The prophet continues: ' He hath exalted me upon a rock: and now He hath lifted up my soul above my enemies.' Is that not a figure of the soul ' built up ' in Jesus Christ? He is that rock on which it is exalted above self, the senses, and nature; above consolations or sufferings; above all that is not *Him* alone! There, with perfect self-mastery, it controls self, rising above self and all else.

"St. Paul also counsels me to be ' *confirmed in the faith*,' in the faith which never permits the soul to slumber but keeps it watchful under the eye of its Master, listening in perfect recollection to His creative word; in its faith in the 'exceeding charity' which, St. Paul tells us, allows God to fill the soul 'unto all the fullness of God.'

"Finally, the Apostle desires me to 'abound in Jesus Christ in thanksgiving,' for everything should end in thanksgiving. 'Father, I give Thee thanks,' was the song of Christ's soul, and He wishes to hear it echoed in mine." [14]

2. While for the majority of Christians Christ is an historical person Who departed from this world twenty centuries ago, or an abstract entity dwelling far off in the highest heaven in an inaccessible eternity, for Sister Elizabeth of the Trinity, as for all saints, Jesus is a concrete everyday reality associated with the smallest details of existence. In short, He is the supreme reality. His invisible but immediate presence is always with the saints. They are constantly conscious of the fact that this Jesus is close beside them—Jesus, the son of God and of Mary—giving them His grace, enlightening and upholding them, reproving them, if need be, saving them, and giving them eternal life.

To understand this doctrine of the intimate presence of Jesus in the life of the saints, we must remember that, as the Word, Christ is everywhere present, equally with the Father and the Holy Ghost. The Trinity is indivisible. With the Father and the Holy Ghost, the Word fills time and space; there is not an atom of the universe that is not penetrated with His divine presence. Were He to withdraw Himself all creation would fall back into nothingness.

As the Word Incarnate He is present in dazzling glory in heaven, filling the blessed with joy by the beauty of His Face as Christ, and in the Blessed Sacrament He is present in His veiled Humanity. "But He Whom the elect contemplate in the Vision, and with Whom the souls on earth have communion by faith, is one and the same." [15] He is the life of both, imparting to the multitude of the predestined the light of glory which

[14] *Last Retreat*, 13th day.   [15] Letter to her aunts ·R., 1903.

beatifies them, and giving Himself to the Church militant by faith and by the sacraments. Day and night virtue goes out of Him,[16] sanctifying the elect, and contact with Him is constantly divinizing the souls of the saints. The Humanity of Christ, the " organ of the Word " and the universal instrument of all graces which descend into souls from the Trinity, brings to all grace, light, strength, and those charismata of all kinds which the Church must have to fulfill her mission on earth. In the supernatural order, we have being, movement, and life in Christ; without Him we have nothing. " Sine me; nihil." [17]

Catholic theology has strongly emphasized this concept in a doctrine of major importance in the economy of our spiritual life: the grace of Christ as Head of the Mystical Body. The Trinitarian life of our Baptism develops in us only " in Christ Jesus: *In Christo Jesu*." [18]

The activity of Sister Elizabeth's soul was based on this doctrine. She loved to seek constant refuge in the grace of that Christ Who dwelt in her in the center of her soul. " I feel that He is giving me eternal life." [19] She had formed the habit of going to everything " in Him," beseeching Him to clothe her with His divine purity, to make her truly " virginal," to lift her soul above all the stress of earth and to maintain her in calm and peace as though she already dwelt in eternity.

" Let us stay in recollection close to *Him Who is*, close to the Unchangeable, Whose love is ever over us. We are ' she who is not.' Let us go to Him Who would have us be wholly His, and Who envelops us so completely that we no longer live, but He lives in us." [20] " It is so sweet and so gentle, that divine presence of the Master; it gives such strength to the soul. To believe that God loves us to the extent of dwelling in us, of becoming the companion of our exile, the confidant, the friend of every moment is the intimacy of the child with its mother, of the wife with her husband. That is the life of the Carmelite:

[16] *Luke* VI, 19.
[17] *John* XV, 5.
[18] *Eph.* I, 3; frequently elsewhere in St. Paul.
[19] To her Prioress. [20] Letter to M. G., 1901.

union, the brilliant sun, under which she sees infinite horizons open out." [21]

This intimate communion with Christ in the center of the soul had become the central point on which her faith and charity, her life of prayer and adoration, converged. " ' Abide in Me.' This command is given, this desire expressed by the Word of God. ' Abide in Me '; not for a few moments, a few passing hours, but *abide* permanently, habitually. Abide in Me, pray in Me, adore in Me, love in Me, suffer in Me, work in Me, act in Me. Abide in Me whatever the person or action you are concerned with." [22]

A favorite attitude of hers was to recollect herself before this " exceeding charity " [23] of Christ, and to allow Him to pour Himself into her. " St. Paul says that we ' are no more strangers and foreigners but fellow citizens with the saints and the domestics of God.' [24] We already live in the supernatural world by faith. His love, His ' exceeding charity,' to quote the great Apostle again—there you have my vision on earth. Shall we ever understand how greatly we are loved? To me, that seems to be truly the knowledge of the saints. In his magnificent Epistles, the sole theme of St. Paul's preaching is this mystery of the charity of Christ. That ' the Father of our Lord Jesus Christ . . . would grant you, according to the riches of His glory to be strengthened by His spirit with might unto the inward man. That Christ may dwell by faith in your hearts: that being rooted and founded in charity, you may be able to comprehend, with all the saints, what is the breadth, and length, and height, and depth. To know also the charity of Christ which surpasseth all knowledge, that you may be filled unto all the fullness of God.' [25] Since our Lord dwells in our souls, His prayer is ours. I wish to share in it constantly, to keep myself as a little jug at the spring, at the fountain of life, in order that I may be able subsequently to give Him to souls, by permitting the waters of His charity to overflow." [26]

[21] Letter to G. de G., 1903.
[22] *Heaven on Earth*, 2nd prayer.
[23] *Eph.* II, 4.
[24] *Eph.* II, 19.
[25] *Eph.* III, 14-19.
[26] Letter to the Abbé Ch., Dec. 25, 1904.

The passages written by Sister Elizabeth on this presence of Jesus within us are so strongly expressed that, were we to take them too literally, we should have to conclude that she is thinking of a real, material indwelling of Jesus within us. She herself puts her mother on guard against such an exaggeration: " You only possess the Sacred Humanity when you receive Holy Communion; but the Divinity, that Essence which the blessed adore in heaven, that is in your soul." [27]

Having made this reservation, she freely yields to the longings of her soul, which always lead her back to its center, there to live in closest fellowship with the Master and to let Him save her. " He is in us in order to sanctify us. So let us ask Him to be Himself our sanctity. When our Lord was on earth, we are told in the Gospel, ' virtue went out from Him.' [28] At His touch, the sick recovered their health, the dead were restored to life. Now He is ever living—in His adorable Sacrament. And in our souls. He it is Who has said: ' If any man love Me, he will keep My word, and My Father will love him; and We will come to him and make Our abode with him.' [29] Since He is there, let us keep Him company as friend with friend. It is this divinely intimate union which is, as it were, the essence of the life at Carmel." [30]

" Deep within itself the soul possesses a Savior Who comes to purify it at every moment." [31] " The divine Adorer is within us. Therefore we have His prayer. Let us offer it. Let us share in it, pray with His soul." [32]

3. What is really characteristic of Sister Elizabeth is her distinctly personal devotion to the soul of Christ.

Others are drawn to honor our Lord in some particular mystery, to venerate one particular part of His sacred body. Elizabeth's interior devotion goes straight to the soul of Christ, the masterpiece of the Trinity.

---

[27] Letter to her mother, June 1906.
[28] *Luke* VI, 19.
[29] *John* XIV, 23.
[30] Letter to Madame A., November 24, 1904.
[31] To the same, November 24, 1905. [32] Letter to G. de G., September 1903.

Because of His personal union with the Word of God, everything about Christ is most worthy of adoration, both in Himself and in each of His mysteries. After the hypostatic union what is noblest in the Incarnate Word is the soul of Jesus. The combined activity of the angels and saints does not equal the smallest act of virtue of the soul of Christ, clothed as it is in a fullness of grace which is, in a manner, infinite and which renders it worthy of the uncreated Person of the Incarnate Word. In it the Trinity is well pleased. The soul of Christ contains depths of light, love, and divine beauty, the intuitive contemplation of which will constitute the greatest joy of eternity after the vision of God. Was it not because of this that, in the presence of His disciples, Jesus said: " Now this is eternal life. That they may know Thee, the only true God, and Jesus Christ Whom Thou hast sent? " [33]

4. Sister Elizabeth of the Trinity could understand how utterly we possess Christ. " I feel that all the treasures of the soul of Christ are mine." [34] She wrote that her favorite book, as a Carmelite, was the soul of Christ. [35]

The first evening after she entered the Carmel, Mother Germaine found her silent and recollected beside the great crucifix that stands in the garden.

" What are you doing here, my child? " asked the Prioress. And Sister Elizabeth answered: " I have passed into the soul of my Christ." [36]

She chose as a watchword for her religious life: " To be identified with every movement of the soul of Christ."

As her spiritual life developed, this identification with the most interior motions of the soul of her Master became impressively real. All the efforts of her interior life resolved themselves into one: " to enter into the movement of His divine Soul," [37] and allow herself to be borne away with Christ into the bosom of the Father.

[33] *John* XVII, 3.   [34] Letter to Canon A., Sept. 11, 1901.
[35] Questionnaire filled out by her a week after she entered Carmel.
[36] This incident was related by Mother Germaine herself.
[37] Letter to Madame A., September 29, 1902.

In her prayer to the Holy Trinity, to which we must be constantly returning in order to grasp the secret movement of her spiritual life, the outstanding features of this devotion to the soul of Christ are clearly evident. It is a splendid summary of her whole teaching upon this point: " O my Christ, Whom I love, crucified by love . . . I beseech Thee to clothe me with Thyself, to identify my soul with all the movements of Thine own. Immerse me in Thyself; possess me wholly; substitute Thyself for me, that my life may be but a radiance of Thine own."

5. One excellent effect of this devotion was to identify Sister Elizabeth with Our Lord's most inward feelings towards His Father.

As theologians know, the soul of Christ was constantly day and night possessed by a twofold yearning: for the redemption of the world and for the glory of His Father. In the last analysis, He became incarnate only for this; to save souls and, after having cleansed them from their sins in His blood, to make them adorers of the Trinity.

This primary concern for His Father's glory is strikingly revealed in the smallest acts and gestures of the life of Jesus. His first thought on entering the world is for His Father: " Sacrifice and oblation of men, Thou didst not desire. . . . Behold I come " to be immolated to Thy Glory.[38] Only one incident from the childhood and hidden life of our Lord has been preserved for us: the finding of Him in the temple, and His reply to His Mother: " Did you not know that I must be about My Father's business? " [39] This single sentence, enfolded in thirty years of silence, illuminates the whole mystery of Jesus, with a lingering flash. Like Mary, we must know that the Son came *in the first place* for His Father's glory. The pronouncements of His public life leave us in no doubt on that head. Equal to His Father as God—" I and the Father are One " [40]—as Man, He shows submission and reverence for Him in His every act. " I do always the things that please Him." [41]

---

[38] *Ps.* XXXIX, 7-8.　　[39] *Luke* II, 49.　　[40] *John* X, 30.　　[41] *John* VIII, 29.

If we take the scene with the Samaritan woman as an example and analyze it carefully, we shall see that the culminating point of this episode, which changed the religious history of the human race, appears in that secret desire of the heart of Christ: to find " adorers in spirit and truth. For the Father also seeketh such "—" *Pater quaerit.*" [42]

But we could quote the whole Gospel of St. John, and especially the prayer of Christ the High Priest, which is the supreme revelation of His Heart and in which the Church will find food for her contemplative life until the end of time. In it the Master glances back over His life, then sums it all up in the two words: " *Glorificavi Te.* I have glorified Thee." [43] When dying, it is to His Father, that Jesus crucified addressed His last words.[44] He has scarcely risen again before He is speaking of " My Father, and your Father, My God and your God." [45] St. Paul shows Him to us dwelling in eternity, " always living to make intercession for us " [46] before His Father's face, until " the end when He shall have delivered up the kingdom to God and the Father," [47]—His final action at the end of time.

Sister Elizabeth of the Trinity had an exceptional awareness of the primary place that the thought of the glory of the Father held in the soul of Christ, Who was the " most perfect Praise of Glory of the Father " and of the Trinity. She left only a few writings on the subject, but they are explicit and wholly in accord with the highest development of her thought. " In that beautiful discourse after the Last Supper, which is, as it were, a last love song of the soul of our divine Master, He addresses these beautiful words to the Father: ' I have glorified Thee on earth, I have finished the work which Thou gavest Me to do.' [48] We who belong to Him as His brides and who ought, therefore, to be completely identified with Him, should, so it seems to me, repeat these words at the close of each day. Perhaps you will say to me: ' How are we to glorify Him? ' It is

[42] *John* IV, 23.
[43] *John* XVII, 4.
[44] *Luke* XXIII, 46.
[45] *John* XX, 17.
[46] *Heb.* VII, 25.
[47] *I Cor.* XV, 24
[48] *John* XVII, 4.

very simple. Our Lord revealed the secret to us when He said: 'My meat is to do the will of Him that sent Me.' " [49]

Thus, while in her interior life Sister Elizabeth was endeavoring to "be identified" with each movement of the soul of Christ, a mysterious transformation took place. The "*mihi autem vivere Christus est*" [50] of St. Paul was realized in her and gave her a motto which well expresses the special character of her devotion to the Son of God: "To show Christ forth in the sight of the Father." This is the highest ideal of the Christian.

" 'I count all things to be but loss, for the excellent knowledge of Jesus Christ, my Lord: for whom I have suffered the loss of all things and count them but as dung, that I may gain Christ: and may be found in Him, not having my justice . . . but that . . . which is of God, justice in faith that I may know Him . . . and the fellowship of His sufferings, being made conformable to His death . . . I follow after, if I may by any means apprehend wherein I am also apprehended by Christ Jesus . . . One thing I do is forgetting the things that are behind and stretching forth myself to those that are before, I press toward the mark, to the prize of the supernal vocation of God in Christ Jesus.' The Apostle has often revealed the grandeur of this vocation: God, ' chose us in Him before the foundation of the world that we should be holy and unspotted in His sight in charity.' 'We . . . being predestinated according to the purpose of Him Who worketh all things according to the counsel of His will, that we may be unto the praise of His glory.' How are we to respond to the dignity of our vocation? This is the secret: ' *Mihi autem vivere Christus est! Vivo enim, jam non ego, vivit vero in me Christus.*' We must be transformed into Jesus Christ. It is still St. Paul who teaches me. ' Those whom God foreknew He also predestinated to be made conformable to the image of His Son.'

" Hence I must study this divine model, so thoroughly identi-

---

[49] Letter to Madame A., 1906; *John* IV, 34.
[50] *Phil.* I, 21.

fying myself with Him that I can incessantly show Him forth in the sight of His Father.

"To begin with, what were His first words on entering the world? 'Behold I come to Thy will, O God.' To me, it seems that this prayer should be like the heart-beat of the bride: Behold, we come, Father, to do Thy will. This first oblation of the divine Master was a real one; His life was but its consequence. He delighted in saying: 'My meat is to do the will of Him that sent Me.' That should be the meat of the bride, and, at the same time, the sword that immolates her: 'My Father, if it be possible let this chalice pass from Me. Nevertheless, not as I will but as Thou wilt.' Then, serenely peaceful, she goes to meet all sacrifices with her Master; rejoicing at having been known by the Father since He crucified her with His Son. 'I have purchased thy testimonies for an inheritance forever: because they are the joy of my heart.' That is the song in the Master's soul, and it should have a perfect echo in His bride's. By constant fidelity to these 'testimonies'—both in thought and in act—she will bear witness to the truth and will be able to say: 'He that sent Me is with Me and He hath not left Me alone. For I do always the things that please Him.' By never leaving Him, by keeping in close contact with Him, the secret *virtue* will go forth from her which delivers and saves souls. Detached, freed from self and all things, she will follow her Master to the mountain, to join with His soul in 'the prayer of God.'

"Then, still through the Divine adorer—through Him Who was the perfect 'Praise of Glory' of the Father,—she will offer the sacrifice of praise always to God, that is to say, the fruit of lips confessing to His Name. And she 'shall speak of the might of Thy terrible acts and shall declare Thy greatness.' In the hour of humiliation, of failure, she will remember the short sentence: '*Jesus autem tacebat*,' and she, too, will be silent, keeping all her strength for the Lord—the strength we draw from silence. When she is abandoned, forsaken, and in such anguish as drew from Christ the loud cry: 'Why hast Thou forsaken me?' she will be mindful of that prayer: 'That they may have

My joy filled in themselves.' And drinking to the very dregs the chalice given by the Father, she will find a heavenly sweetness in its bitterness. Then, after having repeated again and again: 'I thirst'—thirst to possess Thee in glory—she will sing: 'It is consummated . . . Into thy hands I commend my spirit.' Then the Father will come to take her into His heritage where 'in Thy light we shall see light.' 'Know ye also that the Lord hath made his holy one wonderful,' sang David. Yes, in the case of such a soul God's Holy One is made wonderful indeed, for He has destroyed all else to clothe it with Himself, and it has conformed its life to the words of the Precursor: 'He must increase, but I must decrease.' "[51]

"I find my soul's joy (in will, not in emotion) in all that sacrifices, destroys, abases self that I may give place to my divine Master: 'I live, now not I: Christ liveth in me.' I desire to live my own life no longer but to be transformed into Christ, so that my life may be rather divine than human and that the Father bending over me may recognize the image of His Beloved Son, in Whom He set all His pleasure."[52]

"Let us be Christ Himself, and go to the Father in the movement of His divine soul."[53]

6. A second motive animated Christ's soul, day and night: the longing for our redemption.

Whether He walked alone and thoughtful along the roads of Palestine, or whether the crowds of Jerusalem pressed upon Him on every side, Jesus was always alone with the Father, and busied about our salvation. Never for an instant did He take from us that gaze which, because it was the gaze of the Christ, saw everything: heaven, hell, the destinies of His Church, and of each individual soul, even to the smallest detail. His vision of the world equalled the Trinity's—not in intensity of light but in breadth. Nothing was hidden from Him, in the past, the present or the future. Jesus' knowledge of all these things was effective for our salvation. Equal to His Father by

---

[51] *Last Retreat*, 14th day.
[52] *Heaven on Earth*, 5th prayer.   [53] Letter, Sept. 29, 1902.

His Divine Nature, the God-Man was indeed wholly ours. "One" with His Father, "One" with His brethren: there we have the whole mystery of Jesus. Christ is completed in us.

Christian thought has dwelt lovingly on the analysis of this consideration of "Christ in us," mentioned by St. Paul, the foremost doctor of the Mystical Body of Christ, and we can trace a twofold line of thought.

The speculation of the Greek Fathers delighted in the contemplation of that mysterious unity which binds Christians to one another and to Christ and finds its supreme exemplar in the unity of the Trinity.

Western thought has turned its considerations less to the Trinity than to the suffering members of the Savior. St. Augustine, faithfully echoing St. Paul, has left us an exposition of this idea in unsurpassed and classic passages.

To this latter line of thought we must assign the already famous words in which Sister Elizabeth of the Trinity expressed her very personal conception of her role in the Mystical Body: "To be to Christ another humanity wherein He renews His Mystery."

Two days after she had composed the prayer from which this phrase is taken, she explained her thought more at length: "'*Vivo jam non ego; vivit vero in me Christus.*' There you have my dream as a Carmelite; also, I think, your dream as a priest. Above all, it is our Lord's dream and I beg Him to realize it completely in our souls. Let us be to Him, as it were, another humanity in which He may renew His whole mystery. I have asked Him to take up His abode in me as Adorer, as Restorer and as Savior. I cannot tell you what peace this gives to my soul, to think that He supplies for my insufficiency and that even though I should fall at every moment, He is there to lift me up and carry me further into Himself—into that divine Essence in which we already dwell by grace and in which I long to bury myself so deeply that nothing can ever draw me forth." [54]

[54] Letter to the Abbé Ch., November 23, 1904.

This doctrine of the Mystical Body, by which she lived, carries us far beyond the petty views which sometimes stifle religious in their narrow community life. The wide expanses of the Church's life become her preoccupation: " How we feel the need of sanctifying ourselves, of forgetting self in order to be wholly occupied with the Church's interests! Poor France! How I love to cover her with the blood of the Just One, of Him who ever lives to intercede and beg mercy for us! What a sublime mission the Carmelite has! She ought to be a mediator with Jesus Christ, to be another humanity in which He may perpetuate His life of reparation and sacrifice, of praise and adoration." [55]

One cannot but admire the apostolic fruitfulness of a soul which can thus rise to the habitual vision of the whole Christ. Whoever lives in charity, teaches St. Thomas, enters into communion with all the good that is done in the world.[56] True contemplatives understand these things. St. Teresa of the Child Jesus cherished the dream of working for the spiritual welfare of the Church until the end of the world, and it was the ambition of Sister Elizabeth of the Trinity to " tell every soul " the secret of happiness and sanctity hidden in the depths of themselves by the Divine Indwelling.

A true Carmelite spends herself all day in saving souls by means of prayer and silent immolation. Then, when evening comes, before taking her necessary sleep, she flies to the all-powerful intercession of the Co-Redemptrix, and beseeches our Lady to take her place while she sleeps, in her work of intercession for poor sinners, and to continue effectively the destruction of evil in the world.

That is what Sister Elizabeth did, forgetting her own suffering and rising above herself in her one longing to " wear herself out " for love of Christ; to " shed her blood, drop by drop " " for His Body which is the Church." [57] That was what she called " being another humanity to Christ."

[55] Letter to Canon A., January 1906.
[56] *In Symbolum Apostolorum*—" Sanctorum Communionem."
[57] *Col.* I, 24.

7. To be another Christ, but on the Cross: such was Elizabeth's last dream. " For a long time Christ crucified was the subject of her prayer," wrote Father Vallée, who knew her well. Later on, after the great graces concerning the Indwelling of the Trinity, she returned to her crucified Lord, no longer only to contemplate Him, but to imitate His death. " ' *Configuratus morti ejus*.' [58] That is what still haunts me and gives strength to my soul in its suffering. If you knew the sensation of destruction I feel in my whole being! The road to Calvary is opening before me, and I am utterly joyful to walk it as a bride beside my crucified Lord." [59]

To her mother, whose heart was torn at the thought of losing her, she addresses a few words of comfort, reminding her of the redemptive significance of suffering. " It is the Good God who is pleased to immolate His little victim. This Mass that He is saying with me and of which His love is the priest, may last a long time yet, but the time in the hand of Him Who is sacrificing her does not seem long to the little victim. She can say that even if she walks the path of suffering, still she is on the way of happiness, that true happiness which no man can take from her.

" ' I rejoice,' says St. Paul, ' to fill up those things that are wanting of the sufferings of Christ, in my flesh, for His body which is the Church.' [60] Your mother's heart should feel a divine joy when you think that the Master has deigned to choose your daughter, the fruit of your womb, to be associated with His great work of redemption, in order that He may suffer in her, as it were, an extension of His Passion. The bride belongs to the Bridegroom. Mine has taken me. He wishes me to be another humanity in which He can still suffer for His Father's glory, to help the needs of His Church." [61]

" How happy I should be if my Master also desired that I should shed my blood for Him! But what I ask of Him especially is that martyrdom of love which consumed my holy Mother Teresa, whom the Church proclaims ' Victim of divine

[58] *Phil*. III, 10.
[59] Letter to Canon A., July 1906.
[60] *Col*. I, 24.
[61] Letter to her mother, Sept. 10, 1906

love.' And since the Truth has said that the greatest proof of love is to give one's life for the one loved, I give Him mine, that He may do with it as He pleases; if I am not a martyr by blood, I wish to be one for love." [62]

"Rejoice in the thought that from all eternity we have been known of the Father, as St. Paul says, and that He wishes to find in us the image of His crucified Son. If you knew how necessary suffering is in order that God's work may be done in the soul! The good God has an immense desire to enrich us with His graces, but it is we who determine the amount in proportion as we allow ourselves to be immolated by Him— immolated, like the Master, in joy, in thanksgiving, saying with Him: 'The chalice which my Father hath given, shall I not drink it?' [63] He called the hour of His Passion 'His hour,' that for which He had come, that for which He yearned with all His strength. When a great suffering, or a very small sacrifice is offered us, let us think quickly that it is 'our hour,' the hour to prove our love for Him who, as St. Paul says, loved us exceedingly." [64]

Like all the saints, Sister Elizabeth of the Trinity knew the value of suffering and knew that union with God is accomplished only on the Cross. She frequently exults in this blessed suffering, in all the crucifixions of life which imprint on her body and soul the image of the Crucified. "There is something so great, so divine in suffering. It seems to me that if the blessed could be envious of anything, it would be of that treasure. It is such a powerful lever on the heart of God. And then, do you not find it sweet to give to Him Whom you love? The Cross is the heritage of Carmel: 'Either to suffer or to die,' cried St. Teresa; and when our Lord appeared to Our Holy Father St. John of the Cross and asked him what he desired in recompense for all the sufferings that he had endured for His sake, the saint replied: 'Lord, to suffer and be despised for your love.'" [65]

Not that pain left her insensible, but that she was able to draw strength to suffer from the thought of her crucified Master.

---

[62] To the same, July 1906.
[63] *John* XVIII, 11.
[64] Letter to her mother, September 1906.
[65] Letter to Madame A., August 1904.

She has herself told us her secret: "I will tell you what I do when I am a little tired: I look at the Crucified. When I see how He delivered Himself for me, it seems to me that I cannot do less for Him than spend myself, wear myself out, in order to return to Him a little of what He has given to me. In the morning, at holy Mass, let us communicate in His spirit of sacrifice. We are His brides, we ought to resemble Him. If we are faithful in living His life, if we are identified with every movement of the soul of the Crucified, we shall simply have no longer any need to fear our weakness, for He will be our strength; and who can pluck us out of His hand?" [66]

The last eight months of her life were a veritable martyrdom. She delighted to plunge herself into the suffering, dating letters and notes: "From the palace of beatitude and pain." "I am tasting, experiencing joys hitherto unknown; the joy of suffering. BEFORE I DIE, IT IS MY DREAM TO BE TRANSFORMED INTO JESUS CRUCIFIED." [67]

So her last song was a hymn to suffering: a true "Praise of Glory" is a soul that is crucified.

---

[66] To the same, February 1903.
[67] Letter to G. de G., end of October 1906.

Chapter VI

JANUA COELI

1. Our Lady of Carmel. 2. Our Lady of the Incarnation. 3. *Janua Coeli.*

Sister Elizabeth could not fail to give the Mother of God an important place in her life.

Devotion to the Mother of Christ is an essential condition of salvation. All the saints have passionately loved Mary, each according to his special grace. In conformity with his mission, St. Paul marked her place in the economy of Redemption by her part in the mystery of Christ, who was " born of a woman,"[1] to be the Savior of the race fallen in Adam. St. John cherished the memory of Christ's last hour, when Jesus on the Cross left him Mary to be his Mother and the Mother of all the predestined. In his Apocalypse, he has revealed to us how, since her death and Assumption, far from losing interest in us, the blessed Virgin makes use of her presence before the face of the Eternal to watch over us the better, always bending over her children throughout the world, more a Mother than ever. St. Augustine shows us how, by her love, she became Mother of *the whole Christ* at the Incarnation. The Greek Fathers have magnificently sung the praises of the " All Holy "—of her who was the living tabernacle of the Incarnate Word, the most pure temple of the Trinity. For twenty centuries, in the East and in the West, with St. Ephrem, St. Cyril, St. Anselm, St. Bonaventure, St. Thomas—to make the list complete we should have to cite all the doctors and all the saints—the Church has never ceased to proclaim Mary's unique and universal mission in the work of our salvation. Mother of God and of men, Mary

---

[1] *Gal.* IV, 4.

fulfills the divine plan through her motherly care for our welfare. There is not one single movement in the whole scheme of the Redemption in which Mary does not have a part, after Jesus and with Him. "Such is the unchangeable will of Him Who has willed that we should have everything through Mary." [2]

The individual characteristics of each saint are retained in his devotion to Mary.

At the sight of the greatness of the Virgin Mother, the ardent soul of St. Bernard, the harpist of Mary, is ever singing, *De Maria nunquam satis*. St. Thomas fixes a theologian's gaze on the divine motherhood, the keystone of all Mary's grandeur. He sees the Mother of the Word reaching to the confines of the Divinity through that motherhood: sharing one and the same Son with the Eternal Father.

We must not reduce Sister Elizabeth's devotion to Our Lady to the too determined form of servitude, as conceived, for example, by the Blessed Grignon de Montfort. We do not even know whether she had read that masterpiece of Marian literature, the *Treatise on True Devotion to the Blessed Virgin*. She goes to our Lady with all her contemplative's devotion and finds in her the perfect realization of her interior ideal. She is especially attracted to Our Lady of the Incarnation, as she adored the Word hidden in her womb, or as she walked the mountain roads to Judea in calm majesty, in such communion with the Word Who dwelt within her that nothing outside could distract her from her inner vision. The aspect of our Lady which Sister Elizabeth most loved was that of her silence and recollection.

It was not always so. For a long time, her piety towards the Blessed Virgin resembled that of many young girls whose spiritual physiognomy does not show any marked characteristics. She went to Our Lady as the guardian of her purity, and on each of her feasts, she renewed her vow of virginity. She turned to Mary in all her needs, much in a way that a child turns to

[2] S. Bernard *Sermo de Nativitate B. V. M.*

its mother as by instinct for protection; and in times of difficulty, she implored her help for her future or for her vocation. For three days she knelt at the feet of Our Lady of Lourdes, begging her to watch over her and offering herself by her hands as a victim for sinners. We may be sure that Elizabeth Catez never left the house to go to a social gathering without first going to the Blessed Virgin to ask her blessing. Mary always hears the prayers of the pure of heart. Her special grace is to form virgin souls like her own, to keep them like herself holy and unspotted in love in the sight of God. To her special protection Elizabeth must have owed the purity of her life.

Her girlhood diary is full of thoughts on Mary. On every occasion, happy or otherwise, she turned to her, beseeching her to intervene in matters which almost make us smile, but the saints see things more clearly than we. One day, after she had been praised and yielded to vanity over it, she asked Our Lady to prevent her going to a children's matinee; the evening before the performance, she developed such a violent earache that she was unable to attend it. At the age of fourteen, accompanied by a little friend, she went on a pilgrimage to the Burgundian sanctuary of Notre Dame d'Etang to obtain the favor of dying young; she departed from this world at the age of twenty-six. And all this without counting prayers and novenas every time she wished to secure some fresh grace. In her girlhood days, Our Lady had place in everything. Let us take some entries from her diary at random:

February 2nd, 1899. " Feast of the Purification. On each feast of Our Lady, I renew my consecration to this good Mother. So today, I have entrusted myself to her and thrown myself into her arms with the most perfect confidence. I have recommended to her my future and my vocation."

March 12th, 1899. " My good Master, I shall die of grief unless You give me this soul. I implore You to give it to me, I do not care at what price of suffering. Mary, Our Lady of Lourdes, Our Lady of Perpetual Help, come to my aid; unless you work a miracle, all is lost. I am counting upon this miracle."

March 24th, 1899. "O Mary, you to whom I pray daily to obtain humility, help me, crush my pride, send me many humiliations, dear Mother."

April 2nd, 1899. "It is all over. How quickly this mission has passed. Before leaving the church, I have entrusted my poor sinner to Our Lady of Perpetual Help; I have promised to invoke her every day for that poor soul. After that, I again consecrated myself to Mary. I have abandoned myself to her with perfect confidence. She has indeed heard my prayers for my vocation. I shall never be able to express sufficiently my love and my gratitude to her. I am so happy that my heart is overflowing with joy; I am revelling in my happiness in advance. O Mother of Perpetual Help, I shall invoke you daily for these two intentions: that you will continue to support my dear Mother, who now understands me so well, and then, that you will support me also, in this way of the Cross upon which I am setting out so happily in the footsteps of Jesus. Mother, obtain for me perseverance, so as to become wholly perfect. Keep my heart pure."

1. As a Carmelite, her piety towards our Blessed Lady developed rapidly into a life of deep intimacy. Because of a normal psychological development which must be noted, in all the saints, the general traits of their spiritual physiognomy will be seen in their devotion to Mary. Thus, Sister Elizabeth of the Trinity who, on her first day in Carmel had wholly "passed into the soul of her Christ," as a result of the same psychological reflexes fastened her contemplative's gaze upon the soul of Mary. Only a few days after she had entered the convent, she wrote to her mother: "I have placed your soul in that of the Mother of Sorrows, and I have asked her to comfort you. At the end of the cloister, we have a statue of the *Mater Dolorosa*, to which I have great devotion. Every evening, I go and talk to her about you. I so love Our Lady's tears."

Carmel is above all Our Lady's Order. "The souls whom God calls to serve Him in our Order must know that their primary and principal obligation as Carmelites is to honor the

Most Holy Virgin Mary with special devotion: first, in her supreme dignity as Mother of God, in all the privileges and grandeurs which this dignity involves, and in the sovereignty which it gives to her in heaven and on earth; second, in the extreme loving-kindness and humility which led this Most Holy Virgin to become the Mother and Patroness of this Order.

"In order to fulfill this duty, each one shall receive Holy Communion at least once a month in honor of the Most Holy Virgin, for the accomplishment of her designs on earth, for the increase of her honor in all souls, and to obtain from her that the members of this Order may love, honor, and serve her, and belong to her in all fullness, according to the merciful designs of her Divine Son and herself." [3]

The reader will have noticed the singular nobility of this devotion to Mary. The Carmelite goes straight to the Mother of God in order to rejoice with her in that Divine Motherhood which explains everything in Mary: privileges, honors, universal sovereignty.

This is the normal attitude of the Carmelite: first and always *God*. There is no need to add "God alone," that goes without saying. The Carmelite's soul takes its stand before the mystery in a light that is wholly divine and radically excludes every other light. Like the Sacred Humanity of Christ and everything else created, she sees the Blessed Virgin only in relation to God. Not until the second glance, as she comes down from "the supreme dignity of Mother of God," does the Carmelite penetrate into that motherhood of grace, "the extreme loving-kindness and humility which led the Most Blessed Virgin to become the Mother and Patroness of her Order." Moreover, the Carmelite must not stop there but, according to the apostolic vocation of the Order, she must pray and sacrifice herself "for the fulfillment of her designs on earth, for the increase of her honor in all souls, and to obtain from her that the members of this Order may love, honor, and serve her, according to the fullness of the merciful designs of her Divine Son."

---

[3] *Papier d'exaction* (Custom Book brought to France, by the Spanish Mothers).

It would be impossible to overemphasize the benefit which Sister Elizabeth of the Trinity received from this well-balanced devotion inculcated in the members of the great religious Orders during the course of their training. A long tradition of sanctity, a word heard during a commentary on the Rule and Constitutions, a daily readjustment brought about by the simple interplay of the common life, which puts everything in its right place, and faithful souls become ever more saturated with the pure spirit of their Order and advance rapidly towards perfection. In the case of Sister Elizabeth of the Trinity, this is particularly evident in the development of her attitude towards Our Lady.

Once she had entered religion, her piety in that respect took on a Carmelite character. If we would understand this form of devotion to Mary, we must bear in mind that in Carmel solitude is everything.

And what a solitude there is in Mary's soul! There is nothing of the merely human in her. She is a pure, luminous, transparent being, detached from everything, whom no affection that is blameworthy, or even too sensible, can ever touch; completely virginal, Virgin of all virgins, unattached to anything. She went through life " alone with the Alone," wishing for no other society than His, whether in joy or in sorrow. What was the solitude of that heart, which could never be held by the things of sense, which passed through the affections of this transitory world " holy and unspotted in charity! " What was the solitude of that soul, ever communing with God alone, mingling, doubtless, in the life of men, but in order to accomplish a divine work: the soul of the Co-Redemptrix becoming constantly more closely identified with every movement of the soul of Christ who was so solitary in the evening on the mountain top or in Gethsemane! How divine was that solitude of the Virgin's soul, borne away with the Word, her Son, to the very confines of the Godhead, and there, associated in all the designs of the Trinity because of her universal place in the scheme of the world's salvation, and yet, there, more than ever, infinitely distant from the God Who was her Son! We stand here on the brink of an abyss which makes us tremble.

At the crowning point of their lives, the saints are the most solitary men on earth. What shall we say of the Blessed Virgin and of Christ? Who can imagine the solitude of the soul of the Word? In the beginning was the Word, and the Word was with God and the Word was God; and the Word was made flesh and dwelt amongst us, and His own received Him not. We have seen Him in His solitude, God walking in the midst of His creation. It is true that He had the society of the Father and of the Spirit of Love, in the unity of the Godhead, but who could have suspected that who saw Him? And so, in due proportion, was it with the soul of Our Lady, so alone amid men at Nazareth, at Bethlehem, at the foot of the Cross; in reality completely hidden in God with Christ whose mystery she pondered in her heart day and night.

2. This Lady of Carmel, a stranger to everything created and adoring the Word hidden within her, is the Lady of the Incarnation, the Virgin whom Sister Elizabeth of the Trinity especially loved. She, too, had as her ideal a life of silent adoration of the God Who was hidden in the depths of her soul.

" Do we think what must have been in the soul of the Blessed Virgin when, after the Incarnation, she possessed within her the Incarnate Word, the gift of God? In what silence, what recollection she must have buried herself in the depths of her soul in order to embrace that God whose mother she was." [4]

" I do not need to make any effort to enter into this mystery of the Divine Indwelling in the Blessed Virgin. I seem to find in it the habitual movement of my own soul which was also that of hers: to adore God hidden within me." [5]

In reading St. John of the Cross, she finds in Mary the perfect model of transforming union, and she dreams of living on earth as Mary did: in silent adoration of the Word and utterly lost in the Trinity. " At present, I am reading some

---

[4] Letter to her sister, November 1903. [5] Letter to her sister.

beautiful pages in our Holy Father, St. John of the Cross, on the transformation of the soul into the Three Divine Persons. To what heights of glory we are called! Oh, I quite understand the silence and the recollection of the saints who could not emerge from their contemplation! In that state God could lead them to the divine summits where Oneness is achieved between Him and the soul that has become His spouse in the mystical sense of the word. Our blessed Father says that the Holy Spirit then raises it to such heights that He makes it capable of producing in God the same spiration of love that the Father produces in the Son and the Son in the Father, the spiration which is none other than the Holy Ghost Himself. To think that God calls us, in virtue of our vocation, to live in this sacred splendor! What an adorable mystery of love! I want to correspond to it by living on earth as Our Lady did who ' kept all these words in her heart '; [6] I want, so to speak, to bury myself in the depths of my soul, there to lose myself in the Trinity which dwells there in order to transform me into Itself. Then my motto, ' my shining ideal,' will be realized: I shall truly be Elizabeth of the Trinity." [7]

She was very fond of a picture she had received, representing Our Lady of the Incarnation, lost in recollection under the influence of the Trinity's operation in her: " In the solitude of our cell, which I call my little paradise—for it is full of Him Who lives in heaven—I shall often look at the precious picture, and I shall unite myself to the soul of the Blessed Virgin when the Father overshadowed her with His power, while the Word became incarnate within her, and the Holy Ghost came upon her to work the great mystery. It is the whole Trinity in action, God yielding, giving Himself. And ought not the life of the Carmelite be lived under this divine action? " [8]

Our Lady of the Incarnation, wholly recollected under the creative action of the Trinity Which was doing ' great things ' in her: there we have the most intimate and the most cherished

[6] *Luke* II, 51.
[7] Letter to the Abbé Ch., November 23, 1903.
[8] Letter to Mme. de S., 1905.

ideal of Elizabeth's devotion to the Mother of God, an ideal to which we might say she was drawn " connaturally," to use the theological expression. The fruit of this long experience of devotion to Mary would later be the beautiful meditation on Our Lady in her retreat *Heaven on Earth*.

" ' *Si scires donum Dei*—If thou didst know the gift of God!' said Christ one evening to the Samaritan woman. Yet what is this gift of God, but Himself? 'He came unto His own and His own received Him not,' declares the beloved disciple. To many a soul might St. John the Baptist still utter the reproach: 'There hath stood one in the midst of you Whom you knew not.' ' If thou didst know the gift of God!'

" There is one created being who knew that gift of God, who lost no particle of it—a creature so pure and luminous that she seemed light itself: *speculum justitiae*. A being whose life was so simple, so lost in God, that there is but little to say of it. *Virgo fidelis*, the faithful Virgin ' who kept all these words in her heart.' She was so lowly, so hidden in the sight of God, in the seclusion of the temple, that the Blessed Trinity took pleasure in her. ' Because He hath regarded the humility of His handmaid for behold henceforth all generations shall call me blessed . . .'

" The Father bending down to this lovely creature, so unaware of her own beauty, chose her for the Mother of Him in time of Whom He is the Father in eternity. Then the Spirit of love, Who presides over all the works of God, overshadowed her; the Virgin uttered her *fiat*, ' Behold the handmaid of the Lord, be it done to me according to thy word,' and the greatest of all mysteries was accomplished. By the descent of the Word into her womb, Mary became God's own forever and ever.

" During the period between the Annunciation and the Nativity, Our Lady seems to me to be the model for interior souls: those whom God has asked to live within themselves, in the depths of the bottomless abyss. In what peace and recollection did Mary live and act! The most trivial actions were sanctified by her, for through them all she constantly adored the Gift of God. Yet that did not prevent her from spending herself for others when charity required it. The Gospel tells us that ' Mary, rising up, went into the hill country with haste to a city of Juda, to visit her cousin Elizabeth.' The ineffable vision which she contemplated within herself did not lessen her charity for others because, says one writer, ' though contemplation is directed to the praise and eternity of the Lord, it possesses and will never lose concord.' " [9]

3. Such lofty conceptions do not burst out by chance. They presuppose a long life of close union with Mary; and this is borne out by evidence.

As a child, Elizabeth's first poems were written to sing the praise of Mary, " guardian of her purity." Her girlhood diary was filled with the thought of Mary. As a nun, she saw Mary as intimately associated with the smallest details of her life. She often signed letters: " Sister Mary-Elizabeth of the Trinity." Her celebrated prayer was composed on the feast of the Presentation, that " much loved feast," which she felt portrayed the habitual attitude of her own heart: the Virgin's oblation to the Trinity, no longer in the Temple at Jerusalem but in that of her soul. " O my God, Trinity whom I adore . . . Give peace to my soul; make it Thy heaven, Thy cherished dwelling place, Thy home of rest. Let me never leave Thee alone, but keep me there . . . adoring Thee and wholly yielded up to Thy creative action."

As this short life drew to its close Elizabeth turned with redoubled tenderness to Our Lady Immaculate, on whose feast she had received the habit. " It is she, the Immaculate Conception, who gave me the habit of Carmel, and I am asking her to clothe me again in that robe of fine linen in which the bride is decked to present herself at the marriage feast of the Lamb." [10]

One night in the infirmary, as her eyes rested on a picture of the Mother of Sorrows hanging on the wall, Sister Elizabeth heard interiorly one of those reproaches that God addresses to the souls of His saints. Remembering a statue of Our Lady of Lourdes, before which as a young girl she had received many

---

[9] *Heaven on Earth*, 12th prayer.   [10] Letter to Canon A., late July 1906.

graces, she asked her mother for it, in order that she who had presided at her reception " might also watch over her departure." From that time on she always called the statue *Janua Coeli*. She was never without it. Utterly exhausted, she would drag herself to the little balcony which looked down over the choir, the statue in her emaciated hands. It was over a foot high and almost too heavy for her in her weakened state, but whenever *Janua Coeli* was seen, *Laudem Gloriae* was not far away.

One day, Elizabeth placed in the Prioress' cell a little cardboard model representing a medieval castle with a drawbridge. Near the closed door was a cut-out figure of Our Lady of Lourdes: it was *Janua Coeli*. At one corner of the parapeted tower floated a little standard bearing this inscription: " Citadel of suffering and holy recollection, the dwelling place of *Laudem Gloriae*, while waiting to enter the Father's house." *Janua Coeli* [11] had become for her the gateway of the Trinity.

During her last hours of agony, her sisters comforted her by reminding her of the presence of the Virgin she so loved. " Our Lady will be there; it is she who will take you by the hand." " Yes, that is true: *Janua Coeli* will let *Laudem Gloriae* pass."

The day before her death, she was heard murmuring: " In two days, I shall be in the bosom of my Three. *Laetatus sum in his quae dicta sunt mihi.*' " [12] " It is Our Lady, that luminous being, all pure with God's purity, who will take me by the hand to lead me into heaven, that dazzling heaven."

She wished to place her last retreat on earth under the protection of *Janua Coeli*, and she entered into it the evening of August 15th, as " into the novitiate of heaven to prepare to receive the habit of glory." [13] On the first day of retreat, Sister Elizabeth turned to Mary to ask that the supreme desire of her soul might be realized—that she might be identified with Christ crucified by love and become according to His likeness a perfect

---

[11] " Gate of Heaven," one of the titles by which the Blessed Virgin is invoked in the Litany.

[12] *Ps.* CXXI, 1: " I rejoiced at the things that were said to me."

[13] Note to a sister in Carmel, August 15, 1906.

"Praise of Glory" of the Trinity. "'Not that any man hath seen the Father, but the Son and he to whom it shall please the Son to reveal Him.' It might be added that none has penetrated the mystery of Christ in all its depths, unless it has been Our Lady. John and Magdalen did see very far into this mystery, and St. Paul often speaks of the 'knowledge' he had received of it, yet all the saints dwell in shadows compared with Our Lady's light! The secret she kept and pondered in her heart is unspeakable, no tongue can tell it, no pen express it.

"This Mother will so shape my soul that her little child may be a living, striking image of her Firstborn, the Son of the Eternal, the perfect 'Praise of Glory' of His Father." [14]

Towards the end of her retreat, Sister Elizabeth composed a beautiful prayer to Mary, a spontaneous outburst from her heart. It is faultless in doctrine and remarkably deep, being written at the fullest development of her thoughts on Our Lady. There are certain pages written by the saints which we should read on our knees:

"After Jesus Christ, of course, and as far away as the infinite is from the finite, there exists a created being who was also the great 'Praise of Glory' of the Most Holy Trinity. She corresponded fully to the divine vocation of which the Apostle speaks; she was always holy, unspotted, blameless in the sight of the thrice holy God.

"Her soul is so simple, its movements are so profound that they cannot be detected; she seems to reproduce on earth the life of the Divinity, the simple Being. And she is so transparent, so luminous that she might be taken for the light itself. Yet she is but the mirror of the sun of justice, *speculum justitiae*.

"'His Mother kept all these words in her heart.' Her whole history can be summed up in these few words. It was within her own heart that she dwelt, and so deeply did she enter it that no human eye can follow her. When I read in the Gospel that Mary 'went into the hill country with haste into a city of Juda' to perform her charitable office to her cousin Elizabeth,

---

[14] *Last Retreat*, 1st day.

I picture her to myself as she passes—beautiful, calm, majestic, absorbed in communion with the Word of God within her. Her prayer, like His, was always: '*Ecce*—Here I am!' Who? 'The handmaid of the Lord,' the last of His creatures, she, His Mother! Her humility was so genuine! For she was always forgetful of self, unconscious of self, delivered from self. So she could sing: 'He that is mighty hath done great things to me; henceforth all generations shall call me blessed.'

" The Queen of Virgins is the Queen of Martyrs too; but it was within her heart that the sword transpierced her, for with her everything took place within her soul. Oh, how beautiful she is to contemplate during her long martyrdom, enveloped in a majesty both strong and sweet, for she has learned from the Word Himself how they should suffer who are chosen as victims by the Father; these whom He has elected as associates in the great work of redemption, ' those whom He foreknew and predestinated to be made conformable to His Son,' crucified by love.

" She is there, at the foot of the Cross, *standing* in her strength and courage, and my Master says to me: '*Ecce Mater tua.*' He gives her to me for my Mother! And now that He has returned to the Father, that He has put me in His place on the Cross, so that I may ' fill up those things which are wanting of the sufferings of Christ for His Body which is the Church,' Mary is there still to teach me to suffer as He did, to tell me, to make me hear those last outpourings of His soul, which only His Mother could catch.

" When I shall have said my ' *Consummatum est*,' it will be she again, *Janua Coeli*, who will take me into the eternal courts, as she utters the mysterious words: ' *Laetatus sum in his quae dicta sunt mihi, in domum Domini ibimus.*' "

CHAPTER VII

SISTER ELIZABETH OF THE TRINITY AND THE SOULS OF PRIESTS

> "*The priest is another Christ, working for the glory of the Father.*"

1. Friendship with Priests. 2. The Priest of the Mass. 3. Association with the Apostolate of the Priest. 4. The Priest and the direction of souls.

A contemplative cannot let her soul be shut up in the narrow confines of convent walls. Carried along on the great stream of the Church's thought, her spiritual life is characterized by the same perspectives as the Redemption. The contemplative is constantly covering the world with her co-redeeming prayer. This is what our Lady did in the Cenacle. While the first apostles went forth to labor and to die, Mary, silent in prayer, accompanied them to all their battles for Christ. Will anyone dare suggest that the all-powerful intercession of the Mother of God was not more efficacious in securing the extension of Christ's kingdom than the heroic labors of a St. Peter or a St. Paul? During its centuries of struggle the Church Militant will always remember that it was born of contemplative prayer in the Cenacle, and its action on souls will always be based on the prayer of its saints.

Most of the great religious families have seen the matter in this light, and it is customary for the most apostolic Orders to support the ministry of the brothers by the continual prayer of the nuns. Thus, before founding his Order of Preachers, St. Dominic first established the contemplative Sisters, the "Preacheresses" of Notre Dame de Prouille, whose mission was, by a life of supplication and sacrifice, to support the labors of the Preachers.

In this regard, Sister Elizabeth of the Trinity found in Carmel one of the dearest traditions of her Order, and one which is most fruitful for the spiritual welfare of the Church. The daughters of St. Teresa offer their silent sacrifices for priests, first of all.

Sister Elizabeth always professed a cultus for the priesthood. Did she offer her life for priests? Her parish priest, who was for a long time her confessor, was convinced that she did.[1] While no positive evidence allows us to affirm this as a fact, many documents do exist to show that, as a Carmelite, she gave priests a special place in her prayers.

When a priest recommended his ministry to her, she took her promise to pray very seriously: "Reverend Father . . . Since the last time we talked together, I have been very united to you, especially during the Divine Office. I promise to make a special intention for you at Terce, so that the Spirit of Love, He who seals and consummates the unity in the Trinity, may pour Himself abundantly upon you and that He may bear you in the light of faith to those heights where life is only peace, love, union, lighted up even now by the rays of the divine Sun."[2]

1. Sister Elizabeth of the Trinity's attitude for every priest, including those related to her, was one of the most profound respect; the man in him disappeared before the Christ.

In conversations with them she never showed the slightest trace of any feminine sentimentality. "She was just a soul, and that was all," we are told by a young priest who was a family connection, and to whom most of her letters of this kind—perhaps a dozen in all—were addressed. "From the beginning of the conversation, it was 'God alone,' and we never came down from this wholly supernatural atmosphere." Sister Elizabeth had so high and so pure an idea of the priesthood!

We can follow the slightest movements of her soul in her correspondence with this seminarian whom she accompanied to his priesthood and later followed in his apostolate.

---

[1] He mentioned this detail to me himself.
[2] Letter to the Abbé J., February 11, 1902.

The first meeting was entirely supernatural. She wrote of it to her sister: " . . . I had a completely supernatural conversation in the parlor with the Abbé Ch. I think that there was a fusion between the soul of the priest and that of the Carmelite." [3]

Thus began a spiritual friendship which ended only with her death . . . " Before I enter into the great silence of Lent, I want to answer your kind letter, and my soul feels the need of telling you that it is in communion with yours, that it may let itself be taken up and carried away, completely absorbed by Him Whose love wraps us round and who wants to make us perfect in One with Him. I thought of you when, in Father Vallée, I read these words on contemplation: ' The contemplative is a being who lives in the radiance of the face of Christ; who enters into the mystery of God, not in the light that shines from human thought but in that shed by the word of the Word Incarnate.'

" Do you not have the same passionate longing to listen to Him? At times, one feels so strongly the need of silence, that one would wish to do nothing but remain like Magdalen at the Master's feet, eager to hear all, to penetrate ever more deeply into that mystery of charity which He came to reveal to us. Yet do you not find that in action, when we are apparently doing Martha's work, the soul can remain buried in its contemplation like Magdalen, staying very near Him? It is thus that I understand the apostolate both for the Carmelite and for the priest. In this way, both can radiate God and give Him to souls if they remain at the source of divine life. It seems to me that we must draw very close to the Master, commune with His soul, become identified with its every movement, and then go forth as He did to do the will of the Father." [4]

The same supernatural tone animates all her letters. There are no commonplace polite expressions. With the very first sentence, the two souls are placed in God and never come down.

[3] Letter to her sister, September 1902.
[4] Letter to the Abbé Ch., February 24, 1903.

"'Having loved His own that were in the world, He loved them unto the end.'[5] It seems to me that nothing so speaks to us of the love in God's Heart as the Eucharist. It is union, consummation, God in us and we in Him. Is it not heaven on earth? Heaven in faith while we await the face to face vision for which we so long! Then we shall be satisfied when His glory shall appear,[6] when we shall see Him in His light. Do you not find that it rests the soul to think of that meeting, when it shall behold Him who is its one love? Everything vanishes in that thought and one seems to enter upon the mystery of God. . . . As you say in your letter, this mystery is so completely '*ours.*'

"Pray for me that I may live as a true bride; that I may be completely at my Master's disposal and ever on the watch in faith so that He may take me wherever He pleases. I want constantly to keep close to Him Who knows all the mystery so that I may hear everything from Him. 'The speech of the Word is the infusion of the Gift.' It is just so, is it not, that He speaks to our souls in silence: this dear silence is so blessed. From Ascension to Pentecost, we were in retreat in the Cenacle, awaiting the Holy Ghost. It was so good. During this whole Octave, we have the Blessed Sacrament exposed in the oratory. Those are divine hours that we spend in that little corner of heaven, where we possess the vision in substance under the humble Host. Yes, He Whom the blessed contemplate in glory and Whom we adore in faith is truly one and the same. The other day, someone wrote me such a beautiful thought that I send it to you: 'Faith is vision in darkness.' Why should it not be so for us, since God is in us and asks only to take possession of us as He took possession of the saints? Only they are always attentive. As Father Vallée says: 'They keep silence: they are recollected, and their one activity is to become beings who are ever receiving.'

"Let us combine to work for the pleasure of Him Who has loved us exceedingly, as St. Paul tells us.[7] Let us make a home for Him in our souls, a home that is perfectly peaceful, where

---

[5] *John* XIII, 1.   [6] *Ps.* XVI, 15.   [7] *Eph.* II, 4.

the song of love and thanksgiving is always being sung. And let it be a silent place, echoing the great silence which exists in God. And, as you said to me, let us draw near to the pure and radiant Virgin, that she may lead us to Him Whose mystery she has so deeply penetrated. May our life be a continual communion, a perfectly simple movement towards God. Pray to the Queen of Carmel for me. I, on my part, am praying for you, and assure you that I remain with you in adoration and love." [8]

There is not a trace of sentimentality in these lines, which breathe a wholly unearthly purity.

When the time came for ordination to the diaconate, Sister Elizabeth wrote to assure the seminarian, in the name of the Dijon Carmel, that he was not forgotten. "' *Misericordias Domini in aeternum cantabo.*' [9] Our Mother is engaged this evening and has told me to write to you, so that you may have a few lines from Carmel to let you know how united we are to you on this great day. For my part, I am withdrawing in recollection into the center of my soul, where the Holy Spirit dwells. I am asking Him, this Spirit of Love, who ' searcheth all things, yea the deep things of God,' [10] to give Himself to you abundantly and to shine upon your soul, so that in the great light you may go to receive that holy unction of which the Apostle of love speaks. With you, I am singing a hymn of thanksgiving and then keeping silence in order to adore the mystery that is overshadowing your whole being. The whole Trinity is bending down and hovering over you to bring forth in you ' the glory of His grace.' " [11]

" St. Paul tells us in his Epistle to the Romans that those whom God ' foreknew, He also predestinated to be made conformable to the image of His Son.' [12] It seems to me that you are surely concerned here. Are you not that predestined soul whom God has chosen to be His priest? I believe that in His

---

[8] Letter to the Abbé Ch., June 14, 1903.
[9] *Ps.* LXXXVIII, 2.
[10] *I Cor.* II, 10.
[11] Letter to the Abbé Ch., April 1905.
[12] *Rom.* VII, 29.

work of love, the Father is bending over your soul, working upon it with His Divine Hand, His delicate touch, so that the resemblance to the Divine Ideal may become ever closer, until the day when the Church will say to you: ' *Tu es sacerdos in aeternum.*' [13] Then everything in you will be, so to speak, a copy of Jesus Christ, the great High Priest, and *you will be able to reproduce Him unceasingly in the sight of His Father*, and in that of souls. What a grand destiny! The ' super-eminent virtue ' of God is flowing into your being, to transform and divinize it. What recollection, what loving attention to God is demanded for this divine work!" [14]

When at last the day comes for ordination to the priesthood, unable to put her feelings into words, Sister Elizabeth's soul takes refuge in more intense prayer. " I have asked Reverend Mother's permission to write to you in order to tell you that I am closely united to you in spirit during these last days before your ordination. But now that we are approaching the great mystery being prepared for you, I can only be silent . . . and adore the exceeding love of our God. With Our Lady, you can sing your Magnificat, and rejoice in God your Savior; for He that is mighty is doing great things in you and His mercy endureth forever. Then like Mary, keep all that in your heart. Be very close to her, for this ' priestly ' Virgin is also the Mother of Divine Grace, and in her love she wishes to prepare you to become that ' faithful priest who shall do according to the heart of God ' of whom the Scripture speaks.[15] Like that high-priest, ' without father, without mother, without genealogy, having neither beginning of days nor end of life,' [16] the type of the Son of God, of whom St. Paul speaks in his Epistle to the Hebrews, you also become by the holy unction that being who is no longer of earth, that mediator between God and souls, called to show forth ' the glory of His grace,' while sharing in the super-eminent greatness of His power. When He entered into the world, Jesus, the Eternal Priest, said

[13] *Ps.* CIX, 4.
[14] Letter to the Abbé Ch., Spring 1905.
[15] *I Kings* II, 35.   [16] *Heb.* VII, 3.

to His Father: ' Behold, I come to do Thy will.' [17] I think that in this solemn hour of your entrance into the priesthood that ought to be your prayer, and I wish to make it with you. On Friday at the altar, when for the first time Jesus, the Holy One of God, will become incarnate in the humble Host in your consecrated hands, do not forget her whom God has led to Carmel that there she may be the ' Praise of His Glory.' Ask Him that she may be buried in the depths of His mystery and consumed in the fires of His love. Then offer her to the Father, with the Divine Lamb. Good-bye. If you knew how I am praying for you! May the grace of our Lord Jesus Christ and the charity of God and the Communication of the Holy Ghost be with you." [18]

2. Sister Elizabeth loved especially to think of the priest at the altar at the moment when in his hands the Word Incarnate immolates Himself for the Church. The *sense of Christ*, engraven in her soul by her baptism, made her realize that that is the moment when the priest most particularly exercises his office of mediator in the world. She did not go as far as St. Catherine of Siena, and kiss the footprints of the priest who had given Christ to her in Holy Communion, but with a touching persistence she never failed to beg the priest whom she knew to remember her at the altar and to plunge her soul " in the Blood of the Lamb." [19] " I know that you pray for me each day at Holy Mass. Put me into the chalice so that my soul may be wholly bathed in the Blood of my Lord, for Whom I thirst; so that I may be all pure, all transparent, that the Trinity may be reflected in me as in crystal." [20]

She never fails to implore this great favor when any feasts or anniversaries come around. " Tomorrow is the feast of St. Mary Magdalen; she of whom Truth said, ' She hath loved much.' It is also a feast for my soul, for on that day I keep the anniversary of my baptism. Since you are the priest of love,

---

[17] *Heb.* X, 9.
[18] Letter to the Abbé Ch., June 27, 1905: *II Cor.* XIII, 13.
[19] Letter to Canon A., August 1902.   [20] Letter to Canon A.

I come to ask you, with Reverend Mother's permission, to be kind enough to consecrate me to Him tomorrow in Holy Mass. Baptize me in the Blood of the Lamb so that, utterly untouched by everything that is not He, I may live only to love Him more and more passionately until I reach that happy unity to which God has predestined us in His eternal and unchangeable will. I thank you, Father, and kneel for your blessing." [21]

We find a similar request on the occasion of her private retreat. "This evening, I am setting out on a long journey. For ten days I shall be absolutely alone. I shall have several extra hours of prayer, and shall keep my veil down whenever I go about the monastery. Thus, my life will be more than ever like that of a hermit in the desert. Before burying myself in my Thebaid, I feel a real need to ask the help of your good prayers, particularly of a special intention at the Holy Sacrifice of the Mass. When you consecrate the Host, Jesus, Who alone is holy, will become incarnate; will you consecrate me with Him as a victim of praise to His glory, to the end that all my aspirations, all my movements, all my actions may be a homage rendered to His holiness?

" 'Be holy because I am holy.' [22] These words are the motto of my retreat. They are the light in whose rays I shall walk during my divine journey. St. Paul supplies the commentary when he says: 'God . . . chose us before the foundation of the world that we should be holy and unspotted in His sight in charity.' [23] Here, then, is the secret of that virginal purity: to abide in love, that is, in God, for 'God is charity.' [24]

"Pray much for me during these ten days. I rely entirely on your prayers. I shall even say that it seems to me a very natural thing to do, for the good God brought our souls together in order that we might help each other. . . . Did He not say: 'A brother that is helped by his brother is like a strong city?' [25] This is the mission I entrust to you. Please, Father, say for me the prayer that welled from the great heart of St.

---

[21] Letter to the Abbé Ch., July 21, 1905.
[22] *Lev.* XI, 44.
[23] *Eph.* I, 4.
[24] *I John* IV, 16.
[25] *Prov.* XVIII, 19.

Paul for his dear Ephesians: ' That He the Father would grant you, according to the riches of His glory, to be strengthened by His Spirit with might . . . that Christ may dwell by faith in your hearts; that being rooted and founded in charity, you may be able to comprehend . . . what is the breadth, and length, and height and depth; to know also the charity of Christ which surpasseth all knowledge; that you may be filled unto all the fullness of God.' [26] Let us sanctify the Christ in our hearts, so as to effect what David sang under the inspiration of the Holy Spirit: ' Upon him shall my sanctification flourish.' " [27]

When, in the last phase of her life, Sister Elizabeth found her new name in the Scripture, she turned again to the priest of the Mass. " Give me your help, Father, for I have great need of it. The brighter the light shines, the more I feel my powerlessness. On December 8th, since you are a high priest, will you please consecrate me to the power of His love so that I may in truth be *Laudem Gloriae*. I read that in St. Paul, and I understood that it was my vocation in exile while I await the eternal *Sanctus*." [28]

3. During the celebration of the Mass, the priest does two things which clearly reveal his mission, the whole idea of his mediation between God and man. At the consecration, the priest elevates the Host towards the Trinity; then, at the moment of Communion he turns to the faithful and distributes to them the Bread of Life. To offer Christ to the Trinity and to give Christ to the world: such is his twofold mission on earth.

A Christ-like soul is needed to perform this divine task. That is why the whole Church, and particularly contemplatives, must help the priest acquire that soul. For this reason we have the silent immolation of a multitude of lives; the purest, the most crucified, who dwell in cloisters.

Sister Elizabeth of the Trinity possessed to a high degree this sense of the spiritual needs of the priesthood and of the neces-

[26] *Eph.* III, 14-19.
[27] Letter to the Abbé Ch., October 8, 1905; *Ps.* CXXXI, 18.
[28] To the same, December 1905.

sity of praying for the souls of priests. Naturally, we cannot expect a complete treatise on the theology of the priesthood from a Carmelite. She does not enter into a detailed analysis of all the priestly virtues: piety, chastity, detachment from riches, learning, obedience, zeal for the salvation of souls and the glory of God. That is not her task, nor is it in keeping with her spiritual temperament. In accordance with her usual method, she seizes upon the virtues at their source: union with God. By the normal psychological process of transposition, she projects into the soul of the priest her own interior ideal and finds, moreover, a sublimely concise expression to embody her ideal of the priesthood: the priest is *another Christ working for the Father's glory*. She would have loved the grand words of Pius XI in his masterly encyclical on the priesthood: " Let the priest live like another Christ. *Vivat ut alter Christus*." [29]

According to her particular grace, with delicate tact and complete self-effacement, without the least appearance of teaching her correspondent, but quite simply by letting her own Carmelite soul overflow into that of the priest, Sister Elizabeth of the Trinity is able to remind him of the secret of all apostolic work: without interior life, the priest, busy though he may be, does little good, even if he does not do harm, irreparable harm.

She well knew the words of her spiritual Father, St. John of the Cross, in the " Canticle ": " The smallest act of pure love is more precious in the sight of God and more profitable to the Church and to the soul itself than all other works put together." [30] From this we see that the least spark of pure love is of the highest importance for the Church.

To be an apostle means to communicate Jesus Christ to the world. But we can only do that in the measure in which we possess Him ourselves. In His last discourse to His disciples, the Master Himself taught us the true laws of the apostolate.

" I am the vine, you the branches: he that abideth in me and I in him, the same beareth much fruit. As the branch cannot

---

[29] *Ad Catholici Sacerdotii*, December 20, 1935.
[30] *Spiritual Canticle*, Stanza XXIX.

bear fruit of itself unless it abide in the vine, so neither can you unless you abide in Me. If you abide in Me, and in the measure in which you abide in Me, you shall bring forth very much fruit. . . . You shall ask whatever you will, and it shall be done to you. In this is My Father glorified: that you bring forth very much fruit. As My Father hath loved Me, I also have loved you. Abide in My love." [31] The last discourse of our Lord is the charter of the Christian Apostolate.

Solicitous, like her Master, about the interior life, Sister Elizabeth of the Trinity could not fail to emphasize the necessity of a priest's having this union with our Lord if, in his turn, he would give Him to souls. In her mind, the apostle is first and foremost a man of prayer and silent self-sacrifice, imitating the Crucified, who did not save the world by brilliant works or eloquent discourses, but by His sufferings and His death. It is the aim of her apostolate as a Carmelite to remain associated with the work of the priest on this plane of redemptive immolation and imitation of that death. She is anxious to fill up in her flesh " those things that are wanting to the sufferings of Christ for His body which is the Church," [32] and thus to fill up those mysterious voids in the Passion of Christ that God has left in order that we ourselves might contribute our drop of blood to this glorious work of the world's redemption.

" Let us ask Him to make us genuine in our love, that is, men and women of sacrifice; for it seems to me that sacrifice is nothing but love in action. ' He loved me and delivered Himself for me.' I love this thought: ' The life of a priest—and that of the Carmelite—is an advent which prepares the way for the Incarnation in souls:' In one of the Psalms, David sings: ' A fire shall go before Him.' [33] Is not fire love? And is it not our mission to prepare the ways of the Lord by our union with Him Whom the Apostle calls ' a consuming fire? ' [34] In contact with Him, our soul will become like a flame of love, spreading through

---

[31] *John* XV, 4-9.
[32] *Col.* I, 24.
[33] *Ps.* XCVI, 3.
[34] *Heb.* XII, 29.

all the members of the body of Christ which is the Church. Then we shall console the heart of our Master, and showing us to the Father, He will be able to say: 'I am glorified in them.' " [35]

Her apostle's soul penetrated the profound meaning of the dogma of the Communion of Saints, through which each individual is associated in the spiritual welfare of the entire Church. Conscious of this truth she could, in order to judge her personal part as a contemplative in the Mystical Body as a whole, rise without false humility to this lofty truth of the unity which binds all the members of the Church Militant and the Church Triumphant in the WHOLE CHRIST from Whom it proceeds to the Trinity. Far removed from trifles and petty sentimentalities, her grand contemplative's mind moved easily in the vast expanse of the divine plan.

"Do you not think that for souls there is no question of distance, or separation, but that it is truly a case of realizing Our Lord's prayer: 'Father, that they may be made perfect in One?' [36] To me it seems that the souls on earth and those glorified in the light of the vision are very near to one another, since they all share in the communion of the same God, the same Father, Who gives Himself to the former in faith and mystery, and satisfies the latter with His divine glory. But He is the same, and we bear Him within us. He inclines Himself to us in all His love, day and night, in His longing to impart Himself to us, to infuse His divine life into us, so as to make us deified beings, able to radiate Him everywhere. What power over souls does that apostle have who remains ever at the fountain of living water! Then he can overflow on those around him without ever becoming empty himself; for his soul is in communion with the Infinite. I pray much for you, that God may seize upon all the powers of your soul, that He may cause you to partake of His whole mystery, that everything in you may be divine and stamped with His seal, so that you may be

[35] To the Abbé B., 1902: *John* XVII, 10.
[36] *John* XVII, 23.

another Christ, working for the Father's glory. You pray for me, too, I hope? I want to work for the glory of God, and for that I must be wholly filled with Him. Then I shall be all-powerful. A look, a desire will become a prayer that cannot be resisted and that can obtain everything, since it is, so to speak, God Whom we offer to God. May our souls be but one in Him. While you carry Him to souls, I, like Magdalen, will stay close to the Master in silent adoration, asking Him to render your word fruitful in souls. Apostle, Carmelite; it is all one. Let us belong wholly to Him and be flooded with the divine sap. May He be the life of our life, the soul of our soul, and may we day and night consciously rest beneath His divine action." [37]

There is perfect balance in this doctrine of the apostolate of the Carmelite associated with that of the priest in the Church. While the priest takes Christ to souls by his word, by the Sacraments and other forms of his ministry, the Carmelite, like Magdalen, remains silently at the Master's feet, or, better still, like the Virgin Co-Redemptrix beside the Cross, interiorly identified with all the movements of the soul of the Crucified and dying with Him for the same end: the redemption of souls.

4. It may be truly said that the priest occupies a primordial place in the Christian life. The priest, being associated with God in the government of the Church, becomes in St. Paul's words, " God's coadjutor." [38] Sister Elizabeth of the Trinity wrote: " You are the dispenser of the gifts of God, and the Almighty, Whose immensity envelops the universe, seems to have need of you in order to give Himself to souls." [39] We do not sufficiently reflect on this fact.

The world receives Christ by the hands of the priest. By his ministry, the child is born to the life of Christ at the moment of Baptism. He grows up, is strengthened by the priest at his Confirmation; at the hand of the priest he is fed by God, morning after morning; still by means of the priest, he rises from his sins once more to enjoy the divine life. When the hour comes

---

[37] Letter to the Abbé B., June 22 (no year).
[38] *I Cor.* III, 9. [39] Letter to the Abbé B. (undated).

for him to settle in life, the priest draws nigh to place Christ in the new home. Finally, at the close, when all is ending, a last gesture of blessing descends upon the aged in the hour of death: " Go forth Christian soul . . . to the Christ of thy Baptism! " It is the priest who opens for him the gates of heaven. So from the cradle to the grave, the priest is always there.

Nor is this influence of the priest which accompanies man all his life limited to individuals; it extends to nations. The priest alone has received from Christ the commission to teach all nations " even to the uttermost parts of the earth." [40] By means of his preaching and his learning, he renders intellects docile to the "sweet yoke of Christ." [41] " If we consider the truths taught by the priest," remarks Pope Pius XI in his Encyclical *Ad Catholici Sacerdotii,* " if we are willing to weigh their inner power, it is easy to understand what a great benefit for the moral elevation and the tranquillity of peoples the priest's influence is. It is he—and often he alone—who reminds the great and the lowly of the shortness of life, the transitory character of the goods of this world, the true spiritual and eternal values, the truth of the judgments of God, the incorruptible sanctity of that divine glance which searches all hearts to render to each according to his works. In truth, the priest is indeed the mediator placed between God and men, to bring down upon the latter the good things that come from God, and to raise to Him the prayer that appeases His anger." [42]

What shall we say of the priest's action on the most spiritual souls in the Church? They, above all, need his wise guidance lest they should wander from the " narrow way " bordered by precipices, which leads to divine union. St. John of the Cross has left severe pages and hard warnings to incompetent directors who are lacking in knowledge and virtue. A good director of souls is so rare and so precious! " He should be chosen from among a thousand," advises St. Francis de Sales. St. Teresa, who had suffered much in that respect, always cherished a grateful memory of those learned and pious priests in whom

[40] *Acts* I, 8.   [41] *Matt.* XI, 30.   [42] December 20, 1935.

God had provided her with an indispensable support during difficult periods of her spiritual life and while she was making her foundations. On account of the benefit she had derived in such circumstances from certain great theologians of the Order of St. Dominic, she used to say that she was " a Dominican at heart."

This taste for sound doctrine and wise direction has remained traditional in Carmel. On this point, as on others, Sister Elizabeth showed herself a true daughter of St. Teresa.

As a child and as a young girl, she went regularly to confession to her parish priest, who was also her director. She even thought him " too kind," and for a time considered asking more austere direction from a Jesuit Father. We read in her diary for February 6, 1899: " Friday, Saturday and Sunday will be the days of perpetual adoration in our parish Church. My former confessor is going to preach. I shall be very glad to see him again and talk to him about my vocation. How often I have thought regretfully of his strong and severe direction! Our present priest is very good, even too good. He is wanting in severity and lets me off too lightly. The other day, I spoke to Mother about leaving him and taking Father Chesnay who preached the retreat and whom I should be glad to have as a director, but she was displeased and I shall not mention it.

" *Friday, Feb. 10th.*—I went to Confession today and was really content. I spoke about the retreat to my director. I told him all my resolutions and all the graces God had showered upon me during those days. He advised me to accuse myself of my failures to keep my resolutions every time I go to confession. He said that I shall thus make much progress."

At Dijon, she took the opportunity to attend spiritual conferences and retreats given by the Jesuit Fathers, consulting them occasionally for the good of her soul and faithfully following their advice.

She much admired and appreciated Father Vallee's teaching, " so deep and so luminous."[43] The influence of that eminent

---

[43] To Mme. A., September 29, 1902.

religious is apparent in some of the essential features of her spiritual physiognomy: the practice of silence and belief in Love; dwelling in the depths of the soul with Him Who is there and Whose constant desire is to cleanse and save us. Three months before her death, Sister Elizabeth of the Trinity once more sought advice of the Dominican, asking him to draw up in writing for her a practical program of conformity to Christ Crucified, the dominant thought of her last days.

". . . I think it may well be that next year I shall greet you on the feast of St. Dominic in the inheritance of the saints in light. This year I must still withdraw into the heaven of my soul to keep the feast quite interiorly with you. I want to tell you I am doing that. I want also, Father, to ask your prayers that I may be perfectly faithful, perfectly attentive, and that I may climb my Calvary as behooves a bride of the Crucified. 'Those whom God foreknew He also predestinated to be made conformable to the image of His Son.' How I love that great thought of St. Paul! It rests my soul. I think how, in his 'exceeding charity,' He has known me, called me, justified me, and while I wait for Him to glorify me I want to be the unceasing 'Praise of His Glory.' Father, ask that for your little child. Five years ago today—do you remember?—I knocked at the door of Carmel, and you were there to bless my first steps in holy solitude. Now I am knocking at the eternal gates and I ask you to bend over my soul once more and to bless it on the threshold of 'the Father's house.' When I am in the great home of love, in the bosom of the 'Three' to whom you turned my soul, I shall not forget all that you have been to me, and, in my turn, I shall want to give to my Father from whom I have received so much.

"May I venture to express a wish? I should be so glad to have a few lines from you, to tell me how I should realize the divine plan: 'to be made conformable to the likeness of Christ crucified.'

"Good-bye, Reverend Father. I ask you to bless me in the name of the 'Three,' and to consecrate me to 'Them,' as a little victim of praise."

We do not find Sister Elizabeth running from one director to another, like so many restless souls. With simplicity and docility she was content with the confessors whom Providence sent her in Carmel. She did not hesitate, however, on occasion to have recourse to an extraordinary confessor. Thus, on the eve of her profession, her disturbed soul recovered its perfect peace only after the assurance of a discreet and wise religious who came specially on her account.

Throughout her life, she retained a filial and grateful affection for the good Canon, a family friend, who had been the confidant of her first secret.

"If the Carmelite Rule imposes silence on my pen, I assure you that my heart and soul are not kept from going to you. They often break enclosure. I think our Lord forgives me, for I make the journey with Him and in Him. Pray for your little Carmelite that this year may be one of greater fidelity and love. I do so want to console my Master by remaining ever united to Him. I am going to tell you a secret: my dream is to be 'the praise of His glory.' I read that in St. Paul, and my Bridegroom has made me understand that it is my vocation here in exile while waiting to go and sing the eternal *Sanctus* in the city of the saints. But this calls for great fidelity since, in order to be a 'Praise of Glory,' I must be dead to all that is not He, so that I may be moved only by His touch, and poor Elizabeth still does foolish things where her Master is concerned. But, like a tender Father, He forgives her; His divine look purifies her. Like St. Paul, she tries to forget those things that are behind and stretch forth to those that are before . . ."[44]

"How we feel the need of sanctifying ourselves, of forgetting ourselves, in order to be wholly occupied with the Church's interests. Poor France! How I love to cover her with the blood of the Just One; of Him who ever lives to intercede and beg for mercy for us! What a sublime mission the Carmelite has! She ought to be a mediator with Jesus Christ, to be another humanity for Him in which He may perpetuate His life of

[44] *Phil.* III, 13.

reparation and sacrifice, of praise and adoration. Ask Him that I may respond fully to my vocation and not abuse the graces which He lavishes on me. If you knew how I fear that sometimes! Then I cast myself on Him Whom St. John calls 'The Faithful and True,' and I beseech Him to be my fidelity . . . The Sunday after the Epiphany will be the third anniversary of my bridal with the Lamb. When in the Mass you consecrate the Host in which Jesus becomes incarnate, will you also consecrate your little child to Him Who is Almighty Love that He may transform her into the ' praise of His glory.' " [45]

Thus, faithful to the Master's will and to the Church's wisdom, the Carmelite asks the priest to help her in the different phases of her spiritual life and to lead her to union with God. That is the whole meaning of the priesthood: by word, prayer and the Sacraments, above all by the Mass, " to form Christ " in the world of souls, and " by Him, with Him and in Him " to " make them perfect in one " with God.

One thing which Sister Elizabeth of the Trinity never suspected was the divine atmosphere into which she led the souls of the priests who had the happiness of coming into contact with her and who, one and all, were impressed by a feeling of her very high sanctity.[46] It is often so with the priestly ministry. By a wonderful return of the divine wisdom, the priest who devotes himself to souls is sanctified by them. Those who have experienced it know this. While the priest is given to souls by God to guide and save them, so also, in the designs of Providence, souls are placed near the priest in order to reveal to him, or recall to him, the way that leads to the heights. Master Bañez, the celebrated professor of the University of Salamanca and the faithful supporter of St. Teresa, owed to his interviews with the holy Foundress some of those lofty conceptions which made him so great a contemplative theologian. St. John of the Cross, on his part, added to his *Spiritual Canticle* a sublime verse on the divine beauty after

[45] Letter to Canon A., January 1906.
[46] From evidence received. (Her confessor cherishes a veritable cultus for her.)

hearing the spiritual secrets of a Carmelite nun at Beas. Who can tell how many supernatural undertakings and apostolic works have been similarly inspired in the course of the Church's history?

Many are the priests who have gained from the writings of Sister Elizabeth of the Trinity that fixed gaze upon the spiritual summits which makes all things new! It is the humble Carmelite's grateful way of repaying the priesthood a little for what she had received from it. From heaven more than ever does she continue her Carmelite vocation in association with the apostolate of the priest, in order to hasten " the day of Christ," [47] when God shall be " all in all " [48] to the " praise of His glory." [49]

---

[47] *Phil.* I, 10.
[48] *I Cor.* XV, 28.
[49] *Eph.* I, 12.

CHAPTER VIII

THE GIFTS OF THE HOLY GHOST [1]

"All the soul's acts come simultaneously from it and from God."

1. The function of the gifts of the Holy Ghost. 2. The spirit of fear. 3. The spirit of fortitude. 4. The spirit of piety. 5. The spirit of counsel. 6. The spirit of knowledge. 7. The spirit of understanding. 8. The spirit of wisdom.

1. The study of the gifts of the Holy Ghost deals with the highest operations of the spiritual life and touches the loftiest peaks of mystical theology. This *deiform* activity, which indues souls in "the ways of the Trinity," is the supreme triumph of grace, and is seen in all its splendor only at the close of the lives of the saints when self, having, as it were, disappeared, God seems to have reserved for Himself alone the entire motivation of their conduct. The soul has been admitted to dwell in the intimacy of the Divine Persons; it shares the life of the Trinity. In St. John's words, it has "fellowship"[2] with the Father, the Son and the Holy Spirit and is "one" with them.[3] It is the full development of the grace of Baptism.

In the beginning, this is not the case. The Christian moves "in the family of God" rather like an adopted child who has not yet become used to its new home. The baptized soul only imperfectly possesses this life which is, in its essence, deiform. It does not yet know how to behave so as to live "like God." And so, the Divine Persons must come to teach it how to live in the bosom of the family of the Trinity, like God Himself, and,

---

[1] Owing to the major importance of the activity of the gifts of the Holy Ghost, in the spiritual life, we have given the theological exposition in greater detail.

[2] *I John* I, 3.

[3] *John* XVII, 21.

more particularly, " like the Word," since conformity to the Son marks the final goal of our predestination in Christ.

The passage from this *human mode* of the Christian virtues to the *divine mode* is precisely what constitutes the proper object of the activity of the gifts of the Holy Ghost. As the baptized soul progresses in the spiritual life and the grace of his Baptism develops, then this human being who, in St. Peter's words, has become " a partaker of the divine nature "[4] exactly as it subsists in the unity of the Trinity, should become increasingly conscious of the mystery of his divine sonship, which makes him a " stranger " to all that is not God. The Christian is another Christ, whose inner life is hidden with the only begotten Son in the bosom of the Father, there to be " made one " in a single love. It is the divine nature communicated by the Father to the Word, and by Them to the Holy Ghost and which the souls of the predestined receive through participation. It is of the highest importance that this fundamental truth should be thoroughly understood. As an unescapable consequence, the definition of grace carries with it the whole supernatural sense of the activity of the virtues and of the gifts of the Holy Ghost, which results from it as a property results from the essence. How is it possible to understand that faith renders us partakers of the Word [5] unless we have grasped the truth that, by the grace of adoption, the soul has, in its innermost essence, become conformable to the Trinity? Only this conception of grace, which is at once the most traditional and the deepest, explains how, under the special action of the Divine Persons, it is possible to live even on earth, " with the soul living in eternity," " in the manner of the Father, the Son and the Holy Ghost," at least as far as the obscurities of faith and the difficulties of the present life permit, these latter being always an insurmountable obstacle to the full and continuous actual exercise of charity. The word " participation "[6] includes and defines every possible shade of the deiform life in souls, from

[4] *II Peter* 1, 4.
[5] Cf. *Summa Theologica*, I, q. 38, a. 1.
[6] A participation which is formal, analogical, and inadequate.

the first steps of the newly baptized child to the most divine acts of " the earth's rare perfect souls," [7] those who are permanently established on the peaks of transforming union, the normal prelude to the life of heaven. Grace is ordained to the deiform mode of glory; hence, by its most essential law, it leads the elect ever nearer to that perfect life in the image of God, of which the Blessed Trinity is the principle and the exemplar for every single baptized soul. " Be you perfect as also your heavenly Father is perfect," [8] said our Lord; that is, live after the manner of a Divine Person. The whole progress of the spiritual life consists precisely in divesting ourselves more and more of this human manner of practicing the virtues, in order to approach by imitation to the most intimate, secret, and divine movement of the Trinitarian life. The soul no longer sees things from the human standpoint, even in the light of faith, but only in the light of the Word, and " as He sees them "; it loves divinely, having no longer even the power to love any created or uncreated good whatsoever, except to love it primarily for God's sake and for His glory alone, somewhat as the Divine Persons love one another and love the universe in one and the same movement of love.

To recall these mysteries of the highest mystical theology is to sketch the whole function of the gifts of the Holy Ghost, the proper effect of which is to lead souls to transforming union, or to keep them there continuously living in the manner of the Trinity.

At first, the action of the Spirit is slow, progressive, and intermittent. Then, if the soul is faithful, this action becomes increasingly frequent and finally constitutes a permanent state. This is the state when, with His gifts dominating the life of the soul, the Holy Ghost is triumphant in the saints. The perfect model is Jesus Christ, every act of Whose will was completely subject to the motion of the Spirit. After Him, the " Virgin most faithful " is the ideal type and more accessible to our weakness since Christ, being God, will always be infinitely beyond us.

---

[7] *Summa Theologica*, III, q. 61, a. 5.   [8] *Matt.* V, 48.

This mystical life, the normal development of the grace of Baptism, becomes the immediate preparation for the deiform life of the blessed. Theology even dares to define it as " eternal life begun." Having " put on " the divine manner of life as far as it is possible to a creature on earth, the soul already maintains itself, as Sister Elizabeth of the Trinity said, " as changeless and as calm, as though it were already in eternity "; in the " fellowship " of the Father, of His Son and of the Holy Ghost. In the deiform light imparted to it, the soul sees God and all things else " after the manner of the Word " in that unique light in which the Father contemplates the Son and His Spirit, and in which each of the Persons of the Trinity beholds creation.

It loves the Divine Persons and its neighbor, as God loves Himself and all the universe, in one and the same Spirit of Love. Thus, by this deiform activity of the theological virtues under the action of the gifts, the soul becomes, in the bold words of St. Thomas: " a sharer of the Word and of Love—*particeps Verbi, particeps Amoris.*" [9] Amid the happenings of daily life, it truly moves in the manner of God.[10] Like Jesus Christ, its Model, its slightest act is guided by the breathing of the Spirit. This " Godlike behavior " continues to be the *proper effect* of the gifts of the Holy Ghost. For the soul, it is life with God in transforming union, " joined to the Lord in one spirit," [11] having no other light, no other love. Of course, this participation must be understood *with all the distinctions required by our irreducible individuality in the presence of the Uncreated.* The soul, kept conscious of its nothingness by the Spirit of fear and of knowledge, is at peace, trusting in the assistance of the Almighty God and Savior, Who will safely keep for it its eternal inheritance.

In their turn, the cardinal virtues enter into this phase of divine transformation, in the measure in which we can find the ideal prototype of them in God. In God, prudence is that

---

[9] *Summa Theologica,* I, q. 38, a. 1.

[10] *III Sent.,* d. XXXIV, q. 1, a. 3: *ut jam non humanitas sed quasi Deus factus participatione operetur.*

[11] *I Cor.* VI, 17.

universal Providence, which "mightily and sweetly"[12] safeguards and directs the smallest events in the world. There is no temperance in God, since there are no animal passions in the Godhead, but a blessed concentration in unity, and a mysterious *circuminsession* of the Divine Persons, resting in one another: the Father in the Son, and both together in Their one Love, and rejoicing in common in their own happiness. God's strength or fortitude is the unchanging tranquillity that maintains the Blessed Trinity above our human disturbances in an unalterable peace. Finally, God's justice consists in the benevolent but faithful observance of the laws freely decreed by His love, for His own glory and for the true welfare of the predestined.

The soul that has learned the divine ways shares to a greater or lesser degree in this deiform life which renders it so pleasing to the Divine Persons. "The Trinity so loves to find Its own image in creatures."[13] The Master, who knew this, said: "Be you therefore perfect as also your heavenly Father is perfect."[14] All these virtues, seen in the "deiform way," imprint on the soul a resemblance to the very life of God. Through grace and by virtue of its properties, the soul truly *enters into a participation of the Uncreated Nature and the divine attributes.*

Then, despising all the happenings and vanities of this world, its prudence takes refuge in the contemplation of divine things alone. In the measure in which the body allows, its temperance puts aside all sensible joys, not even recognizing them any more. It is the "*Nescivi*"[15] of the soul that has found its God and which, possessing Him, is truly and blessedly forgetful of all else. Its fortitude is a certain resemblance to the divine changelessness; nothing has any power to distract or disturb it, still less to turn it away from God. For it, struggles have ceased; God has triumphed in its life. All its powers are directed towards Him, as justice demands, to serve Him and adore Him. In everything it renders honor and glory to God, living with Him in the unity of a single Spirit. The soul that has reached these heights

[12] *Wis.* VIII, 1.
[13] Letter to Canon A., August 1902.
[14] *Matt.* V, 48.
[15] Cf. *Last Retreat*, 2nd day.

finally enters the cycle of the life of the Trinity, and seems to live as God lives, " in an eternal present." [16]

A constant reader of the *Spiritual Canticle* and of the *Living Flame of Love*, Sister Elizabeth of the Trinity stopped only at the description of these higher states. Not that she ignored or despised Carmel's hard road to the summit. On the contrary, she held that an implacable asceticism is implied in the description of the loftiest mystical states. The soul that is not dead to all things, " which indulges in useless thoughts or desires," [17] thereby bars the way to the path that leads to the heights. Only a soul " resolved to take a *real share* in the Passion of its Master " [18] and to be made conformable to His death reaches transforming union. A true " Praise of Glory " is crucified in the likeness of the Son. We must recognize, however, that her spirit tends to remain predominantly mystical. We find in her a complete and very personal body of doctrine upon transforming union, the most complete expression of which is found in her last letters and her two retreats, all written at a time when her own life was dominated by the deiform activity of the gifts of the Holy Ghost. This individual and completely irreducible character of the mystical teaching of Sister Elizabeth of the Trinity should not surprise us. The Spirit is essentially multiform and there are many mansions in transforming union; one might say that their variety is infinite, God's glory being the better manifested thereby. We find the different descriptions in the works of the Fathers and Doctors of the Church who have treated of mystical questions according to their temperament, their tastes and their milieu. St. John of the Cross and St. Teresa have left us analyses which, notwithstanding fundamental agreement, show appreciable differences. St. Thomas Aquinas, in accordance with the essentially didactic form of his genius, and making use of the thought of Plotinus, who has the greatest mystical genius of antiquity, managed to include in a curious article a brief, but both complete and profound study of the likeness of

---

[16] *Last Retreat*, 10th day.   [17] *Ibid.*, 2nd day.   [18] *Ibid.*, 5th day.

the divine manner of life with that attainable by "a few of the earth's rare perfect souls."[19] In it we find condensed, as in a little mystical *summa*, the supreme point of his moral teaching and his personal doctrine on transforming union.

Here again, and here above all, it would be puerile to expect of Sister Elizabeth of the Trinity a systematic body of teaching on the existence, the necessity, the nature and the properties of the gifts of the Holy Ghost in the light of transforming union. The Carmelite's vocation is not to give an exposition of the ways of the spiritual life but to follow them in the silence of a life wholly "hidden with Christ in God."[20] It is the theologian's task to discern the doctrinal value of this example and show how it is the concrete realization of the principles of mystical science.

So, in a Carmelite setting, Sister Elizabeth of the Trinity stands forth as the living incarnation of the classical doctrine of the gifts of the Holy Spirit.

It is too often incorrectly thought that souls are moved by the Holy Ghost only in the case of heroic acts, and that such motion is accompanied by extraordinary graces. These graces, however, are pure charismata sometimes granted by God to His servants for the good of the Church, but it is of the highest importance to distinguish them from the activity of the gifts. In themselves they may be disassociated from the latter. The Mother of God, who remains the ideal type, the absolutely perfect exemplar of the faithful soul who is ever docile to the Holy Ghost, never had an ecstasy, and in all probability did not work a single miracle during the course of her life on earth. She passed unnoticed among the women of Nazareth and, nevertheless, the smallest action, the slightest look of the Mother of God was of more value in the co-redemption than the combined sufferings of all the martyrs and even all the merits of the Church Militant up to the end of time. The workings of sanctifying grace belong to an infinitely superior and an essentially Trinitarian order. The more Godlike the principle

---

[19] *Summa Theologica*, I-II, q. 61, a. 5. [20] *Col.* III, 3.

of action, the more meritorious is the activity. The smallest act of Christ, because it was the act of the Person of God, possessed an infinite meritorious, impetratory and satisfactory value. By a smile or at play, Jesus could have redeemed myriads of worlds.

This is an extremely important point of doctrine. It is comforting to see it supported by the saints. Like St. Teresa of the Child Jesus, Sister Elizabeth of the Trinity declared that the highest sanctity does not consist in revelations and miracles or in an extraordinary mode of life but in pure faith, in as genuine and divine a charity as possible shown by the unflagging performance of daily duty. " Everything lies in the intention. We can marvellously sanctify the smallest things, transforming the most ordinary actions of life into divine actions! " [21] Let us not dream of martyrdom or ecstasy. " A soul that lives in union with God does nothing that is not supernatural, and its commonest actions, instead of separating it from God, on the contrary, draw it ever nearer to Him." [22]

She has left us a very thoughtful passage on Our Lady, which shows to what a degree her intuition of these truths had reached: " The most trivial actions were sanctified by her." [23] And in Our Lady of the Incarnation, silent and faithful, lost in adoration of the Word hidden in her womb, Sister Elizabeth had learned to recognize the true model for interior souls who wish to live simply and to be always docile to the slightest motion of the Spirit. There, in her eyes, is authentic sanctity. But " what recollection, what loving attention to God is demanded by this sublime work! St. John of the Cross says that the soul must remain in silence and absolute solitude in order that the Most High may realize all His desires in it. Then He *carries* it, so to speak, as a mother carries her child in her arms, and *taking charge of its direction Himself*, He reigns in it by the abundance and serenity of the peace which He diffuses in it." [24]

[21] Letter to her mother, September 10, 1906.
[22] *Ibid.*
[23] *Heaven on Earth*, 12th prayer. [24] Letter to the Abbé Ch., Spring 1905.

All its acts are its own and, at the same time, they are the acts of God.[25] The soul is at once passive beneath the divine action and acting by its own free will. God does not suppress its personal activity but directs and elevates it in a wholly divine way of His own. This is obviously the characteristic feature of the mystical regime of the gifts. " The soul that enters into, that dwells in ' the deep things of God,' that consequently does all by Him, with Him and in Him,' with that clear gaze that gives it a certain resemblance to the only simple Being ... this soul, by each of its actions, *however commonplace they may be*, becomes more deeply rooted in Him it loves. Everything within it renders homage to the thrice holy God; it may be called a perpetual *Sanctus*, a perpetual ' Praise of Glory.' " [26] This is the perfect life, with the soul constantly docile to the least breathing of the Spirit.

One last general remark is called for. Sanctifying grace brings to the soul at one stroke the whole supernatural organism of the virtues and the gifts, but their free activity does not take the same defined form in every case. Some souls excel in a particular virtue, while the other virtues—though present and coming into play when circumstances require—are less pronounced. Thus fortitude is the shining virtue of martyrs, purity of virgins, luminous faith in the lives of the doctors, pure love of God in the silence of the contemplatives. Similarly, certain gifts of the Holy Ghost appear predominant in the lives of the saints. The gift of counsel is more conspicuous in men called to govern; the gift of knowledge, often accompanied by the gift of tears, in the apostles, who are moved to work for the conversion of their brethren in Christ and deeply affected by the moral distress of the latter. The gift of wisdom radiates in the great contemplatives who, soaring above the created, live for God alone, habitually in the company of the Divine Persons.

It is not surprising that in the life and spiritual teaching of Elizabeth of the Trinity the seven gifts of the Holy Ghost are not so sharply discernible. The gift of fear appears but dimly,

---

[25] Cf. *Heaven on Earth*, 3rd prayer.   [26] *Last Retreat*, 8th day.

as does also the gift of counsel. On the other hand, the gift of fortitude is brilliantly evident in the sufferings which made her last days a terrible Calvary. Those which are most clearly evident in her are the great contemplative gifts of understanding and wisdom, which instinctively direct the movement of her soul towards the depths of the life of the Trinity.

This analysis of the gifts of the Holy Ghost will enable us to penetrate the more secret workings of the love of the Trinity in this soul which was so divinely loved.

2. Her pure soul never knew the stain of mortal sin; consequently there was no trace in her of that servile fear found among worldly people; nor does she appear to have known that dread of hell experienced by so many other holy souls. One aspect of sin alone counted in her eyes; it was an infinite offense against the God of Love. That is what overwhelmed her in the condition of sinners and in her own life; the filial fear of a soul that dreads only the sorrow caused by its sins to a Father Who is infinitely good and deserving of perfect fidelity. " I weep over the sins which have hurt Thee so much." [27]

Rather death than sin! " If ever I should be about to offend mortally the Spouse I love above all things, then, O death, strike me down quickly before I incur this great misfortune." [28] " I feel ready to die rather than offend Thee wilfully, even by venial sin." [29]

Under the influence of this spirit of fear, the soul finds itself trembling before the infinite Majesty that dwells within it and could annihilate it in an instant, a fate it feels it deserves on account of its sins. So long as the soul remains in this attitude of holy fear, almost of holy terror, any movement of self-complacency becomes impossible. With all its strength, it regrets whatever in it may be displeasing to God. This spirit of fear keeps it in the humility which is the guardian of perfect charity. It is a necessary disposition for every creature faced with the Majesty of God; a disposition which constantly animates the blessed in heaven and attains its supreme expression in the soul

[27] *Diary*, March 14, 1899. [28] *Ibid.*, March 10, 1899. [29] *Ibid.*, March 17, 1899.

of Christ as He beholds the dread power of His Father, so infinitely terrifying to sinners.

While we do not find in Sister Elizabeth of the Trinity this reverential fear before the terrible Majesty of God, so poignantly present in the souls of some saints and in the soul of Christ during the Agony of Gethsemane, we can easily discover other effects of it in her life. To the gift of fear is attached that primary beatitude of poverty of spirit which has a special affinity with the first of the seven gifts, the one which renders the soul perfectly docile to the influence of the Holy Ghost. " Blessed are the poor in spirit ": [30] those who are utterly detached from everything, who desire no riches save the Trinity. They desire absolutely nothing else—nothing; nothing in creatures, nothing in the memory and in the senses; poverty, poverty, poverty! Nothing in the understanding except the light of the Word; nothing in the will and in the depths of the soul but the presence of the Trinity Which alone can render it blessed. Under the influence of this spirit of fear, the soul, freed from any thought of love apart from God, flies to its nothingness, empties itself of self, dreads the smallest sin, the slightest imperfection, the least clinging to or reliance upon creatures. In order to realize this blessed and liberating poverty, it desires to walk absolutely " alone with the Alone."

Such was the decidedly Carmelite form taken by the gift of fear in Sister Elizabeth of the Trinity; the Spirit urging her to divest herself of all things so as to take refuge in God alone, above every human motive, in an emptiness free of all created things.

3. The gift of fortitude is a most characteristic gift both in the spiritual physiognomy and in the mystical doctrine of the servant of God.

Her first childish fears soon vanished as she came to know the contemplative's contact with the soul of the Crucified. This is the secret of the extremely rapid transformation of her attitude towards suffering. Her diary shows that she had early

---

[30] *Matt.* V, 3.

gained mastery over herself and over the childish nervousness that made her dread a visit to the dentist. Her ideal had become virile. She looked suffering in the face and even desired it eagerly.

At nineteen she wrote: " I want to live and die ' crucified.' " [31] God hears such prayers. She did well to adopt as the motto of her religious life: " To be identified with every movement of the soul of the Crucified."

The religious life is a real martyrdom. The souls of saints find in it an abundant harvest of crucifying sacrifices, the merit of which may equal, and even surpass, martyrdom by blood. If religious never let pass a single occasion of mortifying human nature and surrender without reserve to the demands of Love, God can reveal to every soul, in the setting of its vocation, the road to Calvary which will lead it, without a single false turn, to perfect conformity with His crucified Son. The absolutely faithful observance of a religious Rule approved by the Church would suffice to lead souls to the highest peaks of holiness. For that reason, Pope John XXII said: " Give me a Friar Preacher who keeps his Rule and his Constitutions, and I will canonize him without any further miracle." As much might be said of the legislation of the Carmel and of every other form of religious life. The perfect fulfillment of humble duty calls for the daily exercise of the gift of fortitude. It is not the extraordinary things they do which make the saints, but the *divine manner* in which they do them. This " heroism of little things " of which St. Teresa of the Child Jesus is perhaps the most striking example in the Church, was realized after a new fashion in the Carmelite of Dijon. Extraordinary mortifications were always forbidden her, but she supplied their place by heroic fidelity to the smallest observance of her Order and knew how to find in the Carmelite Rule " the form of her sanctity " [32] and the secret of " giving her blood, drop by drop, for the Church until she was completely spent." [33]

The fact is that, contrary to what is commonly believed, the

[31] *Diary*, March 31, 1899.
[32] Letter to Canon A., July 15, 1903.   [33] To her Prioress.

gift of fortitude lies less in courageously undertaking great works for God than in patiently bearing life's trials, meeting them with a smile. This strength of soul bursts out gloriously in the saints in the hour of martyrdom and, in the life of Jesus, at the moment of His death on the Cross. Joan of Arc is greater bound to the stake than triumphantly entering Orleans at the head of her army.

We find both these forms of the gift of fortitude in Sister Elizabeth of the Trinity.

In the beginning of her religious life, and in the enthusiasm of her first fervor, she was consumed by an almost insatiable hunger and thirst for sanctity. " I love to live in these days of persecution. How necessary it is to be a saint . . . Ask Him to give me this holiness for which I thirst . . . I want to love Him as the saints and martyrs do." [34] Nor in her case were these merely empty words, as in some souls we meet, who dream of martyrdom for love and can scarcely bear the least annoyances and pinpricks of common life. Sister Elizabeth of the Trinity did not run after the mirage of a chimerical sanctity, but rather, with the practical realism of the saints and enlightened by her crucified Lord, she was wise enough to find in the most trivial actions of ordinary life the best means of testifying to her love of God. " I do not know whether I shall have the happiness of witnessing unto blood for my Bridegroom, but at least if I live my Carmelite life *fully*, I shall have the consolation of spending myself for Him." [35] " Were I asked the secret of happiness, I should say: ' To stop paying the slightest attention to self. To deny self all the time! ' " [36] During the last months those around her saw her go forward to meet suffering " with the majesty of a Queen." [37] Her whole frame was being destroyed, wasted, burned up. It was the hour of the triumph of the gift of fortitude in that martyr's soul. The valiant ' Praise of Glory ' becoming ever more closely identified with the soul

[34] Letter to Canon A., September 11, 1901.
[35] To the same, July 1903.
[36] Letter to Fr. de S., September 11, 1906.
[37] Evidence of a witness.

of the Crucified seemed to exhibit the divine strength of Calvary. Seeing her, the Prioress thought instinctively of the Crucifix. She herself was quite aware of the meaning of this consummation of her life in suffering. To her mother, she wrote: " You are afraid that I am a victim, marked out for suffering. I beg of you not to be sad over it. I do not feel worthy of it. Think what it means to share in the sufferings of my crucified Bridegroom and go to my passion with Him; to be with Him a co-redemptrix! "[38] " More and more I am drawn to suffering. This longing almost exceeds the desire for heaven, though that is very strong. Never has the good God made me understand so clearly how suffering is the greatest love token that He can give to a creature. Truly, at each new pain, I kiss my Master's Cross and say ' Thank you! ' I am not worthy of it. I think how suffering was the companion of His life and I—I do not deserve to be treated as His Father treated Him! "[39]

" The sign by which we know that God is in us and that we are possessed by His Love is that we receive not only patiently but *gratefully* whatever hurts us or makes us suffer. Mother darling, accept every trial, every vexation, every unpleasantness that happens in the light that radiates from the Cross. That is the way to please God and advance in the way of love. Oh! thank Him for me. I am *so* happy! I wish I could sow a little of this happiness among those I love . . . I give you tryst in the shadow of the Cross, there to learn the science of suffering."[40]

Joyous in her will beneath the hand that was crucifying her, Sister Elizabeth loved to take refuge in devotion to the Queen of Martyrs, plunged in the immensity of a sorrow " great as the sea," [41] yet " at the cross her station keeping," [42] filled with a wholly divine joy *plane gaudens*,[43] at the thought of the

[38] Letter to her mother, July 18, 1906.
[39] To the same, September 25, 1906.
[40] *Ibid.*
[41] *Lament.* II. 13.
[42] *Stabat Mater.*
[43] Encyclical " *Ad diem illum*," February 2, 1904.

propitiation of the Trinity by the offering of her Son, and at the sight of the Redemption being wrought before her eyes. One of Elizabeth's last notes to her mother gives us a glimpse of her in this heroic attitude of the gift of fortitude. "There is a Being Who is Love, and Who wishes us to live in His company. He is here staying with me, helping me to suffer, teaching me *to soar above the pain, to rest in Him* . . . That transforms everything." [44]

Obviously, this exceeds the human mode of behavior, and can be explained only by the Spirit of Fortitude Who sustained our Lord on the Cross.

4. The Spirit of Jesus assumes many varied aspects in us. He is the Spirit of fear, of strength, of piety, of counsel, of knowledge, of understanding and of wisdom.

In the gift of fear and the beatitude of the poor in spirit, He incites the soul to absolute detachment, and whispers this watchword to it: "Nothing, Nothing, *Nada*." [45] The soul is to rely only on God Who never fails anyone. Distrustful of itself, it takes refuge in the divine omnipotence. Then the Spirit of fortitude takes possession of it, and makes it declare confidently: "I hunger and thirst for justice." [46] "In Thee, O Lord, have I hoped, let me never be confounded." [47] Ready to endure every kind of martyrdom for its God, the soul can cry with St. Teresa of the Child Jesus: "One kind of martyrdom would not suffice me; I want them all" [48] or with Sister Elizabeth of the Trinity: "I want to love as the saints did, as the martyrs did . . . to love until I die of love." [49] Who can tell the wonders which the Spirit of Jesus can silently accomplish in such souls? He makes His way into the innermost depths of their being, making them cry out to God with unspeakable groanings. The soul, the adopted

---

[44] Letter to her mother, October 20, 1906.
[45] Drawing of St. John of the Cross.
[46] Cf. *Matt.* V, 6.
[47] *Ps.* XXX, 2.
[48] *Autobiography of St. Teresa of the Child Jesus.*
[49] Cf. *Diary*, and letter to Canon A., September 11, 1901.

child of the Trinity, murmurs with a child's tenderness: "*Abba, Father!*"[50] It is the very Spirit of the Son.

Clearly recognizing this divine Fatherhood, Sister Elizabeth loved to consider this grace of adoption in the light of her dear St. Paul. To do so quickened her whole worship of God. She had no rigid method or complicated formulae to paralyze the spontaneous movements of her child's heart. She went to God as a child goes to its Father. There was complete simplicity. For her the Trinity was a loved home, the "Father's house," which we ought never leave,[51] the family circle in which her baptized soul feels entirely at home. All the movements of her soul are directed towards God as towards a dearly loved Father and her sublime prayer to the Trinity is but the outpouring of a child's heart to God. To discover the secret of her life of prayer, we should have to analyze that prayer to the Trinity in the light of the gift of piety. How far we are from the self-interested bargaining which so encumbers many lives of prayer that it would seem as though these souls approached God only to beg help from Him. Here the first place is given to the prayer of silent adoration, the identifying of the soul with every movement of the soul of Christ, the contemplation of the "abysses" of the Trinity. Without effort, Sister Elizabeth's soul soars aloft to the Divine Persons with the very Spirit of the Son. "O my Christ . . . enter my soul as Adorer, as Restorer, as Savior! . . . And Thou, O Father, bend towards Thy poor little creature and overshadow her, beholding in her none other than Thy beloved Son in Whom Thou hast set all Thy pleasure."[52]

Doubtless, as behooves a Carmelite and a co-redemptrix, she also finds a place for the prayer of petition for sinners, but in her life of prayer, adoring praise holds by far the first place. This is the purest spirit of Jesus, the perfect Adorer of the Father, Who came on earth primarily to gather around Him the true worshippers whom "the Father seeketh"[53] and whom the Trinity awaits.

[50] *Rom.* VIII, 15.
[51] *Heaven on Earth*, 1st prayer.
[52] *Prayer to the Trinity.*
[53] *John* IV, 23.

Indeed, the special character of the gift of piety is to urge the religious soul in its relations with God to rise above all considerations of personal interest and every created incentive: to be above both needs and benefits.[54]

While the infused virtue of religion renders to God the worship due to Him as Sovereign Lord, First Cause and Last End of all things, Author of the whole natural and supernatural order, the gift of piety, without keeping account of all this debt based upon the divine liberality, looks only to the Uncreated Excellence of the Eternal. It sets no limit to its praise, save the glory which God finds in Himself, in His Word and in His infinite perfections. In her *Magnificat*, our Lady reveals the exaltation of her soul as it is breathed upon by the Spirit of Piety, when she magnifies God not only because of the grace of her divine Motherhood, for which all generations are to call her " blessed," but above all because He is great in Himself, and because the wonders wrought in His humble handmaid are but the sign that He is mighty and " holy is His Name—*et sanctum nomen ejus.*"[55] Similarly, the reason for praising God and exulting in Him is none other than the greatness of the Divinity which the exterior works manifest in only the slightest degree.

The virtue of religion considers God as Creator and Provider: " Thou art worthy, O Lord our God, to receive glory and honor . . . because Thou hast created all things, and for Thy will they were and have been created."[56] But it also renders to God a cultus of gratitude and praise because He is the Author of Redemption and of the whole supernatural order. " Thou art worthy, O Lord, to take the book and open the seals thereof; because thou wast slain and hast redeemed us to God, in Thy blood, out of every tribe, and tongue, and people and nation. And hast made us to our God a kingdom and priests and we shall reign on the earth."[57]

The gift of piety rises above all these considerations of God's goodness with respect to us, to rest only in the consideration of

---

[54] See the classical theologian of the Gifts of the Holy Ghost—John of St. Thomas, etc.
[55] *Luke* I, 49.   [56] *Apoc.* IV, 11.   [57] *Ibid.*

God as He is in Himself: the unfathomable mystery of the infinite perfections of this Divine Essence within the Trinity. It is not only God's Fatherhood of souls by grace that claims its attention, but like the Word the Spirit of Piety penetrates the profoundest depths of the Godhead, the most hidden riches of the Uncreated Nature to the eternally fruitful Paternity: the generation of a Word, consubstantial with the Father, His image, His glory and His splendor, the Spiration of a common Love consubstantial and co-eternal, which has united and will unite Father, Son and Holy Ghost for all eternity; identical Nature, communicated by the Father to the Son, by the Father and Son to the Holy Ghost, without succession of time, inequality of perfection, or dependence, yet with order and distinction of the Persons in an indivisible Unity.

The incentive of the gift of piety is the Trinity Itself. The soul no longer stops with appreciation of His benefits, but desires to glorify God even as God is to Himself His own praise. The soul *seeks to equal the divine measure*, which sets a deiform seal upon its whole worship of prayer, thanksgiving and above all, adoration. In the words of that profound statement, so familiar to Sister Elizabeth of the Trinity, it *adores God for His own sake*, because He is God. The Church on earth is specially moved by the gift of piety when she sings daily in the Gloria of the Mass: "*Gratias agimus tibi propter magnam gloriam tuam*—we give Thee thanks for Thy great glory." This worship which glorifies the divine Majesty has no reference to any benefit but solely to God's greatness in Himself. The object of this adoring piety is the Godhead in Its own uncreated excellence, infinitely superior to all His gifts. Sister Elizabeth's soul was moved as that of her Mother, St. Teresa, had previously been, when the Office of Prime on Sunday put on her lips the Athanasian Creed, in which an enumeration of the divine perfections hidden within the mystery of the Trinity passes before the contemplative gaze of the Church; Unity in Trinity and Trinity in Unity, without confusion of Persons or division of Substance;

one only Godhead—the Father, Son and Holy Ghost; the glory equal, the majesty co-eternal; equal in power, immensity, eternity.[58]

In the closing hours of her life, completely dominated by the thought of eternity, Sister Elizabeth of the Trinity loved the chapters of the Apocalypse which describe that life of adoration of the heavenly liturgy, in which, dwelling above all transitory things and even above itself, the soul adores God for His Own Sake and, in the words of the Psalmist, adores " the Lord for He is holy." "Adoration! Ah, that word comes from heaven! It seems to me that it can be described as the ecstasy of love; love crushed by the beauty, the strength, the vast grandeur of Him it loves." The soul " knows that He Whom it adores possesses in Himself all happiness and all glory, and ' casting its crown ' before Him, as do the blessed, it despises self, loses sight of self and finds its beatitude in Him Whom it adores." [59]

With the eternal liturgy, the supreme development of the gift of piety, the Church Triumphant, swept by Christ, and in Him, into the praise of the Word, realizes the dearest longing of Sister Elizabeth's adoring soul: the unceasing praise of glory before the throne of the Trinity.

5. The gift of counsel is, above all, a gift of governance. Now Sister Elizabeth of the Trinity was never prioress nor did she have any office involving the care of souls. Her entire religious life was divided between the novitiate and the infirmary. Nevertheless, she possessed this Spirit of God in a high degree. The fact is that, although the gift of counsel is more obviously needed by those holding authority, it is no less necessary for all souls, if they are to order their lives perfectly in accordance with God's designs for them. In the case of superiors, it takes on the form of a prudent and supernatural rule which, even amid the organization of material things, cares above all for the spiritual welfare of the souls of the religious and for the greater glory of God. It inspires in inferiors a

[58] *Quicumque*, at Prime on Sunday.   [59] *Last Retreat*, 8th day.

watchful docility to submit to every manifestation of the will of God as shown by His lawful representatives. Whatever the talents or the defects of these latter, God alone speaks through them, and deserves to be heard.

In Sister Elizabeth's case, the gift of counsel was first evident in this form of perfect docility to her spiritual director. As a girl she sought his advice in reference to everything affecting the welfare of her soul, and faithfully accepted his decisions. As a novice, she had constant—sometimes almost too frequent—recourse to her Prioress, even for mere nothings, in her anxiety to act completely in accord with the divine will. Someone who knew her declared: "It would be enough to suggest: 'Our Reverend Mother said . . .' to send her to the end of the world." [60] The Spirit of Counsel not only leads souls by personal and secret inspirations; it also urges them to let themselves be guided and to remain in peace under the direction of those who have the grace to decide and command.

Later, the gift of counsel was revealed in her in another and a higher form. Certain of her correspondents looked to her for the decisive word which was to set them on the way to union with God. It is surprising how easily Sister Elizabeth could adapt herself to these extremely varied personalities: members of her family, children, young girls, people of the world living in the most diverse conditions, priests. No correspondence could be less stilted or artificial. When she wrote to instruct or to point out a moral, she did so without the slightest trace of pedantry but with great discretion, exquisite tact and a perfect grasp of a situation. If need be, she could wait for years for the opportunity of saying the word of reproach which will completely alter the life of a soul. "God be with You. When I am up yonder, will you let me help you, even reprove you if I see that you are not giving the divine Master everything—just because I love you? May He keep you all His, wholly faithful! In Him, I am always yours." [61]

In illuminating, quiet language she explains the highest spiri-

[60] Evidence of a witness. [61] To a friend.

tual thoughts on the "Praise of Glory" or the mystery of the Trinity, in a way all can understand, and this gives to her spirituality that balance and doctrinal accuracy which has led so many people to make the writings of Sister Elizabeth of the Trinity their daily reading. Such facility of transposition and adaptability are derived directly from the gift of counsel, which enables souls after they have consulted the supreme reasons of the Word's Wisdom to discern the most practical, simple and expeditious means of pushing through life's thousand and one difficulties to reach the heights of divine union.

This was the characteristic form which the Spirit of Counsel took in her case. She was not called upon to govern a community, but to lead a multitude of souls to the depths of the Trinitarian life by the path of absolute abnegation and forgetfulness of self, to that "great silence within which allows God to stamp His image upon souls and to transform them into Himself." [62]

6. With the gifts of knowledge, understanding and wisdom, we reach the deepest psychological processes of the souls of the saints. The activity of the higher gifts in them makes it possible for us to glimpse their most inward feelings when confronted with the *nothingness* of the creature and the ALL of God. Hence, the primary importance of these gifts when studying the soul of a contemplative. In the case of Elizabeth of the Trinity, they furnish the key to her spiritual life and her mystical teaching.

The Spirit of Knowledge gives an understanding of creatures in the light of charity and makes it possible to judge them according to their contingent and temporal properties, and even to rise by them to God.

Under this impulsion, a twofold movement takes place in the soul: it understands the nothingness, the emptiness of the creature, and at the same time, in beholding creation, it sees the footprints of God. Thus, the gift of knowledge drew tears from St. Dominic at the thought of the lot of poor sinners and inspired St. Francis to compose his famous *Canticle to the Sun*

[62] Letter to Sister Odile, October 1906.

at the sight of the pageant of nature. We can trace both these currents in the well-known passage of the *Spiritual Canticle* of St. John of the Cross in which the Saint describes how the sight of created nature is at once a help and a torment to the soul of the mystic. The visible universe reveals the passage of the Beloved, but He, the Invisible, has gone by, and the soul must wait until, transformed into Him, it meets Him again in the Beatific Vision.

In great converts—as St. Augustine, for instance, reveals in his *Confessions*—the gift takes the form of a painful experience of sin. Sister Elizabeth's pure soul never knew this disturbing and tragic aspect of the effects of the gift of knowledge. In harmony with the even tenor of her contemplative life, in her it tended rather to become a powerful means of detachment and perfection. Creatures are deceptive and become an obstacle to the fullness of the divine life. The soul must fly from them, must no longer know them; it must consider all things as dross in order to gain Christ, and forget all in Him. It is the " *Nescivi* " of her Last Retreat, and of her *Heaven on Earth*. Her soul longs to pass creatures by without seeing them, to halt only when it reaches Christ. The whole ascesis of silence is explained in this light. Are all created things put together worth even a look from him who—though it be but once—has felt God?

The gift of knowledge is revealed in the saints under another aspect—positive in form. As was the case in the state of innocence, the sight of creatures irresistibly draws them to God. This powerful voice of the concert of creation sometimes exercises so powerful an effect upon certain contemplative souls that they have been heard to whisper " Hush " at the sight of flowers. Moved by the Spirit of Knowledge, the Psalmist says: " *Caeli enarrant gloriam Dei*—The heavens show forth the glory of God." [68] It is in this latter light that the movements of grace habitually experienced by Sister Elizabeth of the Trinity as she beheld the beauties of nature must be regarded. For her, as for the saints, nature was God's great book. As a

[68] *Ps.* XVIII, 2.

girl, she loved the great lonely woods, the wild grandeur of the Pyrenees, the vast ocean; above all, the boundless spaces of a starry night. Her soul was overcome by an impression of the infinite and, to an intense degree, contact with nature gave her God.

As she grew older, these two effects of the gift of knowledge were mingled in her soul. The wretchedness of the creature and the sense of her own nothingness always cast her upon God alone. " If I look at things from the earthly point of view, I see solitude and even emptiness, for I cannot say that my heart has not suffered." [64] " How good it is in the hours when we feel our wretchedness to go and be saved by Him "; [65] " When we look at the divine world which enfolds us, even here in our exile and in which we can move, how the things of earth disappear! All is as though it were not; it is less than nothing. The saints understood so well what true knowledge is, the knowledge that causes us to go out from ourselves, and to throw ourselves upon God and live by Him alone." [66]

Her soul was thus given that knowledge of the *nothingness* of the creature and the ALL of God, which the Spirit of Jesus gives to those who love Him and which Scripture calls the " knowledge of the holy things." [67]

7. Great contemplatives, like eagles, lift their eyes to the summits. They know that the least light on the Trinity is infinitely more satisfying than the knowledge of the whole universe. What are all the movements of the atoms and creatures that have come from God, beside the silent and eternal generation of the Word hidden in His bosom?

It is the work of the two great contemplative gifts of understanding and wisdom to enable us to enter the inmost recesses of these depths of the Trinity. In this wholly deiform light, the soul sees things as God Himself sees them. St. John of the Cross dares to say that the soul which has attained this degree of

[64] Letter to Canon A., January 4, 1904.
[65] Letter to Madame A., November 24, 1905.
[66] To the same, November 24, 1904.
[67] *Wis.* X, 10.

transforming union becomes a sharer in the mystery of the divine processions: the generation of the Word, the Spiration of Love. In this high light of the gifts, it accomplishes by faith and charity acts reserved to God, and proper to the Divine Persons. It is " made perfect in One," [68] as our Lord promised. The word " participation " indicates both the infinite distance which ever remains between God and His creature and a real communication of the Trinitarian life by grace. The soul shares in the light of the Word and in the movement of uncreated Love: *Particeps Verbi, particeps Amoris*,[69] to use the bold expression of St. Thomas, who is so careful about doctrinal exactness and always so measured in his terms.

The essential effect of the gift of understanding is to enable us to penetrate as deeply as possible into the supernatural truths which faith is content to accept on simple external testimony. This loving and delightful understanding of the highest divine truth, particularly of the mystery of the Trinity, its favorite subject, does not depend upon the keenness of the intellect of the subject, but upon his degree of love and his perfect docility to the breathing of the Spirit.

On earth, the most secret touches of this Spirit will always escape us, as will also what is most divine in the lives of the saints. The glimpses we can see in Sister Elizabeth of the Trinity will show us that this action of the Spirit of Understanding attained its fullness only when, having entered Carmel, she had become acquainted with the writings of St. John of the Cross, and read St. Paul and had suffered the final purifications of the life of faith.

We may group the effects of the gift of understanding under six heads, since a divine reality may be hidden either under accidents, words, figures or analogies, and sensible things, or in its causes or in its effects. Clearly this Spirit is manifested very differently according to the circumstances, the varying temperaments of the saints and their missions. It enables some to penetrate the meaning of the Scriptures, others to discern

---

[68] *John* XVII, 23.
[69] *Summa Theologica*, I, q. XXXVIII, a. 1. See also II-II, q. XXIV, art. 2.

the divine plan in souls; to some it gives a particular knowledge of the soul of Christ, of the mystery of Mary, or an understanding of the Redemption, of Providence, of some particular divine attribute, of the Unity of the Trinity. We should never finish were we to detail the innumerable ways in which this Spirit of Understanding, multiform in essence, can communicate Himself to men and angels according as God in His mercy is pleased to reveal His glory.

With Sister Elizabeth of the Trinity, the gifts of the Holy Ghost, like the phases of her spiritual life, normally took a Carmelite form. In the light of her life, it is easy to gather from her writings numerous passages which reveal the action of the gift of understanding.

Her contemplative's gaze long rested in adoration on the soul of Christ, hidden in the Tabernacle under the Eucharistic accidents. "We possess the vision in substance, under the humble form of the Host." [70]

The gift of understanding opened the Holy Scriptures to her and taught her their meaning. This is one of the most striking aspects of the action of the Spirit of God in her case. She usually proceeds by way of mystical paraphrase, made with rare penetration. Without doing violence to the literal sense, she draws from it *her* wonderful spiritual doctrine. The inspired words serve her as a starting point for magnificent contemplative developments, in which her Carmelite's soul delights. A single word of Holy Scripture sometimes gave her " the light of life " [71] for years. Thus she found in St. Paul the new name which revealed to her; as if by God, her vocation for all eternity—a vocation which was to be begun in time: " the unceasing praise of glory of the Trinity." In the last phase of her life, it is St. Paul again who expressed her final program of transformation into Christ in a text which brought grace to her soul: " Being made conformable to His death." [72] At times, a simple juxtaposition of texts is enough to cause the divine light to break into her soul. " ' Being predestinated according to

---

[70] Letter to the Abbé Ch., June 14, 1903.
[71] *John* VIII. 12.   [72] *Last Retreat*, 3rd day.

the purpose of Him who worketh all things according to the counsel of His will; that we may be unto the praise of His glory.' 'God . . . chose us in Him before the foundation of the world that we should be holy and unspotted *in His sight* in charity.' On comparing these two explanations of the divine 'and eternally immutable plan,' I conclude that, if I am worthily to fulfill my office of *Laudem Gloriae*, I must keep myself, whatever happens, *in the sight of God*. The Apostle also says ' in caritate,' that is to say, in God, for ' *Deus caritas est*,' and it is contact with the Divinity which will make me ' holy and unspotted in His sight.' " [73] To be the " Praise of Glory " by the continual practice of the presence of God; that was her whole vocation. And she understood that from one look into St. Paul.

We can discern in her a second movement of the gift of understanding, common in pure and contemplative souls to whom the smallest things recall symbolically or by analogy the presence of God. " When I see the sun bathing our cloisters in its rays, I think how God fills the soul that seeks only Him." [74] In the eyes of the saints, the whole visible universe takes on a spiritual meaning that leads them to God. They look on the mystical side of things. St. Catherine di Ricci could not see a red rose without thinking of the Blood of the Redemption. Elizabeth of the Trinity came of the line of those virgin souls who seem to have recovered the state of innocence and read God in the book of creation. From the time of her entry into Carmel she easily found God in the most trifling details of her life. " Here everything speaks of Him." [75] " At Carmel, the good God is everywhere." [76] " The Master is so present that one would think He were about to appear on our solitary garden path." [77] When informed of the birth of a little niece, she at once inquired the date of the Baptism, because she wished to be present in spirit when, under the signs of Christian regeneration, the

[73] *Ibid.*
[74] Letter to G. de G., September 14, 1902.
[75] To M-L. M., October 26, 1902.
[76] To her sister, 1901. [77] To her aunts, Easter 1903.

Trinity would come down into that soul. Such is the development of mystical symbolism: " Everything is a sacrament that gives us God." [78]

There is another aspect of the gift of understanding which is particularly noticeable in the case of contemplative theologians. After the hard work of human study, everything suddenly becomes luminous, under an impulse of the Spirit. A new world is seen in a principle or in a universal cause: Christ-the-Priest, the One Mediator between heaven and earth, or Mary the Virgin Co-Redemptrix, bearing spiritually in her womb all the members of the Mystical Body; or again the mystery of identification of God's innumerable attributes in His sovereign simplicity, and the conciliation of the Unity of Essence with the Trinity of Persons, in a Godhead infinitely surpassing the most probing research of all created intelligence. All are truths which the gift of understanding can penetrate effortlessly and fruitfully in the beatifying delight of " an eternal life begun on earth " in the very light of God.

Two things in particular arrested Sister Elizabeth's contemplative gaze: the universal influence of the Trinity present in the depths of souls in order to sanctify them, keeping them " changeless and calm " beneath God's creative action, and the redeeming activity of Christ, dwelling day and night within the soul in order to cleanse it, deify it and save it. These are two cardinal points of her spirituality.

Inversely, the gift of understanding reveals God and His almighty causality of effects, without working the long, discursive journeyings of human thought left to its own resources, but by a simple, comparative gaze and by intuition, " after the manner of God." In almost imperceptible signs and in the smallest events of its life, a soul that is attentive to the Holy Ghost suddenly discovers God's providential plan in its regard. Without dialectic reasoning upon causes, the simple sight of the effect of the justice or the mercy of God lets it perceive the whole mystery of divine predestination, the " exceeding charity " [79] which pursues souls in order to unite them to the beatifying Trinity. Through all, God leads to God.

When we know how little theological training Sister Elizabeth of the Trinity had received, we cannot but marvel at the depth and clarity of the pages she has left us on the mysteries of Christ and of Our Lady, on the indwelling of God in the souls of the just and on the praise of glory which should rise unceasingly to the adorable Trinity.

The thoughtful theologian is obliged to conclude that this supra-technical knowledge can be explained in her case only by her experience of the incommunicable knowledge reserved by God for " the pure of heart." [80]

8. The gift of wisdom is the royal gift; by it souls enter most closely into participation of the deiform mode of divine knowledge. Short of the beatific vision, which is the fullest measure of this gift, it is impossible to rise any higher. It is the gaze of the " Word breathing forth love " communicated to the soul, which judges of everything in the light of the highest and most divine causes, and judges them also for the highest reasons " after the manner of God."

The divinized soul which has been introduced by charity into the intimacy of the Divine Persons and, as it were, into the heart of the Trinity is so moved by the Spirit of Love that it contemplates all things from this center, this indivisible point from which they appear to it as they do to God Himself. Thus does it view the divine attributes, creation, redemption, glory, the hypostatic order, the smallest happenings in the world. So far as is possible to mere creatures, it tends to see from the same angle of vision as that from which God sees Himself and the whole universe. It is the deiform manner of contemplation in the light of the experience of the Deity which fills the soul with ineffable sweetness: *per quandam experientiam dulcedinis.*[81]

To understand this, we must understand that God can only see things in Himself: in His causality. It is not directly in

---

[79] *Eph.* II, 4.
[80] *Matt.* V, 8.
[81] *Summa Theologica*, I-II, q. 112, a. 5.

themselves that He knows His creatures, or in the movement of contingent and temporal causes which govern their activity. He beholds them eternally in His Son. He judges of every event of Providence in the light of His Essence and His Glory.

The soul can enter into participation in the Uncreated Light in two ways: first in an unchangeable manner, measured by the participated eternity, which is the vision of glory in the Word; second, outside of the Word by mystical experience and delightfully felt knowledge of God's sweetness either in the radiance of the light of glory or, in default of that—but in a state of violence—in the order of faith enlightened by the gifts. We cannot overemphasize the fact that mystical experience is, so to speak, exiled here on earth. The true Fatherland of the gifts is heaven, in the abiding joy of beatitude, in the face-to-face vision of the Trinity.

What happens here below in the soul which, so far at least as its state of union permits, judges everything in the light of the Trinity, the effects of Whose presence it feels deep within it? In the highest and most spiritual powers of its being, rendered deiform by sanctifying grace, an activity develops of such order as to permit the soul thus divinized to live in fellowship with the Divine Persons, on the level of a truly Trinitarian experience. Faith has already opened supernatural vistas to it and brought it into contact with the whole of heaven. The gifts of knowledge and understanding have allowed it, at the same time, to realize that the creature is *nothing* and that God is ALL, and to enter into the fathomless riches of the life of the Trinity. Then comes wisdom, the most divine of all the gifts, which will make this soul share, in the highest degree possible on earth, in the experimental knowledge which God enjoys within Himself, in His Word, breathing forth Love. Definitely established by transforming union in this divine atmosphere of the Uncreated Persons, having entered as an adopted child into the family of the Trinity, the soul has it in its power to "enjoy God."[82] Connaturalized in Him, it judges henceforth of all

[82] *Ibid.*, I, q. 43, a. 3 ad 1.

things—in God, in the world and in itself—with its experience of the Godhead. While the gift of knowledge acts by an ascending movement, raising the soul from creatures to God, and the gift of understanding penetrates all God's mysteries from without and within by a simple loving gaze, the gift of wisdom may be said never to leave the very heart of the Trinity. It looks at everything from that indivisible center. Thus deiform, the soul can see things only from their highest and most divine motives. The whole movement of the universe, down to its tiniest atoms, thus lies beneath its gaze in the all-pure light of the Trinity and of the divine attributes, and it beholds them in order, according to the rhythm with which these things proceed from God. Creation, redemption, hypostatic order—it sees all, even evil, ordained to the greater glory of the Trinity. Finally, it looks aloft, rising above justice, mercy, prudence and all the divine attributes. Then it suddenly discovers all these uncreated perfections in their eternal Source: in the Godhead of Father, Son and Holy Ghost which infinitely surpasses all our narrow human concepts and leaves God incomprehensible and ineffable even to the gaze of the blessed, and even to the beatified gaze of Christ. It beholds that God, Who is supereminent in His simplicity, is simultaneously Unity in Trinity, indivisible Essence and fellowship of three living Persons, really distinct according to an order of procession which does not affect their consubstantial Equality. Human eye could never have discovered such a mystery, nor could human ear have caught such harmonies, and the human heart could never have suspected such beatitude had not the Godhead stooped to us by grace in Christ, in order that we might enter into the unfathomable depths of God under the guidance of His own Spirit.

That being true, is there any need of further explanation to show that a soul which lives habitually under these sublime inspirations of the gift of wisdom looks, in every department of life, to see the Supreme Principle in God, and, as Elizabeth of the Trinity remarks, " does not stop to consider secondary causes "?

In this last reflection, she lets us into her deepest secret.

After having studied her writings and the movements of her soul for several years, we are thoroughly convinced that *the gift of wisdom remains the most marked characteristic of her doctrine and her life.*

She had an instinctive sense of the eternal and the divine. She would have needed to do violence to herself to come down to the level of the petty interests which impede so many souls—even those of religious and so-called contemplatives—who cannot rise above their wretched cares or their trivialities. Sister Elizabeth went straight to Christ and the Trinity, without troubling too much about the rare faults resulting from her human frailty. Crucified by duty, she did not hamper herself with a multitude of detailed pious practices but, like Our Lady of the Incarnation, amid the countless tasks of the commonplace daily round she was able to keep her eye fixed upon the heights. After the example of her great sister in Carmel, St. Mary Magdalen di Pazzi, " imitating the Word " in her religious life, Sister Elizabeth found in her Carmelite vocation the means of being with Christ a co-redemptrix of the world and of glorifying the Trinity.

" How sublime is the Carmelite's vocation! She must be a mediatrix with Jesus Christ, being like another humanity in which He may perpetuate His life of reparation, sacrifice, praise, and adoration. Ask Him that I may live up to my vocation." [83]

The saints are people of wide vision. Let us but remember the apostolic cry of St. Teresa of the Child Jesus: " I will spend my heaven in doing good upon earth! . . . No, I can take no rest until the end of the world. But when the angel cries: ' Time is no more,' then I shall rest. I shall be able to rejoice, for the number of the elect will be complete." Sister Elizabeth felt a like ambition stir her soul.

" I wish I could tell all souls what a source of strength, peace and happiness they would find by living in this intimate union," [84] of the Three Divine Persons. Like a true Carmelite,

[83] Letter to Canon A., January 1906.
[84] Letter to her mother, August 2, 1906.

she was animated by an immense desire to advance the glory of God. " I surrender myself to Him for His Church and all His interests. I am solicitous for His honor, like my holy Mother St. Teresa. Ask that her daughter may be also a victim of love, *caritatis victima.*" [85] Living as she did, during a period of persecution, she grieved over her country. " Poor France! I love to cover her with the Blood of the Just One." [86]

In her personal idea of union with God she goes straight to the supreme and exemplary cause, the soul of Christ, and longs to be transformed into Christ so that her life may be rather divine than human, and that the Father may recognize in her the image of His Son.[87] She finds concise and vigorous words to express this Christlike wisdom: " Let us go to everything with the Blessed Mother's dispositions." [88] And we have this phrase which shows what is to Wisdom the highest meaning of the Christian life: " To show forth Christ in the sight of the Father." [89] " May I be no longer I but He; and may the Father recognize Him when He looks at me." [90] " When I become completely identified with this Divine Exemplar, dwelling wholly in Him and He in me, I shall fulfill my eternal vocation, for which God chose me in Him *in principio,* and which I shall fulfill *in aeternum* when, in the bosom of the Trinity, I shall be the unceasing ' praise of His glory—*in Laudem gloriae ejus*! " [91]

In this light, we find the adequate answer that solves the problem of evil and the mystery of suffering: *Configuratus morti ejus*—made conformable to His death. That is what haunts me." [92] " I wish to go to my passion with Him in order to be a co-redemptrix with Him! " [93] Such expressions reveal her life.

She took the same attitude with respect to all the divine mysteries. Her whole life was founded " on faith in His exceed-

[85] Letter to Canon A., June 1906.
[86] To the same, January 1906.
[87] Cf. *Heaven on Earth*, 5th prayer.
[88] Letter, 1904.
[89] *Last Retreat*, 14th day.
[90] Letter to Canon A., July 1906.
[91] *Last Retreat*, 1st day.
[92] To Canon A., July 1906.
[93] Letter to her mother, July 18, 1906.

ing charity." It was her vision on earth.[94] "Everything is a sacrament which gives us God."[95] She does not consider suffering in itself, but as an instrument obedient to love,[96] and on her bed of pain, she said over and over: "Our God is a consuming fire and it is His action that I am enduring."[97]

So it was that as her life went on everything appeared to her in an increasingly divine light. When her sisters in Carmel were gathered around her for the last time, by a gracious inspiration of the gift of wisdom, she was heard to murmur in a sort of chant: "In the evening of life, all passes away. Only love remains." This reminds us of the words of St. John of the Cross: "In the evening of life, we shall be judged by love,"[98] and comes back to Our Lord's last commandment of the primacy of charity, which orders everything in the life of a saint.

But the favorite subject of the gift of wisdom is the mystery of the Trinity. To develop this point, we must here reconsider, in this light, that chapter we devoted to the study of the Indwelling of the Trinity, and its central place in the doctrine and life of Sister Elizabeth of the Trinity. Nothing more clearly shows the predominance of the gift of wisdom in her interior life. With her, the continual practice of the presence of God very rapidly became the secret of all her fidelity. A few days before her death, she herself left us this precious testimony: "The belief that a Being whose name is Love is dwelling within us at every moment of the day and night, and that He asks us to live in His company! That, I confide to you, is the secret which has made my life an anticipated heaven."[99]

In her eyes, every movement of the spiritual life resolved itself into that. "My only devotional practice is to enter within, and lose myself in Those Who are there."[100]

---

[94] Letter to the Abbé Ch., December 25, 1904.
[95] Letter to Mme. A., January 1906.
[96] To Madame de S., July 25, 1902.
[97] To her Prioress.
[98] Maxims of St. John of the Cross, IV—Charity N. 70.
[99] Letter to Madame G. de B., 1906.
[100] Letter to G. de G., end of September 1903.

At the close of her short life, established in transforming union, she attained to complete forgetfulness of self. It is the last phase of her spiritual life and the one we have analyzed at the greatest length.[101] Sister Elizabeth had vanished before *Laudem Gloriae*. She no longer signed her letters save with this " new name," and no longer wished to call herself by any other. Rising above the sweetness of the divine presence and beyond herself, she forgets herself entirely so as to be thenceforth only " the unceasing praise of glory of the Trinity." It is the triumph of the gift of wisdom. One single thought dominates everything: the glory of the Trinity. Anything that does not concur in this work of glorifying God or that threatens to retard it is mercilessly cast aside. In the beatifying joy of this presence of the Divine Persons within her which makes her life an anticipated heaven there is no egoistic falling back upon self in order to " enjoy God." It is above all a question of God's glory; and in the " heaven of her soul " her essential office is to sing, day and night, as the blessed do in the " heaven of glory " the praise of the Trinity. Under the impulse of the gift of wisdom, in close connection with the exercise and growth of charity, everything in life takes on the rhythm befitting a " Praise of Glory."

" A ' Praise of Glory ' is a silent soul, a lyre beneath the mysterious *touch of the Holy Ghost* from which He can draw divine harmonies. Knowing that suffering is a string which produces still more exquisite tones, this soul rejoices at having it on its instrument, that it may thus more sweetly move the Heart of its God. A ' Praise of Glory ' is a soul that contemplates God in faith and in simplicity; it reflects all that He is and is a bottomless abyss into which He can flow and outpour Himself. It is a crystal through which He can shine and view His own perfections and splendor. A soul which thus permits the Divine Being to satisfy within it His craving to communicate all He is and has is truly the ' Praise of Glory ' of all His

---

[101] See Ch. I, Section II; and especially Ch. IV, " The Praise of Glory." This latter we feel is *the most important* for a real understanding of the doctrine and life of Sister Elizabeth of the Trinity.

gifts. Finally, a 'Praise of Glory' is one who is always giving thanks; whose acts, movements, thoughts, aspirations, while more deeply establishing her in love, are like an echo of the eternal *Sanctus*. In the heaven of glory, the blessed rest not day or night saying: 'Holy, Holy, Holy, Lord God Almighty . . . and falling down adore Him who liveth forever and ever.' In the heaven of her soul, the 'Praise of Glory' begins now the task which will be hers for all eternity . . . *for she is under the influence of the Holy Ghost Who effects all her action*, and although she may sometimes be unconscious of it, for human weakness prevents souls from keeping their attention fixed on God without distractions, she sings and adores perpetually, and has, so to speak, become absorbed in praise and love, in her passion for the glory of her God." [102]

---

[102] *Heaven on Earth*, 13th prayer.

CHAPTER IX

PRAYER TO THE TRINITY
(COMMENTARY) *

> "*O my 'Three,' my All, my Beatitude, infinite Solitude, Immensity wherein I lose myself . . .*"

To watch a soul at prayer is to surprise it at the moment of its closest intimacy with God, like the priest at the altar. Prayer sums up life of a soul: as the prayer is, so is the life. All the doctrinal genius of St. Thomas Aquinas breaks forth in the Office of the Blessed Sacrament. Not even the Incarnate Word Himself escapes this law of our human psychology, for His Prayer as High Priest is the supreme revelation of the Heart of Christ. Nothing better reveals His love for His Father and His redeeming charity towards His brethren than the circular movement of that soul which speaks to His Father of His glory and of the consummation of all in One: the whole mystery of Christ is in it.

The same is true of the prayer of all the saints. Unlike her Holy Mother, Teresa, Sister Elizabeth of the Trinity did not write a treatise on prayer, but her sublime prayer: " O my God, Trinity Whom I adore . . ." bears the richest testimony to her wholly Carmelite conception of the life of prayer: an unceasing communing with the Trinity. " Prayer does not mean binding ourselves to recite a certain number of vocal prayers daily but the raising of the soul to God through all circumstances, which establishes us in a kind of continual communion with the Most Holy Trinity, quite simply by doing everything in Its sight." [1]

---
* For the text of this prayer, see pp. 53-54.
[1] Letter to G. de G., February 1905.

The prayer in question, which has already become widely known, was composed on the day when all Carmelites renew their vows. It poured from her heart, in one outburst, without a single correction, and is the synthesis of her interior life. All the essential features of her soul are perfectly portrayed in it: the great devotion of her life—the Trinity; the special form of her prayer—adoration; her tender passionate love for the Lord Whom she loves " until she could die of love," and Whom she especially loved on the Cross; finally, the irresistible flight to the Three, her beatitude, her all, infinite Solitude wherein she lost her soul. Mary is not named, but we feel she is there just the same by the date written in Sister Elizabeth's hand, November 21, 1904, the Feast of the Presentation.

It is to be noted that only the final development is lacking: the vast horizons of her life as a " Praise of Glory," then unsuspected.

Faced with such a prayer, one of the most beautiful in Christian literature, we hesitated a long time before attempting a commentary. We felt a little of the embarrassment of the exegete or the theologian seeking to explain the priestly prayer of Our Lord, for all human exegetic or theological commentaries no matter how sublime they may be must forever despair of succeeding in translating the wholly divine simplicity of the last prayer of Jesus for unity. But then we thought of that multitude of contemplative souls who have become so attached to this prayer to the Trinity and who find in it a whole program of interior life and the secret of forgetting self. One Carmelite wrote to us: " Every word makes one pray. This prayer has as recollecting an effect upon my soul as the finest mystical treatises."

Since we have made a close study of this privileged soul over a period of some years, perhaps our commentary will be of some use in revealing its true and very profound meaning.

While we do not wish to subdivide too rigidly the movement of this deeply contemplative soul, it seems possible to distinguish five principal aspects of this prayer:

1. A first spontaneous uplifting of the soul to that Trinity

Which had become her whole life: " O my God, Trinity Whom I adore . . . ! "

2. A description of the spiritual climate in which her contemplative life developed at the center of her soul in an atmosphere of unchangeable peace: " Give peace to my soul. . ."

3. A turning, in passionate tenderness, to Christ, Whom she would love " until I die of very love." The words crowd upon one another, showing the impetuosity of the feelings of one who longs eagerly to be identified with every movement of the soul of Christ: " O my Christ, Whom I love . . . ! "

4. Then a sudden appeal to each of the Three Divine Persons in succession, towards Whom her life is directed: " O Eternal Word! . . . O Consuming Fire! . . . And Thou, O Father! . . ." She dwells particularly upon the Word, Whose Incarnation renders Him more accessible to our human eyes. Her soul is fascinated by this " Eternal Word, Utterance of my God." She invokes the " Spirit of Love " but in order that He may accomplish in her, as it were, an incarnation of the Word, to Whom she desires to be another humanity, wherein the Father may see the face of His Christ, in whom " He has set all His pleasure." For this prayer, like her life, is truly centered on Christ.

5. A last cry, with which this prayer to the Trinity concludes. Her artist's soul takes up again the theme with which she began: " O my God, Trinity Whom I adore! " but develops it more fully in a strongly accentuated movement which carries her soul into the very depths of the Trinity: " O my Three . . . I yield myself to Thee as Thy prey."

* . * *

I. O MY GOD, TRINITY WHOM I ADORE

O my God!—Her soul goes straight, not to the divine perfections but to the essence, the source of all the attributes: to *God* Himself.

Trinity:—Not the God of philosophers and scholars, but the God of Christians and mystics: Father, Word, Love.

Some souls, such as St. Catherine of Siena, are more specially drawn to the Father; others, like St. Gertrude and St. Margaret Mary, to the Son; still others to the Holy Ghost. The Church acknowledges all these forms of prayer to be legitimate, since she herself in her liturgy addresses each, Father, Son and Holy Ghost, in turn. The worship is rendered to the Persons Who, in the Trinity, remain infinitely distinct. Like a true theologian, St. Thomas had devotion to "the Trinity in Unity," which sums up, in an all-embracing phrase, the whole essence of the mystery.

Sister Elizabeth of the Trinity was not so much struck by this intimate aspect of the mystery in itself, as concerned to find therein the blessed and explicit term of her life of union: "The Blessed Trinity is our dwelling place, our home, our Father's house, which we should never leave."[2] We would understand better if we could have heard how tenderly she spoke of her "Three" with her hands pressed to her heart, as to a loved presence: "I do so love this mystery; it is an abyss in which I lose myself!"

Whom I adore:—Adoration is the proper form of this life of prayer. It desires to imitate the blessed in the heavenly city, as described for us in the last chapters of the Apocalypse, "with palms in their hands, who fall down and adore before the throne of the Lamb."

With this life of prayer, wherein adoration predominates, we are far removed from those multitudes of begging souls, who never seem to approach God save with hands outstretched to receive! Like a true contemplative with an understanding of God, Sister Elizabeth begins at once by paying Him homage because of His infinite perfections or, to use her favorite expression, "for His Own Sake." Her deeply religious soul quite naturally takes the most fundamental attitude towards God: adoration. The prayer of petition thinks of the need to be relieved; thanksgiving keeps looking back upon the benefits received; expiation is mingled with the remembrance of past

[2] *Heaven on Earth*, 1st prayer.

sins; adoration alone contemplates God Himself, in the uncreated excellence of His Essence and of His Persons. The soul forgets everything before the glory of its God. " Adoration . . . can be defined as the ecstasy of love; love crushed by the beauty, the strength, the vast grandeur of Him it loves." [3]

Help me to become utterly forgetful of self:—The great obstacle for the Carmelite, as for every contemplative soul, is self. " Self-love only dies a quarter of an hour after we do," St. Francis of Sales said smiling, and the saints have waged their fiercest battles against themselves in order to destroy that stubbornly tenacious *self*. We can never be astonished at its persistent obstinacy even in the greatest souls, those dearest to God, until the day when, by a wholly gratuitous grace, He is pleased to deliver them from themselves.

Since Sister Elizabeth of the Trinity was called by her special vocation to become a model and patron of interior souls, she had to learn by her own experience the great danger to those souls whom God wills are to be recollected deep within themselves, there to live by Him alone. For a long time, her spiritual life was hampered by her poor " self." She suffered in consequence and nothing could deliver her from it. That sovereign deliverance of souls can only be the triumph of grace, and one of the final effects of the gifts of the Holy Ghost. Hence, it is not by chance, but under the influence of a very personal feeling, that in the second sentence of this prayer, she looks back to herself, making this last lament of a " self " which will shortly die. " Help me to become utterly forgetful of self." Three days after composing this prayer, she returned to the same thought: " The saints completely understood true knowledge, which enables us to leave everything, particularly self, in order to cast ourselves upon God and live only by Him." [4]

Utterly:—Let us realize what this means. " Utterly forgetful ": the impulse towards God never obstructed, either by external events or internal fluctuations. Sister Elizabeth of the

---
[3] *Last Retreat*, 8th day.
[4] Letter to Madame A., November 24, 1904.

Trinity aims high; it is a question of reaching that blessed transformation in Christ expressed in St. Paul's bold sentence: "I live now not I, but Christ liveth in me." "What a going out from self does that imply! What a dying! This great saint wrote to the Colossians: 'You are dead; and your life is hid with Christ in God.' This is the condition: we must be dead; otherwise, we may be hidden in God at certain times, but we do not habitually live in the Divinity, because our feelings, our self-seeking and the rest draw us forth from Him."[5] And again: "I have isolated, separated, stripped myself of all things, natural and supernatural, even as regards the gifts of God. For unless a soul has destroyed and become emancipated from self, it must necessarily, at certain times, be commonplace and natural, and that is unworthy of a child of God, a bride of Christ, and a temple of the Holy Ghost."[6]

Help me:—This perfect and final deliverance is the supreme triumph of grace over nature in the saints. Sister Elizabeth humbly begs for it: "Help me."

We know that God heard the prayer of His humble servant. A year later, she could write to a friend:

"It may seem difficult to forget yourself. If you only knew how simple it is! I am going to tell you my secret. Think about this God Who dwells within you, Whose temple you are. It is St. Paul who says that, so we may believe it. Little by little, the soul becomes accustomed to live in His sweet company. It realizes that it bears within itself a little heaven in which the God of love has established His abode. Then it is as though it breathed a divine air. I would even say that only the body remains on earth, and that the soul dwells in Him Who is the Unchangeable. And here is how it is done: it is not by looking at our miseries that we shall be cleansed, but by gazing upon Him Who is all purity and sanctity."[7]

That I may bury myself in Thee:—Having become completely detached from itself and having reached the pure sum-

---
[5] *Last Retreat*, 6th day.
[6] *Ibid.*, 10th day.   [7] Letter to Madame A., November 24, 1905.

mits of Mount Carmel, the soul at last enters into the cycle of the life of the Trinity; it is buried in God. This divine intimacy had become so familiar to Sister Elizabeth of the Trinity that it seemed to her as though God were going to appear to her as she passed through the cloisters. " God in me and I in Him! Oh, that is my Life! "

As changeless and as peaceful as though my soul were already in eternity:—One of the results of this essentially contemplative spirituality is to withdraw the soul from its petty preoccupations and from self so as to establish it permanently in an atmosphere of eternity. Should not every Christian soul consider itself in exile on earth, since the grace of Baptism has deposited in it the germ of that changeless existence which by faith it already lives in the light of the Word? One word of the Creed, inexpressibly significant, clearly indicates the fundamental attitude of every believing soul with regard to this transitory world. *Expecto*: " I look for the life; the world to come." This sense of eternity dominated the soul of the servant of God increasingly as the years went by. Her whole soul began to dwell in that beyond, invisible but so near. In the last months, she was heard to murmur: " He no longer speaks to me save of eternity."

Changeless and peaceful:—Peace holds a foremost place in this spiritual doctrine. Sister Elizabeth returns to it three times in this short prayer: " As changeless and as peaceful as though my soul were already in eternity "; " may nothing disturb my peace "; " give peace to my soul." That peace which surpasses all feeling does not come from the world but originates in a divine attribute. " May nothing disturb my peace or draw me out of Thee, O my immutable Lord." St. Augustine has left us a celebrated definition of peace: the tranquillity of order—" *Pax est tranquillitas ordinis.*" Spiritual peace is a harmony of the powers in unity, the simultaneous focusing of their effort on one and the same end. Its principle is God, Who is loved in all things, and above all things. Theologians know that peace is one of the interior effects of charity. For a soul to be perfectly ordered to God: that is peace.

Sister Elizabeth of the Trinity has given us some equivalent descriptions: "To 'keep our strength' for the Lord is to keep our whole being in unity by interior silence; to collect all our powers, to occupy them in the one work of love."[8] "If my desires, my fears, my joys or my sorrows, if all the impulses coming from these four passions are not completely subjected to God, there will be turmoil within me; therefore the slumber of all the powers, the unity of the whole being are needed."[9] Then the soul need no longer fear either turmoil outside or tempests within."[10] "The will must be sweetly lost in that of God, so that the inclinations and faculties may be moved in and by this love alone."[11] Far from being an obstacle, creatures only root it more deeply in the Master's love.[12] It is in the unity of powers all kept for Christ that there is unchanging peace.

May I penetrate more deeply every moment into the depths of Thy Mystery:—This petition reveals the holy Carmelite's soul, her desire to realize more fully every day the primary meaning of all religious life: to tend to perfection. This anxiety for what is most perfect, which St. Teresa made the object of a special vow, is found in an eminent degree in her daughter. We must admit that the predominating impression left upon us, after several years of contact with the soul of Sister Elizabeth of the Trinity, is the ever-increasing rapidity of her eager progress towards God. One of the Carmelites of Dijon, who was very intimate with her and of whom the servant of God said: "We are like the two rooms of one apartment," told us that the end of her life especially was a wonderful spiritual ascension. From the beginning of the last eight months in the infirmary she said: "We could no longer follow her." It is in this light that we must understand this phrase which so well expresses her longing for complete perfection: "May I penetrate more deeply every moment into the depths of Thy Mystery." It was a settled conviction with her that "every moment is given us

---

[8] *Last Retreat*, 2nd day.
[9] *Ibid.*, 10th day.
[10] *Ibid.*, 2nd day.
[11] *Heaven on Earth*, 7th prayer.
[12] Cf. *Last Retreat*, 8th day.

in order that we may become more firmly rooted in God, so that the likeness to our divine Model may become more striking, the union closer." She never changed her mind. In the retreat she composed for her sister, as a last legacy, she returned to it with a richly compressed conciseness which defines the spiritual life as " eternal life begun and ever in progress."

II. GIVE PEACE TO MY SOUL

A fresh aspect of this prayer enables us to enter into her deeply personal conception of the interior life. Not that she discovered a doctrine unknown to Christian teaching, but she was able to penetrate the profound meaning of Our Lord's words: " The Kingdom of God is *within* you." Obviously she has received from God the grace of recalling souls to this point of the pure Gospel teaching. Might we not say of Sister Elizabeth of the Trinity what she herself wrote of Mary, the pattern of her own interior life: " It was within her own heart that she dwelt." Her special grace was to live the Trinitarian grace of her Baptism in all its fullness in the depths of her soul and to invite souls to return to the true sources of the divine life.

Make it Thy heaven:—The soul that is established in peace and freed from self becomes the scene of wonders of grace and is for God a true heaven, a " cherished dwelling place," His " home of rest." The loftiness of this inner life with the divine Persons must be noted. Ordinary perspectives are reversed. The majority of souls seek union with God from the praiseworthy desire of becoming saints, but do they always think sufficiently of the supreme reason for all sanctity, God's joy and His greater glory? They make every effort to reach God without succeeding in becoming completely forgetful of themselves. Great dangers lurk in this method of spirituality, which is a sort of sanctification of self. Here, on the contrary, the truth of God's primacy stands out.

The soul is a living temple, in which the Most Holy Trinity receives a ceaseless cultus of adoration, thanksgiving, praise, and love. The Divine Persons rejoice in one another in the center of this soul where They dwell together; where the Father begets the Son, and the Father and the Son breathe forth one and the same Love. The soul becomes a heaven for God. At the thought of this divine loving-kindness which finds its delights in living among the children of men, Sister Elizabeth of the Trinity later described the " Praise of Glory " as " a soul which permits the divine Being to satisfy within it His craving to communicate all He is and has." [13]

Let me never leave Thee there alone:—Here we see the necessary personal collaboration: " Keep me there all absorbed in Thee, in living faith, adoring Thee and wholly yielded up to Thy creative action."

Strictly speaking, God is never alone, either in Himself or in souls. The fellowship of the Three Persons is self-sufficient. The Father, Son and Holy Ghost dwell together now, as " in the beginning " and They ever shall " world without end," finding light, love and joy to an infinite degree in the depths of Their Essence and in a perfect friendship. Hence, God is never alone and the theology of the Trinity justly remarks that, in the strict sense of the term, it is forbidden and dangerous to call God " the Solitary."

This life of God " within " Himself so fully constitutes His joy that if, by an impossibility, this plurality of Persons did not exist in the life of the Trinity, our God would remain the Eternal Solitary, even amid an infinite multitude of men and angels, called by grace to share His infinite life, somewhat as a human being possessed of understanding and will would be alone as he walked in a garden, notwithstanding the presence of innumerable plants and animals.[14]

In an overflow of pure goodness, and in His " exceeding charity," God has willed to find His delights among the children of men. He has been seen amidst His creation; the Word has been made flesh and has dwelt amongst us. We belong to the number of those privileged souls to whom it has been given to

---

[13] *Heaven on Earth*, 13th prayer.

[14] See the profound explanation of St. Thomas: *Summa Theologica*, I, q. 31, a. 3 ad 1.

become "the children of God," and to be able to have communion with the "Word," predestined to live "in fellowship" with Him. "In fellowship"—that expression of St. John, so dear to Sister Elizabeth of the Trinity—explains to us the meaning of her prayer: "Let me never leave Thee there alone."

But keep me there all absorbed in Thee:—Her ascesis and her mysticism consisted precisely in keeping herself free and detached from all else, that she might live in the center of her soul, "in the presence of the living God."

In living faith:—"A Carmelite is a soul of faith." The servant of God often came back to the first of the theological virtues for her own private spiritual life. "The program for my retreat will be to keep myself by faith and love under the unction of the Holy One." To rest "in living faith" is to go beyond the formulae which express to our mind the truths to be believed; it is, rather, to dwell in God.

Adoring Thee:—Always the same essential attitude of adoration in the presence of God.

Wholly yielded up to Thy creative action:—Sister Elizabeth of the Trinity was one of those souls who surrender without reserve to the action of the Holy Ghost, convinced that the spiritual life consists less in multiplying personal efforts than in letting oneself be possessed by God. Her constant and increasingly apparent concern was to "believe in Love"; to allow herself to be transformed by Him. It is of the highest importance to become thoroughly imbued, as she was, with the truth that the first motion towards sanctity comes from God, and belongs, first and foremost, to the effects of His grace; that is to say, to His gratuitous love. Is it not a true characteristic of God's love for us that it is creative? To allow ourselves to be loved, then, means to allow God to act in the innermost depths of our being, to allow Him to work in us all the wonders of His grace and His glory.

Sister Elizabeth had grasped the meaning of the answer we should make to that Love which asks only to work in us, which is, to seek to be "wholly yielded up to Thy creative action."

III. O MY CHRIST, WHOM I LOVE

Now we see the way to the Trinity: Christ. He seems to appear suddenly but the truth is that He is at the center of Sister Elizabeth's prayer as He was at the center of her life.

O My Christ Whom I Love:—As soon as He appears, it is no longer a matter of loving, but of loving " until I die of very love." Even before this she had written in her diary: " I long to make Him known, to make Him loved the world over." Five years had gone by since then, years lived in daily intimacy as a bride of Christ.

Her devotion to Christ goes straight to the essential: to Christ " crucified by love "; to Him Who had told her, the evening of her profession day, that He had chosen her to live her whole life in silence and in love. She had surrendered herself: " *Fain would I be the bride of Thy Heart*," and on that morning, " the happiest of her life," she had become the spouse of Christ until death. Thenceforth, there would be no other life in her but Christ.

Fain would I cover Thee with glory:—" The woman is the glory of the man." [15] Like a faithful spouse Sister Elizabeth sets herself still more eagerly to advance His honor. God has not yet revealed to her her supreme vocation of being a " praise of glory," but He is leading her on to it. There will come a day when this activity will absorb everything in her soul for the glory of the Trinity and of her Christ.

Yet I realize my weakness:—It is encouraging to know that, like ourselves, the saints felt themselves weak. Did not our Lord Himself will to accept succor from the angel of the Agony and from the Cyrenean? Confronted with a superhuman ideal, the saints did not shrink back. Rather they knew how to call to their aid the " Strong One," Whose secret virtue is ever there to cleanse us, save us, deify us, and transform us into Himself. " He is ever living in our souls, ever at work there. Let us allow ourselves to be built up by Him. May He be the soul of

---

[15] *I Cor.* XI, 7.

our soul, the life of our life, so that we can say with St. Paul: 'To me to live is Christ.' "[16] Far from surprising or checking them, their wretchedness and weakness only throw them upon God and upon Jesus Christ. Hear this sublime crescendo expressing the confidence of saints: " I beg Thee to clothe me with Thyself, to identify my soul with all the movements of Thine own." Then the words pile up, burst out, to express the overflowing feeling: " I beg Thee . . . immerse me in Thyself; possess me wholly; substitute Thyself for me, that my life may be but a radiance of Thine own." " Enter my soul as Adorer, as Restorer, as Savior." She is completely transformed into Christ; the motto engraved on her " beautiful profession crucifix " is realized: " I live now not I, but Christ liveth in me: *Vivo jam non ego, vivit in me Christus.*"

IV. O ETERNAL WORD!

The face of the Crucified leads to the radiant splendor of the Word. It is a theme familiar to mystical writers. All true devotion to our Lord is directed *principally* to His Godhead; the Sacred Humanity is but a road. We are here following along the way of perfectly balanced tradition. After having halted a while in the redeeming wounds of Him who is " crucified by love," the thought leaps up to the Word.

O Eternal Word, Utterance of my God! I long to pass my life in listening to Thee:—What do all the wonders of nature and of grace matter for the soul that has met with the Word? Such creatures are not the Word, and " it is He we seek." Do not the very heavens which proclaim His glory yet hide Him from our sight? " Eternal Word! Utterance of My God! I long to pass my life in listening to Thee! " Thou wilt tell me the whole secret hidden in the bosom of the Father: the mystery of the Three in One.

I long to become docile, that I may learn all from Thee:— Now the servant of God reveals to us the source of her highest spiritual lights: God's school. It would be hard to find a soul

[16] Letter to Madame A., November 9, 1902.

who owed less to books. At the most, she had fed upon a very few spiritual works: the *Spiritual Canticle* and the *Living Flame* of her Father, St. John of the Cross, " who penetrates so deeply into the Godhead," and the Epistles of St. Paul. As she confided in a whisper to her Prioress: " What He teaches me within is ineffable." On her part, Mother Germaine was quite convinced that Sister Elizabeth of the Trinity was, above all, the pupil and the hearer of the Word.

Through all darkness, all privations, all helplessness:—Here we recognize the way of " Nothingness " which leads to the summit of Carmel. In order to attain to divine union, the contemplative, particularly the Carmelite, is called upon to experience the long and painful purifications of the " nights "; after having left all for Christ, to feel Him vanish, not for a day or for a few months but for years, for a whole lifetime perhaps, and to remain faithful, never taking back the sacrifice and never murmuring. These short words hide a great experience endured; let souls given to prayer seek God not by way of consolations, but in naked faith and absolute detachment. Let them remain faithful therein: " through all darkness, all privations and all weakness."

I crave to keep Thee ever with me and to dwell beneath thy lustrous beams:—Sister Elizabeth of the Trinity, too, in the early days of her entrance into mystical ways had known the intoxicating joys of the presence of God. Then, for a long time, she had to seek her God in pure faith. " After these ecstasies, these high raptures, during which the soul forgets everything and sees only God, how hard and trying ordinary prayer seems! What an effort it is to unite one's powers! How much it costs and how difficult it seems! " For all that, it is not the time to abandon the life of prayer. It is the blessed hour that leads to transforming union in the silence of the night. Then more than ever, the soul must keep its gaze fixed upon God and dwell in peace beneath the " lustrous beams " of the dark, translucent night. It must allow itself to be more and more passively drawn by the Word: " O my beloved Star, so hold me that I cannot wander from Thy light!" Like the moth, let me be lost in the blaze of Thy great light.

Spirit of Love:—To be in the bosom of the Trinity the Personal Love of the Father and the Son: such is the whole mystery of the Holy Ghost, the true "Spirit of Love," in Whom God loves Himself and the whole universe. The innermost nature of this Divine Person, equal to the Father and the Son, from Whom He proceeds, is to be their substantial and coeternal Love in one and the same Triune life.

Here again, the servant of God merely mentions a fundamental derivative principle of the dogma of the Trinity, that which has the most profound meaning for the contemplative who even on earth would live by this mystery of a God Who is personal Love. Her private concern is of a more practical order. Her prayer is not an outpouring of the intra-Trinitarian life, but the movement of a contemplative soul who finds in that mystery of the Trinity her All, her Beatitude, the infinite Solitude wherein she loses herself. She invokes the Spirit of Love because of His sanctifying office in respect of souls which are striving for union with God. "O consuming Fire, descend within me and reproduce in me, as it were, an incarnation of the Word." She had previously begged Christ to identify her with every movement of His own soul, to substitute Himself for her, that her life might be but a radiance of His life. The same thought is continued when she appeals to the Father and the Holy Ghost, showing how wholly her desire to be transformed into Christ is the center of this essentially Trinitarian prayer. Nothing shows more emphatically the degree to which Jesus had become her life.

Reproduce in me, as it were, an incarnation of the Word: — A bold expression which must be clearly understood. Note the words: *as it were.* On no account must the petition be taken too literally; strictly speaking, it would be an impossibility. It is the language of a soul wholly possessed by Christ and dreaming of becoming "another Christ: *alter Christus.*"

May I be to Him another humanity, wherein He renews His

mystery:—A luminous sentence which sheds light upon all the rest. She herself explained it three days later when writing to a young priest: "May I be to Him another humanity," that is, "May He continue in me His life of reparation, sacrifice, praise and adoration . . . I have asked Him to come into me as Adorer, as Restorer and as Savior."

And Thou, O Father:—Now the Father is here, the Beginning of all the Godhead. He is Father! that is His mystery and His special character in the bosom of the Three. He is the Beginning without beginning, whence flows, as from an infinitely fruitful source, the whole life of the Trinity *within Itself*. The supreme light of the face-to-face vision will be to find in Him, as in its eternal origin, the whole mystery of the Trinity in Unity.

But at the grace-filled hour when Sister Elizabeth composed her prayer, this particular point was not directly involved. Beholding that divine Fatherhood, she saw above all her own nothingness. "O Father, bend towards Thy poor little creature." Reminding herself of the mystery of Our Lady of the Incarnation, the aspect under which she preferred to think of Mary, she adds "and overshadow her," that is, protect her. Finally returning as always to Christ, she whispers: "Behold in her none other than thy Beloved Son in Whom Thou hast set all Thy pleasures."

O MY THREE!

The prayer closes. A last uplifting of her soul carries her to the "Three" to Whom she has vowed her life. "O my Three, my All, my Beatitude, infinite Solitude, Immensity wherein I lose myself! I yield myself to Thee as Thy prey. Merge Thyself in me that I may be immersed in Thee until I depart to contemplate in Thy light the abyss of thy greatness!"

The prayer with which it opens has been granted: she loses sight of herself. The soul is transformed in God.

Epilogue

HER MISSION

> 1. *"My mission will be to keep souls in that great inner silence."*
> 2. *"I bequeath you this vocation which was mine in the bosom of the Church: THE PRAISE OF GLORY OF THE MOST HOLY TRINITY."*

1. The great interior silence. 2. The Praise of Glory of the Trinity.

At the time of their departure from this world, the great servants of God were aware that their apostolic activity in the service of the Church, far from ceasing at death, would be more intensive after their souls had entered the abode of glory. Had they not their master's example and the memory of His promise to His Apostles: " It is expedient for you that I go . . . When I depart, I shall send the Spirit unto you." St. Paul has left us the description of that eternal activity of Christ, *always living* before the Father's face; to adore and to glorify Him, indeed, but also *to make intercession for us.*[1] Who would dare think that since her glorious Assumption, the Mother of men has turned away from our earthly trials or that in her eternal mystery amid the joys of the Beatific Vision the Mother of God does not solicitously remain at the service of her other children by her all-powerful intercession, constantly bending over the nations of the world in order to " bring them forth " to Christ, more than ever a Mother!

It is not exceptional to find upon the lips of great founders of religious orders such words as those spoken by St. Dominic to his sons as they wept at his approaching death: " I shall be

[1] *Heb.* VII, 25.

more useful to you up there." The whole world has heard the wish of "the greatest saint of modern times," [2] St. Teresa of the Child Jesus: "In heaven, I shall not be idle. I will spend my heaven in doing good upon earth." Her humble sister at Dijon let fall the same apostolic cry: "Believe that, above, in the home of love, I shall take an active interest in you. I shall ask for a grace of union, of intimacy with the Master; that is what has made my life an anticipated heaven." A few days before her death, moved by the Holy Ghost, her failing hand pencilled to a lay sister the celebrated passage: "IT SEEMS TO ME THAT IN HEAVEN MY MISSION WILL BE TO DRAW SOULS, by helping them to go out of themselves in order to adhere to God by a very simple, wholly loving movement and to maintain them in THAT GREAT INNER SILENCE which allows God to imprint Himself on them and to transform them into Himself."

Prophetic words, which we have seen realized by the rapid and worldwide circulation of the SOUVENIRS.

1. In heaven, each saint has his mission, in harmony with the scheme of the Redemption and in reward for the merits he acquired on earth. Until the end of the world, they will all continue to work for the extension of the Kingdom of God and for the formation of the "*totus Christus.*" The Mother of the Incarnate Word functions as universal Mediatrix of all graces without exception while the other saints have their own rather special provinces, according to their place in the providential economy. Thus the founders of religious orders watch especially over the members of their institutes, a St. Joan of Arc over her country, a bishop over his diocese, a parish priest over his parish, a father or mother over their children. The providential mission of Sister Elizabeth of the Trinity is not to intervene in the government of the world in any striking way but to draw souls into the ways of silence and recollection for the greater glory of the Trinity. "It seems to me that in heaven my mission will be to draw souls."

"*By helping them to go out of themselves.*" This is the grace

---

[2] Pius X to a Missionary Bishop.

of graces. How many souls never succeed in getting out of the thousand "labyrinthine ways" of *self*! The most fervent sigh over it and despair of so doing. In vain do they endeavor to free themselves by their own efforts which avail nothing. This is beyond men's strength and calls for the grace of God. Hence it is a very precious grace which the servant of God promises to all those interior souls imprisoned in their own egoism. From heaven, her silent intervention leads them to that complete liberation which casts them wholly upon Christ.

The soul detaches itself only in order to unite itself to God; to adhere to Him. This is the positive and fundamental aspect of the interior mission fulfilled by Sister Elizabeth of the Trinity. Already her spiritual writings have borne much fruit in the most diverse Catholic circles, her call to the interior life being addressed to all members of the Church. Nevertheless, it must be recognized that the silent Carmelite of Dijon seems to have received a more particular mission with respect to contemplatives, in order to detach them from themselves—and sometimes from their trivial preoccupations—and draw them into the great stream of divine life which gives them power over the heart of God for men's redemption.

Now for a multitude of interior souls, everything is so complicated in their spiritual life! Some seek God by means of excessive mortifications, others by an extremely literal and mechanical fidelity to detail which does not easily hear the breathing of the Spirit. Sister Elizabeth reminds all these souls, whose will is good but who sometimes are badly informed, that we must go to God "by a very simple and wholly loving movement." Simplicity is effected only by love. A soul that in perfect charity seeks only the glory of God whatever happens is a simple soul which goes straight to Him. "'*Deus ignis consumens*—our God is a consuming fire'; that is, a fire of love which destroys, which transforms into itself whatever it touches. The mystical death of which St. Paul spoke becomes very simple and sweet to souls who yield themselves up to the action of its flames within the depths of their being. They think far less of the work of destruction and detachment left to them to accomplish than of plunging into the furnace of love burning within them, which is the Holy Ghost Himself, the same Love which in the Blessed Trinity is the bond between the Father and His Word. Such souls enter into Him by a living faith and there in simplicity and peace they are raised by Him above all things and above all sensible devotion into the 'sacred darkness' and transformed into the divine image. As St. John expresses it, they live 'in fellowship' with the Three adorable Persons Whose life they share. That is the contemplative life." [3]

Then the soul is kept in that *great interior silence*, so dear to Sister Elizabeth of the Trinity and the center towards which her whole spiritual teaching converges. After the chapter devoted to the *Ascesis of Silence*, there is no need to insist upon this fundamental point. Today, activity carries all before it. People no longer think of anything but external action. Souls no longer know how to be silent in order to listen to God. In this modern world, where everything is noise and tumult, is there a more urgent mission than that entrusted by Divine Providence to the holy Carmelite of Dijon—the mission of leading souls back to the path of recollection and keeping them "*in that great inner silence which allows God to imprint Himself upon them and to transform them into Himself*"? She has taught us that the " soul which reserves something for self in its interior kingdom, whose powers are not all 'enclosed' in God, cannot be a perfect 'Praise of Glory' . . . A soul which listens to *self*, which is preoccupied with its sensibilities, which indulges in useless thoughts or desires, scatters its forces. It is not completely under God's sway. Its lyre is not in tune, so that when the Divine Master strikes it, He cannot draw forth celestial harmonies; it is too human, and discordant." [4]

Everything within us must be put to silence; the outward senses as regards earthly things; the interior powers with respect to all the din within. There must be silence of the eyes, silence of the imagination and the memory, above all silence of the

[3] *Heaven on Earth*, 6th prayer.   [4] *Last Retreat*, 2nd day.

heart. "I must guard against being withdrawn from this holy interior silence, by keeping myself always in the same state, the same isolation, the same retirement, the same detachment. If my desires, my fears, my joys or my sorrows, if all the impulses coming from these four passions are not completely subjected to God, I shall not be silent;[5] there will be turmoil within me. Therefore calm, the slumber of the powers, the unity of the whole being, are needed."[6] In their turn, the highest spiritual faculties must enter into this great interior silence; silence of the understanding, no useless thought; silence of the judgment, which means so radical a liberation from the excessively critical modern mind; above all, silence of the will which begets in the soul the great silence of love.

Once it is established in souls, this "great inner silence" allows God to imprint Himself upon them and to transform them into Himself. The supreme object of all human life, transforming union, is attained. "Then the Master has full liberty—liberty to infuse Himself into the soul, to give Himself 'according to the measure of the giving of Christ,' and the soul, thus simplified and unified, becomes the throne of Him Who changes not, because unity is the throne of the Blessed Trinity."[7]

2. A highly important posthumous document reveals to us another and still more essential aspect of the providential mission of the servant of God. After her death a small envelope was found. It was carefully sealed with red wax and bore these words: "Secrets for our Mother." It was the last confidence in the hour when the saints see everything in the light of eternity.

"Mother, when you read these lines, your little 'Praise of Glory' will no longer be singing on earth but will be dwelling in the immense fire of love . . . This hour is so serious and solemn that I do not want to wait to tell you things which I fear to diminish by trying to express in words . . . What your child means to do is to reveal what she feels, or to speak more

---

[5] In the retreat itself, the word is *solitary*.
[6] *Last Retreat*, 10th day.   [7] *Ibid.*, 2nd day.

correctly, what God, in these hours of deep recollection of unifying contact, is making her understand. . . . Reverend Mother, consecrated my Mother from all eternity, now that I am going away, *I bequeath to you this vocation which was mine in the bosom of the Church Militant and which I shall fulfill unceasingly in the Church Triumphant: the Praise of Glory of the Most Holy Trinity."*

The glory of the Trinity: there is the last testament of the saintly Carmelite to all souls who would follow her footsteps in the ways of the interior life. That praise of glory of the Trinity which was her " vocation in exile " and remains " her office through all eternity " " before the face of God," is related to the highest purpose of God with respect to every creature. Everything in God's handiwork is ordained to this glory: " *Universa propter Se operatus est Deus.*—The Lord hath made all things for Himself." [8] If He sent His Son into the world, it was before all else to repair the damage caused to His glory by sin. Jesus Himself summed up His earthly mission in a word: " *Pater glorificavi Te*: Father, I have glorified Thee." [9]

We are now in a position to grasp in all its fullness the mystical doctrine of Sister Elizabeth of the Trinity.

The adorable Trinity is the supreme Good towards which all souls and the world of pure spirits tend. It is in order that we may enter into " fellowship " with the Divine Persons that the Father created the universe and sent His Son into it. The whole mystery of the Church and of the Mother of God, the Mediatrix of Grace, is to lead *the whole Christ* to the contemplation of the Trinity. The vision of the Trinity in unity; there we have man's sublime destiny.[10] On earth, he painfully makes his way through " Christ crucified by love," but only to establish himself eternally in God. By way of all the crosses, all the " nights," all the mystical deaths of the Church Militant, souls are silently climbing towards the Unchanging Trinity, the source of all

[8] *Prov.* XVI, 4.
[9] *John* XVII, 4.
[10] Cf. *I Sent.* I, II, L—(Expositio textus)—*Cognitio Trinitatis in unitate est fructus et finis totius vitae nostrae.*

beatitude. Only those come to the vision of God who are made "perfect in One"; those who in this ascent have the courage to abandon all that is not akin to God, that they may rejoice in that Being upon Whom all depends, in His isolation, His simplicity, His purity; towards Whom all look; from Whom is being, life, and thought. "There is a Being Who is Love, and Who wishes us to dwell in His company."[11] "This Infinite Love Who envelops us desires to associate us even here below with all His blessedness. It is the whole Trinity that abides within us, all that mystery which we shall behold in the vision of heaven."[12]

To the soul that has by faith caught sight of these glories of the Trinity, all the rest appears but vanity. It is aware that in its innermost self it "possesses a supreme Good in comparison with which all others are nothing. Thus, every joy which befalls the soul invites it to prefer the joy which it possesses within itself, with which no other can compare."[13] With what love and longing does this happy soul which has met this Good seek to be united with It! It loves God with a love stronger than death; with eager yearning, it despises all other love, and other attractions that might have been able to lead it astray momentarily. To be deprived of everything created is no hardship for him who has God within him. He only is deserving of pity who is deprived of the vision of that supreme Beauty. Hence, we must leave all in order to possess this Divine Treasure, become absolutely detached from the fascination of passing attractions which threaten to turn the soul aside from its end; we must know nothing of earth, and must flee "alone with the Alone," becoming as strangers to all else. The soul's true fatherland is there in the bosom of the tranquil Trinity, in silence and recollection. "The Trinity, then, is our dwelling place, our home, our Father's house which we should never leave."[14]

[11] Letter to her mother, October 20, 1903.
[12] Letter to G. de G., August 20, 1903.
[13] *Heaven on Earth*, 11th prayer.
[14] *Ibid.*, 1st prayer.

A higher phase of the spiritual life is entered upon when the soul, triumphing over self and entirely forgetful of self, no longer lives but for God, like the blessed in heaven, in unceasing praise of His glory. In its every movement, its every aspiration as in every one of its acts, be these ever so commonplace, that soul is, so to speak, a perpetual *Sanctus*, a continual " praise of glory." [15] It is beginning in time what will be its office through all eternity and no matter what it does, it is constantly recollected deep within itself, in that most secret sanctuary of its life, whither it has retired with its God.

" O thou soul, most beautiful of creatures, who so longest to know the place where thy Beloved is, that thou mayest seek Him and be united to Him; thou art thyself that very tabernacle where He dwells, the secret chamber of His retreat where He is hidden. Rejoice therefore and exult because thy Beloved, thy Treasure, thy sole hope is so near as to be within thee; and to speak truly, thou canst not be without Him." [16]

Nevertheless, let this soul be on its guard. It is not only for its joy that God abides within it, but primarily for His glory. " The Trinity so loves to find Its own image and likeness in Its creation! " Thus the glory of the Trinity must finally raise the soul above itself and its own joy. " Since my soul is a heaven, wherein I dwell while awaiting the heavenly Jerusalem, this heaven, too, must sing the glory of the Eternal, nothing but the glory of the Eternal." [17] That, in the last analysis, is what the spiritual doctrine of Sister Elizabeth of the Trinity seeks to lead souls to do: to live after the manner of the immutable Trinity in an eternal present, ever adoring It for Its own sake by means of a steadfast gaze that becomes ever more simple and more unitive, until they become the splendor of Its glory or, in other words, the ceaseless praise of the glory of Its perfections.[18]

While St. Teresa of the Child Jesus has drawn innumerable

---

[15] *Last Retreat*, 8th day.
[16] St. John of the Cross, *Spiritual Canticle*, Stanza I.
[17] *Last Retreat*, 7th day.
[18] *Ibid.*, 16th day.

souls after her in her offering as victim to the Merciful Love of God, it seems to be the mission of Sister Elizabeth of the Trinity to raise up in the Church a multitude of "Praises of Glory" of the Trinity.

"I BEQUEATH TO YOU THIS VOCATION WHICH WAS MINE IN THE BOSOM OF THE CHURCH MILITANT, AND WHICH I SHALL FULFILL UNCEASINGLY IN THE CHURCH TRIUMPHANT:

THE PRAISE OF GLORY OF THE MOST HOLY TRINITY."

APPENDIX I

LAST SPIRITUAL COUNSELS [1]

"Now I will answer your questions."

Here comes Sabeth at last, with her pencil, to pay her dear Fr —— a visit. I say " with her pencil," for, as far as our hearts go, we have already lived together for a long time and we shall always be together. How I love these evening visits! They are like a prelude to that communion reaching from heaven to earth, which will one day exist between our souls. I feel as if I were bending over you like a mother over her favorite child. I raise my eyes and look at God; then I lower them on you, shedding on you the rays of His love. I say nothing to Him about you, but He understands me and prefers my silence. My darling child, I wish I were a saint so that I could help you on earth while waiting until I can do so from Paradise. What would I not suffer to obtain for you the grace of fortitude you need!

Now I will answer your questions.

Let us speak first of *humility*. I have read splendid passages on this subject. One devout writer says that " nothing can disturb the humble man, who possesses invincible peace because he has thrown himself so low that no one will descend that far to look for him." He says too that " the humble soul finds its keenest joy in the feeling of its powerlessness before God."

Pride is not a thing that can be destroyed with one bold sword stroke, though some heroic acts of humility, such as we see in the lives of the saints, doubtless weaken it considerably, if they do not destroy it.

Rather, we must die daily. " Quotidie morior," [2] " I die daily," cried St. Paul. This doctrine of dying to self—the law for every

---

[1] This letter, written September 11, 1906 (but a few weeks before her death) to a girlhood friend, reveals the whole experience of her interior life, expressed as the saints write: with the simplicity of the Gospel.

[2] *I Cor.* XV, 31.

Christian soul ever since Christ said: " If any man will come after Me, let him deny himself and take up his cross " [3]—this doctrine, which seems so austere, is sweet and delightful when we consider the consummation of this death, which substitutes the life of God for our life of sin and misery. This is what St. Paul meant when he wrote: " Stripping yourselves of the old man with his deeds and putting on the new . . . according to the image of Him that created him." [4] This image is God Himself. Do you remember how plainly He expressed it on the day of creation: " Let us make man to Our image and likeness " ? [5]

Oh! truly, if we thought more about the origin of our soul, the things of this world would seem so petty that we should have only contempt for them. St. Peter wrote in one of his Epistles that we are " made partakers of the Divine nature." [6] And St. Paul counsels us to hold (firmly) to the end " the beginning of His substance " [7] which He has given to us.

It seems to me that the soul that realizes its own grandeur enters into that holy liberty of the children of God [8] of which the Apostle speaks—that is, it goes beyond all things, even beyond itself.

I think, too, that the freest soul is the most self-forgetful. If anyone asked me the secret of happiness, I would say that it is to pay no attention whatever to self, to deny self all the time. There is a good way of killing pride: starving it out. Remember, pride is love of ourselves. The love of God, then, must be so strong that it extinguishes all other love in us.

St. Augustine says that we have two cities within us: the city of God and the city of self. In proportion as the first is enlarged, the second will be destroyed. A soul that lives in faith in the presence of God, that has the " single eye " [9] of which Christ speaks in the Gospel—that is, a pure intention directed solely to God—would also be a humble soul. It would recognize the gifts He had bestowed upon it, for humility is truth, but would appropriate nothing to self, referring all to God, as did the Blessed Virgin. All the movements of pride you feel within you become faults only when your will consents to them; otherwise, though you may suffer greatly as a result of them, you do not offend the good God. The

---

[3] *Matt.* XVI, 24.
[4] *Col.* III, 9-10.
[5] *Gen.* I, 26.
[6] *II Peter* I, 4.
[7] *Heb.* III, 14.
[8] *Rom.* VIII, 21.
[9] *Matt.* VI, 22.

faults into which you tell me you slip inadvertently no doubt denote a store of self-love, but that, my dear little friend, is to an extent a very part of us. What the good God asks of you is never *voluntarily* to dwell on any thought of pride and never to perform an action inspired by that same pride, for that would not be good. But if you find you have done such a thing, you must not be discouraged, for it is pride itself which is irritated; but, like Magdalen, confess your misery at the Master's feet and ask Him to free you of it. He so loves to see a soul recognize its own helplessness! Then, as a great saint has said: "The abyss of God's immensity is confronted with the abyss of the creature's nothingness, and God embraces this nothingness." [10]

It is not pride, my dear, to think that you do not want an easy life. Indeed, I believe that God wills that your life should be lived in a sphere where the divine air is breathed. If you knew how I pity souls who live for nothing higher than the world and its trivialities! They seem like slaves to me and I should like to say to them: "Shake off the yoke that weighs you down! Why wear fetters that chain you to self and to things less than self?" The happy ones of this world, I think, are those with enough self-contempt and self-forgetfulness to choose the cross for their lot. What blissful peace we enjoy when we place our happiness in suffering! "I . . . fill up those things that are wanting of the sufferings of Christ, in my flesh, for His Body, which is the Church" [11]—that is what constitutes the Apostle's joy! This thought obsesses me and I confess to you that it gives me a profound, secret happiness to think that God has chosen to associate me with the Passion of His Christ. The road to Calvary which I climb daily seems to me rather the path of beatitude.

Have you ever seen any of those pictures showing death mowing the harvest with his sickle? Well, that is my condition. I seem to feel him destroying me. It is sometimes painful for nature and I assure you that, if I stayed on a natural plane, I should feel only my cowardice in suffering. But this is the human way of looking at it and I quickly "open the eye of my soul to the light of faith," which tells me that it is Love Who is destroying me, Who is slowly wearing me away. Then I feel an immense joy and yield myself as His prey.

To attain the ideal life of the soul, I believe that we must always

---

[10] St. Angela of Foligno.   [11] *Col.* I, 24.

live supernaturally, that is, we must never act "naturally." We must grasp the fact that God is deep within us and go to everything with Him. Then no action is trivial, no matter how commonplace it is, because we are not living in these things but going beyond them. A supernatural soul never considers secondary causes, but only God. The more its life is simplified, the more it resembles the life of the blessed, the more then is it freed from itself and from everything else. It finds everything reduced to unity, to the "one thing necessary" [12] of which the Master spoke to Magdalen. Then the soul is truly great, truly free, for it has "enclosed its will in God's."

When we meditate on our eternal predestination visible things seem so contemptible! Listen to what St. Paul says: "Whom He foreknew, He also predestinated to be made conformable to the image of His Son." [13] That is not all. You will see, my darling, that you are among the number of the predestinated. "And whom He predestinated, them He also called." [14] It is Baptism that made you a child of adoption, that stamped you with the seal of the Blessed Trinity. "And whom He called, them he also justified." [15] How often have you been justified by the sacrament of Penance and by God's many touches on your soul, without your even knowing it! "And whom He justified, them He also glorified." [16] That is what awaits you in eternity. But remember that our degree of glory will be the degree of grace in which God finds us at the moment of death. Allow Him to complete the work of His predestination in you and, to do that listen to St. Paul again, who will give you a rule of life: "Walk ye in [Jesus Christ], rooted and built up in Him, and confirmed in the faith . . . abounding in Him in thanksgiving." [17]

Yes, little child of my soul and my heart, walk in Jesus Christ. You need that spacious way; you are not meant for the narrow by-ways of this world. *Be rooted in Him.* For this you must be uprooted from self, or act as if you were by denying self wherever you meet it. Be *built up* in Him, far above all that is passing, up where all is pure and luminous. Be confirmed in the faith, that is, act by the light of God alone and never by your own impressions and imagination. Believe that He loves you and that He desires to help you Himself in your struggles. Believe in His love, in His

[12] *Luke* X, 42. [14] *Rom.* VIII, 30. [16] *Ibid.*
[13] *Rom.* VIII, 29. [15] *Ibid.* [17] *Col.* II, 6-7.

"exceeding charity," [18] as St. Paul says. Nourish your soul with the great truths of faith which show us how rich we are and the end for which God created us. If you live in these truths, your devotion will not be emotional exaltation *as you fear* but true devotion. The truth, the truth of love, is so beautiful! He "loved me and delivered Himself for me." [19] That, dear child, is the truth! Finally, "abound in thanksgiving." That is the last point of the rule and is but the consequence of the others. If you are rooted in Jesus Christ, confirmed in your faith, your life will be a constant thanksgiving, in the charity of the children of God. I wonder how a soul which has fathomed the love of God's heart for it can ever be anything but joyful, whatever its suffering or grief. Remember, He chose you in Him before the foundation of the world, that you should be holy and unspotted in His sight in charity.[20] That is St. Paul speaking again. And so you must not fear the struggle, or temptation. "When I am weak," declared the Apostle, "then am I powerful"; for then "the power of Christ may dwell in me." [21]

I wonder what our Reverend Mother will think of this long epistle. She does not let me write at all now, as I am extremely weak and constantly feel faint. This letter may be the last your Sabeth will send you. It has taken her a great many days to write and that will explain its incoherence, yet I cannot bring myself to leave you this evening. I am alone; it is half-past seven; the community is at recreation and I feel as if I were almost in heaven already here in my little cell, alone with Him, bearing my cross with my Master. My happiness increases with my sufferings. If you only knew what sweetness there is at the bottom of the chalice prepared by our Father in heaven!

Adieu, my dearest Fr ——! I can write no more but in the silence of our visits together you will fill in, you will understand all I leave unsaid. I take you in my arms and caress you as a mother fondles her baby. God keep you, my darling! May He protect you under the shadow of His wings [22] from all evil.

Sr. M. Elizabeth of the Trinity
Laudem Gloriae

This will be my new name in heaven . . .

---

[18] *Eph.* II, 4.
[19] *Gal.* II, 20.
[20] *Eph.* I, 4.
[21] *II Cor.* XII, 9-10.
[22] *Ps.* XVI, 9.

APPENDIX II

HEAVEN ON EARTH

> "*I have found my heaven on earth, since heaven is God and God is in my soul.*"
>
> "*The day I understood that, everything became clear to me. I wish I could whisper this secret to those I love.*"

How We Can Find Heaven on Earth [1]

First Prayer

"*The Trinity: Our Home*"

"Father, I will that where I am, they also whom Thou hast given Me be with Me; that they may see My glory which Thou hast given Me, because Thou hast loved Me before the creation of the world." [2] Such is Christ's last desire, His supreme prayer, before returning to the Father. He wills that where He is, we too may be, not only through all eternity but even in time, which is eternity begun and ever in progress.

Where, then, are we to be with Him, that His divine ideal may be realized? "The hiding place of the Son of God is in the bosom of the Father, which is the divine Essence, transcending all mortal vision, and hidden from all human understanding, as Isaias said: 'Verily, Thou art a hidden God!'" [3] Yet it is His will that we

---

[1] Sister Elizabeth of the Trinity composed this retreat during the summer of 1906, a few months before her death, in response to the request of a greatly loved soul—her sister—who had begged to be initiated into the secret of her interior life. Both in this and in the *Last Retreat*, the subtitles are ours.

[2] *John* XVII, 24.

[3] *Is.* XLV, 15; quotation from St. John of the Cross, *Spiritual Canticle*, explanation of 1st stanza.

should abide permanently in Him; that we should dwell where He dwells in the unity of love and that we should be, so to speak, the shadow of Himself.

By Baptism, says St. Paul, "we are buried"[4] in Christ. And again: "God . . . hath made us sit together in the heavenly places, through Jesus Christ: that He might show in the ages to come the abundant riches of His grace."[5] He adds: "Now therefore you are no more strangers and foreigners, but you are fellow citizens with the saints, and domestics of God."[6] The Blessed Trinity, then, is our dwelling-place, our home, our Father's house, which we should never leave.

* * *

Second Prayer
"Abide in Me"

"Abide in Me."[7] This command is given, this desire expressed by the Word of God. "Abide in Me": not for a few moments, a few passing hours, but abide permanently, habitually. Abide in Me, pray in Me, adore in Me, love in Me, suffer in Me, work in Me, act in Me. Abide in Me, whatever the person or action you are concerned with, penetrating ever deeper into this abode. This is the true wilderness into which God leads the soul that He may speak to it.[8] But to grasp the meaning of this mysterious appeal we must do more than listen to it superficially; we must immerse ourselves deeply, and more deeply still, into the Divinity by means of recollection. "I follow after," exclaimed St. Paul.[9] So should we descend daily by this path into the abyss, which is God Himself. Let us glide into its depths with loving confidence. "Deep calleth on deep."[10] It is there, sunk to its lowest depths, that the abyss of our nothingness will find itself face to face with the abyss of the mercy, with the immensity of the All of God. There shall we find the strength to die to self and, losing all trace of self, we shall be transformed in love. "Blessed are they who die in the Lord."[11]

* * *

---

[4] *Rom.* VI, 5.
[5] *Eph.* II, 6-7.
[6] *Eph.* II, 19.
[7] *John* XV, 4.
[8] *Osee* II, 14.
[9] *Phil.* III, 12.
[10] *Ps.* XLI, 8.
[11] *Apoc.* XIV, 13

Third Prayer
"The Kingdom of God Is Within You"

" The kingdom of God is within you." [12]

God has just invited us to abide in Him, that our soul may live in the heritage of His glory; and He now reveals to us that we are not to go outside ourselves to find this inheritance, for the kingdom of God is within us. St. John of the Cross says that it is in the substance of the soul, which is inaccessible to the devil and the world, that God gives Himself to it. Then all the movements of the soul become divine, and though of God, still are the soul's, because Our Lord effects them in it and with it. The same saint also states that the center of the soul is God. When the soul loves, comprehends, and enjoys Him with all its strength, it has attained to its deepest and ultimate center in God. When, however, the soul has not attained to this state, though it be in God, Who is the center of it, still it is not in the deepest center, because there is still room for it to advance. Love unites the soul with God, and the greater its love the deeper does it enter God, and the more it is centered in Him. Thus, a soul which has but one degree of love is already in God, Who is its center; but when its love has attained the highest degree, it will have penetrated to its inmost depth or center, and will be transformed until it becomes most like God. To such a soul, recollected in itself, may be addressed Father Lacordaire's words to St. Mary Magdalen: " Ask no more after the Master of anyone on earth or in heaven, for He is your soul, and your soul is He."

* * *

Fourth Prayer
" If Anyone Love Me "

" If anyone love Me, he will keep My word, and My Father will love him, and We will come to him, and will make Our abode with him." [13]

Again the Master tells us that He desires to dwell within us. " If anyone love Me! " It is this which draws God to His creature; not an emotional love, but a love " strong as death . . . which

---

[12] *Luke* XVII, 21.   [13] *John* XIV, 23.

many waters cannot quench."[14] "I love the Father,"[15] and so "I do always the things that please Him."[16] Thus spoke our blessed Master, and every soul that longs to keep close to Him should live by this word. Such a soul should make the Divine Will its food, its daily bread; it should allow itself to be immolated at the pleasure of the Father, as was the crucified Christ Whom it adores. Every occurrence, every event, each suffering, each joy is a sacrament which gives God to it, so that it ceases to distinguish between them but breaks through them and passes them by to rest in God Himself above all else. It rises to the topmost peak of His heart, even higher than His gifts and His consolations, higher than the joys which come from Him. It is characteristic of love never to seek self, to hold back nothing but to give all to the beloved. Happy the soul that truly loves, for love makes its Lord its Captive!

* * *

Fifth Prayer
"You Are Dead"

"You are dead, and your life is hid with Christ in God."[17]

St. Paul thus lights up for us the path that leads to the abyss. "You are dead." What does this mean but that the soul that aspires to dwell with God in the impregnable fortress of holy recollection must (*in spirit*) be separated, detached, and withdrawn from the thought of all else? "*Quotidie morior.*"[18] The soul finds in itself a simple loving tendency towards God no matter what creatures do. It is unaffected by transitory things, for it steps over them intent upon God. "*Quotidie morior*—I die daily." I master and renounce self more every day so that Christ may increase and be exalted. "*Quotidie morior.*" I find my soul's joy (in will, not in emotion) in all that sacrifices, destroys, abases self, that I may give place to my divine Master. "I live now not I, but Christ liveth in me."[19] I desire to live my own life no longer, but to be transformed into Christ, so that my life may be rather divine than human, and that the Father, bending towards me, may recognize the image of His beloved Son, in Whom He has set all His pleasure.

* * *

[14] *Cant.* VIII, 6-7.
[15] *John* XIV, 31.
[16] *John* VIII, 29.
[17] *Col.* III, 3.
[18] *I Cor.* XV, 31.
[19] *Gal.* II, 20.

Sixth Prayer
"*Our God Is a Consuming Fire*"

"*Deus ignis consumens.*"[20] "Our God," wrote St. Paul, "is a consuming fire," that is, a fire of love which destroys, which transforms into itself whatever it touches.

The mystic death of which St. Paul spoke becomes very simple and sweet to souls who yield themselves up to the action of its flames within the depths of their being. They think far less of the work of destruction and detachment left to them to accomplish than of plunging into the furnace of love burning within them, which is the Holy Ghost Himself—the same Love which in the Blessed Trinity is the bond between the Father and His Word. Such souls enter into Him by a living faith; there, in simplicity and peace, they are raised by Him above all things, above all sensible devotion, into the "sacred darkness," and transformed into the divine image. As St. John expresses it, they live "in fellowship"[21] with the three adorable Persons Whose life they share. That is the contemplative life.

* * *

Seventh Prayer
"*I Am Come to Cast Fire on the Earth*"

"I am come to cast fire on the earth, and what will I, but that it be kindled?"[22]

The Master Himself here tells us of His longing to see the fire of love ignited. All our works and labors are as nothing in His sight: we can give Him nothing, nor can we satisfy His one desire of enhancing the dignity of our soul. Nothing so pleases Him as to see it increase, and nothing can so enhance it as its becoming, in some sort, equal with God. This is why He exacts the tribute of its love, the property of love being to put, as far as possible, the lover and the beloved on a par. The soul which possesses such love appears on a kind of equality with Jesus, because their mutual love makes them share all in common. "I have called you friends, because all things whatsoever I have heard of My Father, I have

---

[20] *Heb.* XII, 29. [21] *1 John* I, 3. [22] *Luke* XII, 49.

made known to you."[23] But to attain to this love the soul must have first surrendered self entirely; the will must be sweetly lost in that of God, so that the inclinations and faculties may be moved in and by this love alone. I do all by love; I suffer all with love. That is what David means when he sings: "I will keep my strength to Thee."[24] Then the soul is so filled, absorbed, and protected by love that it finds the secret of growing in love wherever it may be. Even in its intercourse with the world and amid the cares of this life, it can truly affirm: my sole occupation is love.

* * *

Eighth Prayer
"He that Cometh to God, Must Believe"

"He that cometh to God, must believe."[25] So speaks St. Paul. He also says: "Faith is the substance of things to be hoped for, the evidence of things that appear not."[26] That is to say, faith makes future blessings so certain and so present to us that they are evolved in our soul and subsist there before we actually enjoy them. St. John of the Cross says that faith serves as feet to take us to God, and is possession itself in an obscure manner. Faith alone can enlighten us concerning Him we love, and should be chosen by our soul as the means by which to attain divine union. It fills us with spiritual gifts. Christ, when speaking to the Samaritan woman, alluded to faith when He promised to give those who should believe in Him "a fountain of water, springing up into life everlasting."[27] Thus, faith gives us God even in this life, behind the veil, yet still God Himself. "When that which is perfect is come"—that is, the clear vision—"that which is imperfect"—or the knowledge given by faith—"shall be done away."[28]

"We have known, and have believed the charity which God hath to us."[29] This is our great act of faith, the means of rendering love for love to our God. It is "the mystery which hath been hidden"[30] in the heart of the Father, of which St. Paul speaks, which at last we fathom and which thrills our soul. When it really believes in this "exceeding love" overshadowing it, we may say

[23] *John* XV, 15.   [25] *Heb.* XI, 6.   [27] *John* IV, 14.   [29] *I John* IV, 16.
[24] *Ps.* LVIII, 10.   [26] *Heb.* XI, 1.   [28] *I Cor.* XIII, 10.   [30] *Col.* I, 26.

of it, what was said of Moses, that he " endured as seeing Him that is invisible." [31] The soul no longer stops at tastes or feelings. Thenceforth it cares little whether it feels God or not, whether He sends it joy or suffering; it believes in His Love. The more it is tried, the stronger is its faith, for it overleaps, as it were, all obstacles and finds its rest in the bosom of infinite Love, Which can do naught but works of love. So to this soul, vivified by faith, the Master can whisper in secret the words He once spoke to Mary Magdalen: " Thy faith hath made thee safe, go in peace." [32]

* * *

Ninth Prayer

" Conformable to the Image of His Son "

" For whom He foreknew, He also predestinated to be made conformable to the image of His Son . . . and whom He predestinated, them He also called. And whom He called, them He also justified. And whom He justified, them He also glorified. What shall we then say to these things? If God be for us, who is against us? . . . Who then shall separate us from the love of Christ? " [33] Such is the mystery of predestination, of divine election, as the Apostle saw it. Those " whom He foreknew." Were we not of the number? May not God say to our souls what of old He said by the voice of His prophet: " And I passed by thee and saw thee; and behold thy time was the time of lovers; and I spread my garment over thee . . . and I swore to thee and I entered into a covenant with thee. And thou becamest mine! " [34] Yes, we have become His by Baptism. That is what St. Paul means by the words: " Them He *called.*" We are called to receive the seal of the Blessed Trinity. At the same time when, in St. Peter's words, we were " made partakers of the Divine Nature," [35] we received " the beginning of His substance." [36] Then He *justified* us by His Sacraments and by His direct touches in the deepest center of our soul, justified us also by faith [37] and according to the measure of our faith in the redemption which Jesus Christ has acquired for us. Finally, He wills to *glorify* us and therefore, says St. Paul, " hath made us worthy to be partakers of the lot of the saints in light." [38] But we shall be

[31] *Heb.* XI, 27. [33] *Rom.* VIII, 29-35. [35] *II Peter* I, 4. [37] Cf. *Rom.* V, 1.
[32] *Luke* VII, 50. [34] *Ezech.* XVI, 8. [36] *Heb.* III, 14. [38] *Col.* I, 12.

glorified in the measure in which we have been made conformable to the image of His Divine Son. Let us contemplate this adored image; let us stay unceasingly within its radiance, that it may be impressed upon us. Then let us go to everything with the attitude of soul with which our Master approached all things. Then we shall realize the great desire of God, Who " purposed in Him . . . to re-establish all things in Christ." [39]

* * *

Tenth Prayer

"To Me, to Live Is Christ"

" I count all things to be but loss for the excellent knowledge of Jesus Christ my Lord; for Whom I have suffered the loss of all things, and count them but as dung, that I may gain Christ. . . . That I may know Him . . . and the fellowship of His sufferings, being made conformable to His death . . . I follow after, if I may by any means apprehend, wherein I am also apprehended by Christ Jesus. . . . One thing I do; forgetting the things that are behind, and stretching forth myself to those that are before, I press towards the mark to the prize of the supernal vocation of God in Christ Jesus." [40] That is, I desire nothing but to be identified with Him. " *Mihi vivere Christus est*—To me, to live is Christ." [41] St. Paul's burning soul is clearly revealed in these lines. Let us study this divine Model during this retreat, in which we seek to become more closely conformed to our adored Master or, even more than that, to be so wholly merged in Him that we can say: " I live, now not I; but Christ liveth in me. And that I live now in the flesh: I live in the faith of the Son of God, Who loved me, and delivered Himself for me." [42] His knowledge, the Apostle tells us, is " excellent." [43] The first thing He said upon coming into the world was: " A body thou hast fitted to me: Holocausts for sin did not please thee . . . Then said I: Behold, I come to do Thy Will, O God." [44] For thirty-three years, this Will was so truly His daily bread [45] that, as He commended His soul to His Father, He could say to Him: " All is consummated." [46] Yes, all, absolutely

---

[39] *Eph.* I, 9-10.　　[41] *Phil.* I, 21.　　[43] *Phil.* III, 8.　　[45] *John* IV, 32, 34.
[40] *Phil.* III, 8-14.　　[42] *Gal.* II, 20.　　[44] *Heb.* X, 5, 9.　　[46] *John* XIX, 30.

all Thou didst will has been accomplished; that is why "I have glorified Thee on the earth." [47]

In fact, when speaking to His Apostles of this food of which they knew nothing, Jesus told them that it was the doing of the Will of Him that sent Him.[48] In the same way, He could say: "I am not alone." [49] "He that sent Me is with Me . . . for I do always the things that please Him." [50] Let us lovingly eat this bread of God's Will. If we should sometimes find His Will most painful, we can, of course, say with our beloved Master: "My Father, if it be possible let this chalice pass from Me," but we will immediately add: "nevertheless, not as I will, but as Thou wilt." [51] Then, with calm strength we too will ascend our Calvary with the Crucified One, singing a hymn of thanksgiving to the Father in the depths of our soul, for those who walk this painful way are those whom He foreknew and predestinated to be made conformable to the image of His Divine Son,[52] Love's Crucified One.

* * *

Eleventh Prayer

"*The Adoption of the Children of God*"

"God hath predestinated us unto the adoption of children through Jesus Christ unto Himself, according to the purpose of His will: unto the praise of the glory of His grace, in which He hath graced us in His beloved Son. In Whom we have redemption through His blood, the remission of sins, according to the riches of His grace, which hath superabounded in us, in all wisdom and prudence." [53] A soul which has truly become the child of God is, in the Apostle's words, moved by the Holy Spirit Himself, because "whosoever are led by the Spirit of God, they are the sons of God." [54] And again: "You have not received the spirit of bondage again in fear; but you have received the spirit of adoption of sons, whereby we cry: Abba! Father! For the Spirit Himself giveth testimony to our spirit that we are the sons of God. And if sons, heirs also; heirs indeed of God, and joint-heirs with Christ: yet so, if we suffer with Him, that we may also be glorified with Him." [55] It

---

[47] *John* XVII, 4.
[48] Cf. *John* IV, 34.
[49] *John* VIII, 16.
[50] *John* VIII, 29.
[51] *Matt.* XXVI, 39.
[52] Cf. *Rom.* VIII, 29.
[53] *Eph.* I, 5-8.
[54] *Rom.* VIII, 14.
[55] *Rom.* VIII, 15-17.

was that we might attain to this abyss of glory that God created us in His image and likeness.

"Behold," says St. John, "what manner of charity the Father hath bestowed on us, that we should be called, and should be, the sons of God. . . . We are now the sons of God, and it hath not yet appeared what we shall be. We know that, when He shall appear, we shall be like to Him, because we shall see Him as He is. And everyone that hath this hope in him, sanctifieth himself, as He also is holy." [56]

This is the measure of the sanctity of the children of God—to be holy as God is, to be holy with the holiness of God by living in contact with Him in the depths of the bottomless abyss within themselves. Then the soul appears, to a certain extent, to resemble God, Who, though He takes delight in all things, yet never takes such delight as in Himself, because He possesses within Himself a supreme good in comparison with which all others are nothing. Thus, every joy which befalls the soul invites it to prefer the Good which it possesses within itself, with which no other can compare.

"Our Father, Who art in heaven." [57] We must seek Him, and above all, we must dwell in the little heaven He has made for Himself in the center of our soul. Christ told the Samaritan woman that the Father seeks true adorers "who shall adore Him in spirit and in truth." [58] Let us be those fervent adorers and rejoice His heart. Let us adore Him *in spirit*; that is, with heart and thoughts bent on Him, our mind filled with the knowledge of Him imparted by the light of faith. Let us adore Him *in truth* by our actions, which make us true by our always doing what will please the Father, Whose children we are. In short, "let us adore in spirit and in truth," that is, *by* Jesus Christ and *with* Jesus Christ, for He alone truly adores in spirit and in truth. Then we shall be the children of God and shall learn by experience the truth of what Isaias said: "You shall be carried at the breasts, and upon the knees shall they caress you." [59] In fact, God appears to occupy Himself solely with overwhelming the soul with caresses and marks of affection, like a mother who picks up her baby and feeds it with her milk. Let us listen to our Father's mysterious appeal: "My son, give Me thy heart." [60]

* * *

[56] *I John* III, 1-3.
[57] *Matt.* VI, 9.
[58] *John* IV, 23.
[59] *Is.* LXVI, 12.
[60] *Prov.* XXIII, 26.

Twelfth Prayer
"*Our Lady of the Incarnation*"

"*Si scires donum Dei*—If thou didst know the gift of God,"[61] Christ said one evening to the Samaritan woman. Yet what is this gift of God, but Himself? "He came unto His own and His own received Him not,"[62] declares the beloved Disciple. To many a soul might St. John the Baptist still utter the reproach: "There hath stood one in the midst of you Whom you knew not."[63] "If thou didst know the gift of God!"

There is one created being who did know that gift of God, who lost no particle of it; a creature so pure and luminous that she seemed to be the Light itself: *Speculum justitiae*; a being whose life was so simple, so lost in God, that there is but little to say of it: *Virgo fidelis*, the faithful Virgin, who "kept all these words in her heart."[64] She was so lowly, so hidden in God, in the seclusion of the temple, that she drew upon herself the complacent regard of the Holy Trinity: "Because He hath regarded the humility of His handmaid; for behold from henceforth all generations shall call me blessed."[65] The Father, bending down to this lovely creature, so unaware of her own beauty, chose her for the Mother in time of Him Whose Father He is in eternity. Then the Spirit of Love, Who presides over all the works of God, overshadowed her; the Virgin uttered her *Fiat*: "Behold the handmaid of the Lord; be it done to me according to thy word,"[66] and the greatest of all mysteries was accomplished. By the descent of the Word into her womb, Mary became God's own forever and ever.

During the period between the Annunciation and the Nativity, Our Lady seems to me to be the model of interior souls: those whom God has called to live within themselves, in the depths of the bottomless abyss. In what peace and recollection did Mary live and act! The most trivial actions were sanctified by her, for, through them all, she remained the constant adorer of the Gift of God. Yet that did not prevent her from spending herself for others when charity required it. The Gospel tells us that "Mary, rising up . . . went into the hill country with haste to a city of Juda,"[67] to visit her cousin Elizabeth. Never did the ineffable vision which

[61] *John* IV, 10.
[62] *John* I, 11.
[63] *John* I, 26.
[64] *Luke* II, 51.
[65] *Luke* I, 48.
[66] *Luke* I, 38.
[67] *Luke* I, 39.

she contemplated within herself lessen her charity for others, because, says one writer, "though contemplation is directed to the praise and the eternity of its Lord, it possesses and will never lose concord."

* * *

Thirteenth Prayer
"A Praise of Glory"

We have been "predestinated according to the purpose of Him Who worketh all things according to the counsel of His Will, that we may be unto the praise of His glory." [68]

It is St. Paul who speaks thus—St. Paul, inspired by God Himself. How can we fulfill this great dream of the heart of our God, this immutable desire regarding our souls—in a word, how can we correspond to our vocation and become perfect praises of the glory of the Most Blessed Trinity? In heaven, every soul is a praise of the glory of the Father, the Word, and the Holy Ghost, because each soul is established in pure love, and lives no longer its own life, but the life of God. Then, as St. Paul says, it knows Him as it is known by Him. In other words:

A "Praise of Glory" is a soul that dwells in God, that loves Him with the pure, disinterested love which does not seek self in the sweetness of this love; a soul that loves Him above all His gifts, which would have loved Him as much had it received nothing from Him, and which desires good for the object of its love. But how can we actually wish and will good to God except by accomplishing His Will, since this Will ordains all things for His greater glory? Such a soul should surrender itself fully, blindly to this Will, so that it cannot possibly will anything but what God wills.

A "Praise of Glory" is a silent soul, a lyre beneath the mysterious touch of the Holy Ghost, from which He can draw divine harmonies. Knowing that suffering is a string which produces still more exquisite tones, this soul rejoices at having it on its instrument, that it may thus more sweetly move the heart of its God.

"A Praise of Glory" is a soul that contemplates God in faith and in simplicity. It reflects all that He is and is a fathomless abyss into which He can flow and outpour Himself. It is a crystal through

---

[68] *Eph.* I, 11-12.

which He can shine and view His own perfections and splendor. A soul which thus permits the Divine Being to satisfy within it His craving to communicate all He is and has, is truly the " Praise of Glory " of all His gifts.

Finally, a " Praise of Glory " is one who is always giving thanks; whose acts, movements, thoughts, aspirations, while more deeply establishing her in love, are like an echo of the eternal *Sanctus*.

In the heaven of glory, the blessed rest not day or night, saying: " Holy, holy, holy, Lord God Almighty . . . and falling down, adore Him that liveth for ever and ever." [69]

In the heaven of her soul, the " Praise of Glory " begins now the task which will be hers for all eternity. Her chant is uninterrupted, for she is under the influence of the Holy Ghost, Who effects all her actions and, although she may sometimes be unconscious of it, for human weakness prevents souls from keeping their attention fixed on God without distractions, she sings and adores perpetually and has, so to speak, become absorbed in praise and love, in her passion for the glory of her God.

Let us, in the heaven of our soul, be praises of glory to the Blessed Trinity and praises of love to our Immaculate Mother. One day the veil will be withdrawn, and we shall be brought into the eternal courts; there we shall sing in the bosom of infinite Love, and God will give us " the new name " promised to him that overcometh. What will that name be? *Laudem Gloriae*.[70]

---

[69] *Apoc.* IV, 8, 10.
[70] *Eph.* I, 12.

APPENDIX III

THE LAST RETREAT OF "*LAUDEM GLORIAE*"[1]

"*It is my dream to be 'the Praise of His Glory.'*"

Thursday, August 16, 1906.

First Day
"*Nescivi*"

"*Nescivi!*—I knew not."[2] So sings the bride of the Canticle after having been brought into the inner cellar. That, it seems to me, should also be the song of a "Praise of Glory" on the first day of her retreat, when the Master makes her sound the depths of the bottomless abyss, that she may learn to fulfill the office which will be hers in eternity and which she also ought to perform in time, which is eternity begun and ever in progress.

"*Nescivi!*" I know nothing, I desire to know nothing, but "Him . . . and the fellowship of His sufferings, being made conformable to His death."[3] "Whom He foreknew, He also predestinated to be made conformable to the image of His Son,"[4] Who was crucified by love. When I become completely identified with this Divine Exemplar, dwelling wholly in Him and He in me, I shall fulfill my eternal vocation for which God chose me in Him *in principio* and which I

---

[1] Those who would sound the depths of the mind of Elizabeth of the Trinity must turn to her last retreat. *The Last Retreat of "Laudem Gloriae"*— she herself gave it the title—is, so to speak, her little mystical summa, the quintessence of her spiritual teaching at the highest point of her mystical experience. It is a real treatise on transforming union, as she conceived it along the lines of her vocation of a "Praise of Glory" and as she interiorly lived it. In it she leaves a plan of life to all "praises of glory" who would thereafter follow in her steps along the road of a sanctity which is wholly forgetful of self and wholly devoted to the purest glory of the Trinity.

[2] *Cant.* VI, 11.   [3] *Phil.* III, 10.   [4] *Rom.* VIII, 29.

shall fulfill *in aeternum* when, immersed in the bosom of the Trinity, I shall be the unceasing " praise of His glory—*in laudem gloriae ejus.*" [5]

" Not that any man hath seen the Father," [6] " but the Son and he to whom it shall please the Son to reveal Him." [7] It might be added that no one has penetrated the mystery of Christ in all its depths unless it be Our Lady. John and Magdalen did see very far into this mystery and St. Paul often speaks of the " knowledge " [8] he had received of it, yet all the saints dwell in shadow compared with Our Lady's light! The secret she kept and pondered in her heart [9] is unspeakable; no tongue can tell it, no pen express it.

This Mother of grace will so shape my soul that her little child may be a living, striking image of her " Firstborn," [10] the Son of the Eternal, the perfect Praise of the glory of His Father.

✢ ✢ ✢

Second Day
"In Silence of the Powers"

" My soul is continually in my hands." [11] This was the song of my Master's soul, and that is why, in the midst of all His anguish, He remained calm and strong. " My soul is continually in my hands." What does that mean except perfect self-control in the presence of the Peaceful?

" I will keep my strength to thee," [12] is another of Christ's songs in which I desire to join incessantly. My Rule tells me: " In silence . . . shall your strength be." To keep our strength for the Lord is to keep our whole being in unity by interior silence; to collect all our powers, to occupy them in the one work of love, to have the " single eye " which allows the light of God to enlighten us.

A soul which listens to self, which is preoccupied with its sensibilities, which indulges in useless thoughts or desires, scatters its forces. It is not completely under God's sway. Its lyre is not in tune, so that when the Master strikes it, He cannot draw forth divine harmonies; it is too human and discordant.

[5] *Eph.* I, 12.
[6] *John* VI, 46.
[7] *Matt.* XI, 27.
[8] *Eph.* III, 4.
[9] Cf. *Luke* II, 19.
[10] *Matt.* I, 25.
[11] *Ps.* CXVIII, 109.
[12] *Ps.* LVIII, 10.

The soul which reserves anything for self in its interior kingdom, whose powers are not all "enclosed" in God, cannot be a perfect "Praise of Glory"; it is unfit to sing continually the *canticum magnum* of which St. Paul speaks because it is not in unity. So that, instead of persevering in praise, in simplicity, whatever may happen, it must be continually tuning the strings of its instrument, which are all a little off key.

How necessary is this blessed unity for the soul that craves to live here below the life of the blessed—that is, of simple beings, of spirits! Did not the Divine Master mean to teach this to St. Mary Magdalen when He spoke of the *unum necessarium?* [13] How well that great saint realized it! She had recognized her God by the light of faith under the veil of His humanity and, in silence, in the unity of her powers, she "heard His word" [14] and could sing: "My soul is continually in my hands," and also the little word "*Nescivi!*" Yes! she knew nothing but Him. Whatever noise and bustle there might be around her: "*Nescivi!*" She might be blamed: "*Nescivi!*" Neither care for honor nor exterior things could draw her from her sacred silence.

Thus it is with the soul dwelling in the fortress of holy recollection. By the light of faith it sees its God present, dwelling within it, while, in turn, the soul is so present to Him in its beautiful simplicity that He guards it with jealous care. Then, whatever turmoil there may be outside or whatever tempests within, however its honor may be assailed: "*Nescivi!*" God may hide Himself, withdraw His sensible grace: "*Nescivi!*" "For [Him] I have suffered the loss of all things," [15] it exclaims with St. Paul. Henceforth the Master has full liberty—liberty to infuse Himself into the soul, to give Himself "according to the measure of the giving of Christ," [16] and the soul, thus simplified and unified, becomes the throne of Him Who changes not, because unity is the throne of the Blessed Trinity.

* * *

Third Day

"In the Presence of God"

"In Whom we also are called by lot, being predestinated according to the purpose of Him Who worketh all things according to the

[13] *Luke* X, 42.   [14] *Luke* X, 39.   [15] *Phil.* III, 8.   [16] *Eph.* IV, 7.

counsel of His will. That we may be unto the praise of His glory." [17]

It is St. Paul who makes known to us this divine election—St. Paul, who penetrated so deeply into the " mystery which hath been hidden from eternity in God." [18] Let us listen to him as he enlightens us regarding this vocation to which we are called. God, he says, " chose us *in Him* before the foundation of the world, that we should be holy and unspotted in His sight in charity." [19]

On comparing these two explanations of the divine " and eternally immutable " plan, I conclude that, if I am worthily to fulfill my office of *Laudem Gloriae*, I must keep myself whatever happens in the presence of God. The Apostle also says " *in caritate*," [20] that is to say, in God, for " *Deus caritas est*," [21] and it is contact with the Divinity which will make me " holy and unspotted in His sight." I apply this to the beautiful virtue of simplicity concerning which a pious author has written: " It gives the soul the repose of the abyss," that is, rest in God, the unfathomable abyss, prelude to and echo of that eternal Sabbath of which St. Paul speaks: " For we, who have believed, shall enter into rest." [22]

Glorified souls have this rest in the abyss because they contemplate God in the simplicity of His Essence. " Then I shall know even as I am known," [23] says St. Paul, meaning by intuitive vision, a simple glance. That is why, the saint continues, they " are transformed into the same image from glory to glory, as by the Spirit of the Lord." [24] Then they are a ceaseless praise of glory to the Divine Being, Who contemplates His own splendor in them.

I believe that we should give immense joy to the heart of God by imitating, in the heaven of our soul, this occupation of the blessed, adhering to Him by the simple contemplation which resembles the state of innocence in which man was created.

"To our image and likeness," [25]—such was the plan of the Creator, that He might view Himself in His creature and might see His own perfections and beauty reflected through him as through a pure and flawless crystal. Is not that a kind of extension of His own glory? The soul, by the simplicity of the gaze which it fixes upon its Divine Object, is separated from all around it and, above all, from self. Henceforth, it is resplendent with " the light of the

---

[17] *Eph.* I, 11-12.
[18] *Eph.* III, 9.
[19] *Eph.* I, 4.
[20] *Eph.* I, 4.
[21] *I John* IV, 8.
[22] *Heb.* IV, 3.
[23] *I Cor.* XIII, 12.
[24] *II Cor.* III, 18.
[25] *Gen.* I, 26.

knowledge of the glory of God "[26] mentioned by the Apostle, because it allows the Divinity to reflect Himself in it and all His attributes are communicated to it. Such a soul is truly "the Praise of the Glory" of all His gifts. Whatever happens and during the most commonplace employments, it sings the *canticum magnum*, the *canticum novum*, and this canticle thrills God to His very depths.

"Then shall thy light," we may say to this soul with Isaias, "rise up in darkness, and thy darkness shall be as the noonday. And the Lord will give thee rest continually and will fill thy soul with brightness and deliver thy bones, and thou shalt be like a watered garden, and like a fountain of water, whose waters shall not fail . . . I will lift thee up above the high places of the earth."[27]

* * *

Fourth Day

"Faith"

Yesterday, St. Paul raised the veil a little so that I could catch a glimpse "of the lot of the saints in light "[28] and ascertain how they employ themselves so that I might try, as far as possible, to conform my life to theirs, and fulfill my vocation of *Laudem Gloriae*.

Today, it is St. John, the disciple whom Jesus loved, who will partly open the "eternal gates "[29] for me, that my soul may rest in "Jerusalem, the heavenly city, the blessed vision of peace."[30] He tells me, to begin with, that "the city hath no need of the sun, nor of the moon, to shine in it. For the glory of God hath enlightened it, and the Lamb is the lamp thereof."[31] If I wish my interior city to agree with, to resemble in some measure that of the immortal "King of ages,"[32] and to shine with the great illumination given by God, I must first extinguish every other light, so that in the holy city the Lamb may be its only Lamp.

Here faith, the fair light of faith, appears to me. That, and no other, ought to enlighten me to go to meet the Bridegroom. The Psalmist sings that "He made darkness His covert,"[33] but seems

---

[26] *II Cor.* IV, 6.
[27] *Is.* LVIII, 10-14.
[30] *Office of the Dedication of a Church*: Hymn for I Vespers.
[31] *Apoc.* XXI, 23.
[32] *I Tim.* I, 17.

[28] *Col.* I, 12.
[29] *Ps.* XXIII, 7.

[33] *Ps.* XVII, 12.

to contradict himself by saying elsewhere that He is "clothed with light as with a garment."[34] This apparent contradiction appears to me to mean that I ought to plunge into the sacred darkness, keeping all my powers in night and emptiness. Then I shall meet my Master and the light which clothes Him as a garment will enwrap me too, for He wishes His bride to be luminous with His light and with His light *alone*, "having the glory of God."[35]

It is said of Moses that "he endured as seeing Him that is invisible."[36] Such should be the attitude of a "Praise of Glory" who desires to persevere in her hymn of thanksgiving whatever happens; to be enduring in her faith, as if she saw Him Who is invisible; enduring in her faith in His "exceeding charity." "We have known and have believed the charity, which God hath to us."[37]

"Faith," says St. Paul, "is the substance of things to be hoped for, the evidence of things that appear not."[38] What does it matter to the soul that retires within itself, enlightened by this word, whether it feels or does not feel, whether it is in light or darkness, enjoys or does not enjoy? It is struck by a kind of shame at making any distinction between such things and, despising itself utterly for such want of love, it turns at once to its Master for deliverance. To use the expressive words of a great mystic: "It exalts Him upon the highest summit of the heart," that is to say, above the sweetness and consolations which flow from Him, having resolved to pass by all else in order to be united with Him Whom it loves. To this soul, this enduring believer in the God of love, may be applied the words of the prince of the Apostles: "In Whom . . . believing, [you] shall rejoice with joy unspeakable and glorified."[39]

* * *

Fifth Day
"On the Way to Calvary"

"I saw a great multitude, which no man could number . . . Who are they? . . . These are they who are come out of great tribulation, and have washed their robes, and have made them white in the blood of the Lamb. Therefore they are before the throne of

---

[34] *Ps.* CIII, 2.   [36] *Heb.* XI, 27.   [38] *Heb.* XI, 1.
[35] *Apoc.* XXI, 11.   [37] *I John* IV, 16.   [39] *I Peter* I, 8.

God, and they serve Him day and night in His temple: and He, that sitteth on the throne, shall dwell over them. They shall no more hunger nor thirst, neither shall the sun fall on them, nor any heat. For the Lamb, which is in the midst of the throne, shall rule them, and shall lead them to the fountains of the waters of life, and God shall wipe away all tears from their eyes." [40]

All these elect souls, palm in hand, bathed in the light of God, must needs have first passed through "great tribulation" and known that sorrow "great as the sea," [41] sung by the prophet. Before "beholding the glory of the Lord with open face," [42] they have shared the abjection of His Christ; before being "transformed into the same image from glory to glory," [43] they have been conformed to the image of the Word Incarnate, crucified by love.

The soul that longs to serve God day and night in His temple (by which I understand that inner sanctuary of which St. Paul speaks when he says: "The temple of God is holy, which you are" [44]) must be resolved to take a real share in the Passion of its Master. It is a redeemed soul and in its turn must redeem other souls. Therefore it will sing upon its lyre: "God forbid that I should glory, save in the cross of our Lord Jesus Christ!" [45] "With Christ I am nailed to the cross." [46] And again: "I . . . fill up those things that are wanting of the sufferings of Christ, in my flesh, for His Body, which is the Church." [47]

"The queen stood on thy right hand." [48] Such is the attitude of this soul. It walks the road to Calvary at the right hand of her crucified, crushed, and humbled King Who, strong, calm, and full of majesty, goes to His Passion, to show forth "the glory of His grace," [49] to use St. Paul's strong expression. He desires His bride to join in His work of redemption, and the way of sorrow which she treads seems to her the way of beatitude, not only because it leads there, but also because her holy Teacher makes her understand that she must pass beyond the bitterness of suffering, to find her rest in it, as He did. Then she can serve God day and night in His temple. Neither interior nor exterior trials can make her leave

---

[40] *Apoc.* VII, 9-17.
[41] *Lam.* II, 13.
[42] *II Cor.* III, 18.
[43] *Ibid.*
[44] *I Cor.* III, 17.

[45] *Gal.* VI, 14.
[46] *Gal.* II, 19.
[47] *Col.* I, 24.
[48] *Ps.* XLIV, 10.
[49] *Eph.* I, 6.

the holy fortress in which He has enclosed her. She no longer thirsts or hungers, for in spite of her overwhelming longing for heaven she is satisfied with the food that was her Master's—the will of the Father. She no. longer feels the " sun fall on her "—that is, she does not suffer from suffering, and the " Lamb . . . can lead " her " to the fountains of the waters of life," where He will, as He will, for she looks not at the path whereon she walks, but only at the Shepherd Who guides her.

God, bending down towards this soul, His adopted daughter, so conformed to the image of His Son, " the first-born of every creature," [50] recognizes it as one whom He has predestinated, called, justified; and His Fatherly heart thrills at the thought of perfecting His work, that is, of glorifying the soul by transferring it to His kingdom, there to sing through endless ages " the praise of His glory."

* * *

Sixth Day
" These Souls Are Virgins "

" And I beheld, and lo, a Lamb stood upon Mount Sion, and with Him an hundred forty-four thousand, having His name and the name of His Father written on their foreheads. And I heard a voice from heaven, as the voice of many waters, and as the voice of great thunder; and the voice, which I heard, was as the voice of harpers, harping on their harps. And they sang as it were a new canticle, before the throne, . . . and no man could say the canticle, but those hundred forty-four thousand . . . for they are virgins. These follow the Lamb whithersoever He goeth." [51]

There are some, pure as the light, who even here on earth belong to this generation; they already bear the name of the Lamb and of the Father written on their foreheads. They bear the name of the Lamb by their resemblance and conformity with Him Whom St. John calls the " Faithful and True," [52] Whom he shows us clothed in a robe stained with blood. These Christians are also faithful and true, and their robes are stained with the blood of their perpetual immolation. They bear the name of His Father, because He radiates the beauty of His perfection in them, all His divine attributes being reflected in such souls, which are like so many

---

[50] *Col.* I, 15.   [51] *Apoc.* XIV, 1-4.   [52] *Apoc.* III, 14.

strings of an instrument, vibrating and giving forth the *canticum novum.*

"They follow the Lamb whithersoever He goeth," not only by the wide and level roads but by the thorny paths, among the brambles by the way. "They are virgins"—that is, free, set apart, detached. "Free from all except from their love," separated from all, from self above all, detached from all, both in the supernatural and natural order. What a going out from self does that imply! What a death! As St. Paul says: "I die daily." [53]

This great saint wrote to the Colossians: "You are dead; and your life is hid with Christ in God." [54] There is the condition: we must be *dead*; otherwise, we may be hidden in God at certain times, but we do not habitually *live* in the Divinity, because our feelings, our self-seeking, and the rest draw us forth from Him.

The soul that gazes upon its Master with the single eye which makes the whole body full of light, is kept from the iniquity [55] within it over which the prophet lamented. The Lord makes it enter the "large place" [56] which is nothing else than Himself. There all is pure, all is holy.

Oh, blessed death in God! Oh, sweet and delightful loss of self within Him Whom we love! Henceforth the creature can say: "And I live, now not I; but Christ liveth in me. And that I live now in the flesh: I live in the faith of the Son of God, Who loved me, and delivered Himself for me." [57]

* * *

Seventh Day

"Nothing but the Glory of the Eternal"

Coeli enarrant gloriam Dei.[58] This is what the heavens show forth: "the glory of God."

Since my soul is a heaven wherein I dwell while awaiting the heavenly Jerusalem, this heaven, too, must sing the glory of the Eternal, *nothing* but the glory of the Eternal.

"Day to day uttereth speech." [59] All the light, the communications from God to my soul, are this "day" which "uttereth speech"

---

[53] *I Cor.* XV, 31.
[54] *Col.* III, 3.
[55] Cf. *Ps.* XVII, 24.
[56] *Ps.* XVII, 20.
[57] *Gal.* II, 20.
[58] *Ps.* XVIII, 2.
[59] *Ibid.*, 3.

of His glory "to day." "The commandment of the Lord is lightsome, enlightening the eyes,"[60] sings the Psalmist. Consequently, my fidelity to all His commandments and interior promptings causes me to live in His light; it is also the " speech " which " uttereth " His glory.

But what a sweet mystery! " Lord, he who looks upon Thee doth shine,"[61] cries the prophet. The soul which, by its far-seeing inner gaze, contemplates God through all with a simplicity that separates it from all else, " shines "; it is a " day that uttereth speech " of His glory " to day." " Night to night showeth knowledge."[62] How consoling this is! My helplessness, my repugnances, my ignorance, my very faults themselves declare the glory of the Eternal! And my sufferings of body and soul " show forth the glory of God! "

David sang: " What shall I render to the Lord, for all the things that He hath rendered to me? I will take the chalice of salvation."[63] If I take this chalice, crimsoned with the Blood of my Master, and in joyous thanksgiving mingle my own blood with that of the sacred Victim Who gives it a share of His own infinity, it may bring wonderful glory to the Father; then my suffering is a " speech " that utters the glory of the Eternal.

There (in the soul which shows forth His glory), " He hath set His tabernacle in the sun."[64] The " sun " is the Word—the Bridegroom. If He finds my soul empty of all that is not included in the two words—His love, His glory—He chooses it for His " bride-chamber." He enters it impetuously, rejoicing " as a giant to run the way," so that I cannot hide myself " from His heat."[65] This is the " consuming fire "[66] which will work that blessed transformation described by St. John of the Cross when he said: " Each of them seems to be the other, and they are both but one," a " Praise of Glory " to the Father.

* * *

Eighth Day

" *They Fell Down . . . and Adored . . . and Cast Their Crowns* "

" They rested not day and night, saying: Holy, holy, holy, Lord God Almighty, Who was, and Who is, and Who is to come . . .

[60] *Ibid.*, 9.
[61] *Ps.* XXXIV, 6.
[62] *Ps.* XVIII, 3.
[63] *Ps.* CXV, 12-13.
[64] *Ps.* XVIII, 6.
[65] *Ibid.*, 7.
[66] *Heb.* XII, 29.

[They] fell down before Him . . . and adored Him . . . and cast their crowns before the throne, saying: Thou art worthy, O Lord our God, to receive glory, and honor, and power." [67]

How can I imitate, within the heaven of my soul, the ceaseless occupation of the blessed in the heaven of glory? How can I maintain this constant praise, this uninterrupted adoration? St. Paul enlightens me when he writes to his disciples: "That He [the Father] would grant you, according to the riches of His glory, to be strengthened by His Spirit with might unto the inward man. That Christ may dwell by faith in your hearts; that being rooted and founded in charity . . ." [68]

"To be rooted and founded in charity" is, it seems to me, the necessary condition of worthily fulfilling the office of a *Laudem Gloriae*. The soul that enters into, that dwells in "the deep things of God," [69] and that consequently does all by Him, with Him, and in Him with that clear gaze which gives it a certain resemblance to the one, simple Being—this soul, by its every aspiration, every action, every movement, however commonplace, becomes more deeply rooted in Him it loves. Everything within it renders homage to the thrice-holy God; it may be called a perpetual *Sanctus*, a perpetual "Praise of Glory."

They "fell down . . . and adored . . . and cast their crowns." First of all, the soul should "fall down," should plunge into the abyss of its own nothingness, so sinking into it that, according to the beautiful expression of a mystic, it finds the true, invincible, and perfect peace that naught can trouble, for it has cast itself so low that none will descend to follow it. Then it can adore.

Adoration! Ah! that word comes from heaven! It seems to me that it can be defined as the ecstasy of love; love crushed by the beauty, the strength, the vast grandeur of Him it loves. It falls into a kind of swoon, into a profound and deep silence—silence such as David spoke of when he cried: "Silence is Thy praise." [70] Yes! that is the most perfect praise, for it is sung eternally in the bosom of the tranquil Trinity. It is also "the final effort of the soul that overflows and can speak no more." (Lacordaire)

"Exalt ye the Lord . . . for the Lord our God is holy," [71] as the

[67] *Apoc.* IV, 8-11.
[68] *Eph.* III, 16, 17.
[69] *I Cor.* II, 10.
[70] *Ps.* LXV, 2. (d'Eyragues.)
[71] *Ps.* XCVIII, 9.

Psalm says. And again: " They shall adore Him always for His own sake." [72] A soul which meditates upon these thoughts, which understands their meaning with the " mind of the Lord," [73] as St. Paul says, lives in an anticipated heaven, above all that passes, above itself! It knows that He Whom it adores possesses in Himself all happiness, all glory, and casting its crown before Him, as do the blessed, it despises self, loses sight of self, and finds its beatitude in Him Whom it adores, whatever its sufferings or grief, for it has gone out from self and *passed into* Another. The soul, in this attitude of adoration, resembles the wells spoken of by St. John of the Cross, which receive the waters flowing from Lebanon. And those who look on the soul may exclaim: " The stream of the river maketh the city of God joyful." [74]

* * *

Ninth Day
" Be Ye Holy, Because I . . . Am Holy."

" Be ye holy, because I . . . am holy." [75] Who is He Who can give such a command? He Himself has revealed His name, the name proper to Him, which He alone may own. " God said to Moses: I AM WHO AM; " [76] the One Who lives, the Principle of all beings. " In Him," says the Apostle, " we live, and move, and are." [77]

" Be ye holy, because I . . . am holy " is, it seems to me, the wish expressed on the day of creation by the words of God: " Let us make man to Our image and likeness." [78] The Creator's idea has always been to associate and to identify His creature with Himself. St. Peter writes that we have been " made partakers of the divine nature." [79] St. Paul urges us to " hold the beginning of His substance firm unto the end." [80] And the Apostle of love declares: " We are now the sons of God; and it hath not yet appeared what we shall be. We know, that, when He shall appear, we shall be like Him: because we shall see Him as He is. And everyone that hath this hope in him, sanctifieth himself, as He also is holy." [81]

[72] *Ps.* LXXI, 15.
[73] *Rom.* XI, 34.
[74] *Ps.* XLV, 5.
[75] *Lev.* XIX, 2.
[76] *Exod.* III, 14.
[77] *Acts* XVII, 28.
[78] *Gen.* I, 26.
[79] *II Peter* I, 4.
[80] *Heb.* III, 14.
[81] *I John* III, 2-3.

To be holy, even as God is holy, is the measure for the children of His love. Has not the Master said: " Be you therefore perfect, as also your heavenly Father is perfect " ? [82] God said to Abraham: " Walk before Me and be perfect." [83] This, then, is the means by which to attain the perfection that our heavenly Father requires of us. St. Paul, after having penetrated the divine counsels, reveals this to us clearly in the words: " God chose us in Him before the foundation of the world, that we should be holy and unspotted *in His sight* in charity." [84]

I seek light again from the same saint in order to walk unerringly on this magnificent way of the presence of God, on which the soul travels "alone with the Alone," led by the help of His " right hand," [85] " overshadowed with His shoulders, trusting under his wings . . . , not afraid of the terror of the night, of the arrow that flieth in the day, of the business that walketh about in the dark: of invasion, or of the noonday devil." [86]

" Put off, according to former conversation, the old man . . . and be renewed according to the spirit of your mind: and put on the new man, who according to God is created in justice and holiness of truth." [87] The path is traced for us. We have but to deny ourselves in order to traverse it as God intends us to. To deny self, to die to self, to lose sight of self: is not that the Master's meaning when He says: " If any man will come after Me, let him deny himself, and take up his cross, and follow Me "? [88]

" If you live according to the flesh," continues the Apostle, " you shall die. But if by the spirit you mortify the deeds of the flesh, you shall live." [89] This is the death that God demands, of which St. Paul says: " Death is swallowed up in victory." [90] " O death, I will be thy death! " [91] says the Lord. That is: " Soul, My adopted daughter, look on Me, and thou wilt lose sight of self; flow wholly into Me. Come, die in Me, that I may live in thee!"

* * *

[82] *Matt.* V, 48.
[83] *Gen.* XVII, 1.
[84] *Eph.* I, 4-5.
[85] *Ps.* XIX, 7.
[86] Cf. *Ps.* XC, 4-6.
[87] *Eph.* IV, 22-24.
[88] *Matt.* XVI, 24.
[89] *Rom.* VIII, 13.
[90] *I Cor.* XV, 54.
[91] *Osee* XIII, 14.

Tenth Day
"In an Eternal Present"

"Be you therefore perfect, as also your heavenly Father is perfect."[92] When my Master makes me hear this sentence in the depths of my soul, I realize that He is asking me to live, like the Father, in an eternal present, with no past, no future, but wholly in the unity of my being, in the eternal present. What is this present? David tells me: "For Him they shall always adore."[93] That is the eternal present in which a "Praise of Glory" should abide.

But if her attitude of adorer is to be real, so that she can sing: "I will arise early,"[94] she must also be able to say with St. Paul: "For Him I have suffered the loss of all things."[95] That is, for His sake, and in order that I may incessantly adore Him, I have isolated, separated, stripped myself of all things, natural and supernatural, even as regards the gifts of God. For unless a soul has destroyed and become emancipated from self, it must necessarily at certain times be commonplace and natural, and that is unworthy of a child of God, a bride of Christ, and a temple of the Holy Ghost. As a protection against living according to nature, the soul must have a lively faith, and must keep its eyes fixed upon the Master; then it can say, with the prophet king: "I walked in the innocence of my heart, in the midst of my house."[96] It will adore God "for His own sake," and will dwell like Him in the eternal present in which He lives.

"Be you therefore perfect, as also your heavenly Father is perfect." "God," says St. Denis, "is the great Solitary." My Master bids me imitate this perfection, to render Him homage by living in strict solitude. The Divinity dwells in eternal and profound solitude; He cares for the needs of His creatures without in any way leaving it, for He never goes out from Himself, and this solitude is nothing but His Divinity.

I must guard against being withdrawn from this holy interior silence by keeping myself always in the same state, the same isolation, the same retirement, the same detachment. If my desires, my fears, my joys, or my sorrows, if all the impulses coming from these

[92] *Matt.* V, 48.
[93] *Ps.* LXXI, 15.
[94] *Ps.* LXI, 9.
[95] *Phil.* III, 8.
[96] *Ps.* C, 2.

four passions are not completely subjected to God, I shall not be solitary: there will be turmoil within me. Therefore calm, the slumber of the powers, the unity of the whole being, are needed.

"Hearken, O daughter, ... incline thine ear: and forget thy people and thy father's house. And the King shall greatly desire thy beauty." [97] This injunction is, I feel, a call to keep silence: "Hearken ... incline thine ear." But in order to listen we must forget our "father's house," that is, whatever pertains to the natural life, of which the Apostle says: "If you live according to the flesh, you shall die." [98] To forget our people is more difficult, for this "people" is that world which is, as it were, a part of ourselves. It includes our feelings, memories, impressions, and so forth. In a word, it is *self*. We must forget it, give it up. Then when the soul has broken with it and is wholly delivered from all it means, "the King shall greatly desire" its beauty, for beauty—at least God's beauty—is unity.

* * *

Eleventh Day
"The Trinity Itself Dwells in the Soul"

"The Lord ... brought me forth into a large place ... because He was well pleased with me." [99]

The Creator, seeing that silence reigns within His creature who is deeply recollected in her interior solitude, greatly desires her beauty. He leads her into that immense and infinite solitude, into that "large place" of which the Psalmist sings, which is His very Self: "I will enter into the powers of the Lord." [100] The Lord said by His prophet: "I will allure her, and will lead her into the wilderness: and I will speak to her heart." [101] The soul has now entered that vast solitude in which God will make His voice heard. "The word of God is living and effectual, and more piercing than any two-edged sword: and reaching unto the division of the soul and the spirit, of the joints also and the marrow." [102] It is, then, this word itself which will finish the work of stripping the soul, its characteristic and peculiar property being to effect and create what it makes known, provided the soul yields its consent.

[97] *Ps.* XLIV, 11-12.
[98] *Rom.* VIII, 13.
[99] *Ps.* XVII, 20.
[100] *Ps.* LXX, 16.
[101] *Osee* II, 14.
[102] *Heb.* IV, 12.

To know, however, is not all that is requisite. The soul must keep the word, and by this keeping it is sanctified in the truth, according to the will of the Divine Master: " Sanctify them in truth. Thy word is truth." [103] To those who keep His word He has promised: " My Father will love him, and We will come to him, and will make Our abode *in him*." [104] The Three Persons of the Blessed Trinity dwell within the soul which loves them in truth, that is, by keeping Their word. And when this soul realizes what riches it possesses, all the natural or supernatural joys which might come to it from creatures, or even from God, only induce it to enter within itself to enjoy the substantial good it owns, which is nothing else but God Himself. Therefore, St. John of the Cross declares, " it has a certain resemblance to the Divinity."

" Be you therefore perfect, as also your heavenly Father is perfect." St. Paul tells me that He " worketh all things according to the counsel of His will," [105] and my Master asks me again to render Him homage in this manner: " To do all things according to the counsel of My will." Never to let myself be led by my impressions, by the first impulses of nature, but to control myself by my will. For this will to be free, it must, as one writer puts it, be " enclosed " within the will of God. Then I shall be " led by the spirit of God," [106] as St. Paul says. All that I do will partake of the divine, the eternal, and, like Him Who changes not, I shall dwell here on earth in an eternal present.

* * *

Twelfth Day

" By Him, I Have Access to the Father "

" *Verbum caro factum est, et habitavit in nobis.*" [107] God said: " Be ye holy, because I . . . am holy," but He remained inaccessible and hidden. The creature needed to have Him descend to it, to have Him live its life, so that, setting its feet in His footsteps, it might mount up to Him, sanctifying itself by His sanctity.

" For them do I sanctify myself, that they also may be sanctified in truth." [108] I have now before me " the mystery which hath

---

[103] *John* XVII, 17.
[104] *John* XIV, 23.
[105] *Eph.* I, 11.
[106] *Rom.* VIII, 14.
[107] *John* I, 14.
[108] *John* XVII, 19.

been hidden from ages and generations ... this mystery ... which is Christ, in you the hope of glory," [109] says St. Paul, adding that the mystery had been manifested to him.[110] It is, then, from this great Apostle that I shall learn this wisdom " which surpasseth all knowledge," [111] the charity of Christ.

First, he tells me: " He is my peace," that " by Him we have access ... to the Father," [112] " because in Him it hath well pleased the Father that all fullness should dwell: and through Him to reconcile all things unto Himself, making peace through the Blood of His cross, both as to the things that are on earth, and the things that are in heaven." [113] " And you are filled in Him," continues the Apostle, ". . . buried with Him in baptism, in Whom also you are risen again by the faith of the operation of God ... and you ... He hath quickened together with Him; forgiving you all offences: blotting out the handwriting of the decree that was against us, which was contrary to us. And He hath taken the same out of the way, fastening it to the cross: and despoiling the principalities and powers, He hath exposed them confidently in open show, triumphing over them in Himself " [114] " to present you holy and unspotted and blameless before Him." [115]

That is the work of Christ as regards every soul of good will, the work which His immense love, His " exceeding charity," urges Him to do for me. He desires to be my peace, so that nothing can distract my attention or draw me forth from the invincible fortress of holy recollection. There He will give me " access to the Father " and will keep me as motionless and calm in His presence as though my soul were already in eternity.[116] By the Blood of the cross He will make peace in my little heaven, that it may be indeed the place of repose of the " Three." He will fill me with Himself; He will absorb me into Himself, making me live with Him by His life: " *Mihi vivere Christus est.*" [117]

[109] *Col.* I, 26-27.
[110] *Eph.* III, 4. [112] *Eph.* II, 18. [114] *Col.* II, 10-15.
[111] *Eph.* III, 19. [113] *Col.* I, 19-20. [115] *Col.* I, 22.

[116] Most exceptionally, the thought here was reworked. The first text reads as follows: " The work of Christ as regards every soul of good will and what He desires to do in me is this: to be my peace so that nothing may draw me from the Father's bosom, so that I may rest there as motionless and calm as though my soul were already in eternity."

[117] *Phil.* I, 21.

Though I may continually fall, in trustful faith I will ask Him to raise me, knowing that He will forgive me and with jealous care will cleanse me perfectly. More than that, He will strip me, will deliver me from my miseries, from all that offers an obstacle to the divine action upon me. He will draw my powers to Him and make them captive, triumphing over them as they dwell in Him. Then I shall have passed completely into Him and shall be able to say: " I live, now not I; but Christ liveth in me," [118] and I shall be *holy, unspotted, and blameless* in the Father's sight.

* * *

Thirteenth Day

" Walk in Jesus Christ "

"*Instaurare omnia in Christo.*" [119] Again it is St. Paul who teaches me. He, who has just been immersed in the divine counsels, tells me that God " hath purposed . . . to re-establish all things in Christ." The Apostle comes to my aid again, to help me individually to realize this divine plan, and gives me a rule of life: " Walk in Him [Jesus Christ the Lord], rooted and built up in Him, and confirmed in the faith . . . abounding in Him with thanksgiving." [120]

To walk in Jesus Christ appears to me to mean to go out from self, to lose sight of, to forsake self, that we may enter more deeply into Him every moment—enter so profoundly as to be " rooted " in Him, and that we may boldly challenge all events with the defiant cry: " Who, then, shall separate us from the love of Christ? " [121] When the soul is so deeply fixed in Him as to be *rooted* in Him, the divine sap flows freely through it and destroys whatever in its life was trivial, imperfect, natural. Then, in the Apostle's words, " that which is mortal " will be " swallowed up by life." [122] Thus stripped of self and clothed with Jesus Christ, the soul has nothing to fear either from external contacts or interior difficulties; all such things, far from being an impediment, only root it more firmly in its love for its Master. Whatever happens the soul is ready to adore Him always for His own sake, being free, liberated from self and all else. It can sing with the Psalmist: " If armies in camp should

[118] *Gal.* II, 20.
[119] *Eph.* I, 10.
[120] *Col.* II, 6-7.
[121] *Rom.* VIII, 35.
[122] *II Cor.* V, 4.

stand together against me, my heart shall not fear. If a battle should rise up against me, in this will I be confident. . . . For He hath hidden me in His tabernacle,"[123] that is, in Himself. I think this is the meaning of St. Paul's words, to be "rooted" in Jesus Christ.

Now, what is it to be "built up" in Him? The prophet continues: "He hath exalted me above a rock; and now He hath lifted up my head above my enemies."[124] Is that not a figure of the soul "built up" in Jesus Christ? He is that Rock on which it is exalted above self, the senses, and nature; above consolations or sufferings; above all that is not *Him* alone! There, with perfect self-mastery, it controls self, rising above self and all else.

St. Paul now counsels me to be "confirmed in the faith," in the faith which never permits the soul to slumber, but keeps it watchful under the eye of its Master, listening in perfect recollection to His creative word; in its faith in the "exceeding charity" which, St. Paul tells us, allows God to fill the soul "unto all the fulness of God."[125]

Finally, the Apostle desires me to abound in Jesus Christ in thanksgiving, for everything should end in thanksgiving. "Father, I give Thee thanks,"[126] was the song of Christ's soul, and He wishes to hear it echoed in mine. But I think that the *canticum novum* which will best please and charm my God is that of a soul detached from all things, delivered from self, wherein He can reflect all that He is and He can dispose of it as He will. Such a soul waits to be touched by Him as though it were a lyre, and all the gifts it has received are like so many strings which vibrate to give forth, day and night, the "praise of His glory."

* * *

Fourteenth Day
"To Know Him"

"I count all things to be but loss, for the excellent knowledge of Jesus Christ my Lord; for Whom I have suffered the loss of all things, and count them but as dung, that I may gain Christ: and may be found in Him, not having my justice . . . but that . . . which is of God, justice in faith: that I may know Him . . . and

---

[123] *Ps.* XXVI, 3, 5. [124] *Ps.* XXVI, 6. [125] *Eph.* III, 19. [126] *John* XI, 41.

APPENDIX III: LAST RETREAT OF 'LAUDEM GLORIAE' 251

the fellowship of His sufferings, being made conformable to His death . . . I follow after, if I may by any means apprehend wherein I am also apprehended by Christ Jesus . . . One thing I do: forgetting the things that are behind, and stretching forth myself to those that are before, I press towards the mark, to the prize of the supernal vocation of God in Christ Jesus." [127]

The Apostle has often revealed the grandeur of this vocation: God " chose us in Him before the foundation of the world, that we should be holy and unspotted in His sight in charity." [128] " We . . . being predestinated according to the purpose of Him Who worketh all things according to the counsel of His will. That we may be unto the praise of His glory." [129] How are we to respond to the dignity of our vocation? This is the secret: " *Mihi vivere Christus est.*" [130] " *Vivo enim, jam non ego, vivit vero in me Christus.*" [131] We must be transformed into Jesus Christ. It is still St. Paul who is teaching me: " For whom He foreknew, He also predestinated to be made conformable to the image of His Son." [132] Hence, I must study this divine Model, so thoroughly identifying myself with Him that I can incessantly show Him forth in the sight of His Father.

To begin with, what were His first words on entering the world? " Behold, I come to do Thy will, O God." [133] To me it seems that this prayer should be truly the heartbeat of the bride: Behold, we come, Father, to do Thy will. This first oblation of the divine Master was a real one: His life was but its consequence. He delighted in saying: " My meat is to do the will of Him that sent Me." [134] This should be the meat of the bride and, at the same time, the sword that immolates her.

" My Father, if it be possible let this chalice pass from Me. Nevertheless, not as I will but as Thou wilt." [135] Then, serenely peaceful, she goes to meet all sacrifices with her Master, rejoicing at *having been known* by the Father, since He crucifies her with His Son. " I have purchased Thy testimonies for an inheritance forever because they are the joy of my heart." [136] Behold the song in the Master's soul, and it should have a perfect echo in His bride's. By constant fidelity to these " testimonies," both in thought

[127] *Phil.* III, 8-14.
[128] *Eph.* I, 4.
[129] *Eph.* I, 11-12.
[130] *Phil.* I, 21.
[131] *Gal.* II, 20.
[132] *Rom.* VIII, 29.
[133] *Heb.* X, 9.
[134] *John* IV, 34.
[135] *Matt.* XXVI, 39.
[136] *Ps.* CXVIII, 111.

and in act, she will bear witness to the truth and will be able to say: "He that sent Me is with Me and He hath not left Me alone. For I do always the things that please Him." [137] By never leaving Him, by keeping in close contact with Him, the secret virtue will go forth from her which delivers and saves souls. Detached, freed from self and all things, she will follow her Master to the mountain, to join with His soul in "the prayer of God." [138] Then, still through the divine Adorer—through Him Who was the perfect "Praise of Glory" of the Father—she will "offer the sacrifice of praise always to God, that is to say, the fruit of lips confessing to His Name." [139] And like the Psalmist she "shall speak of the might of Thy terrible acts and shall declare Thy greatness." [140]

In the hour of humiliation, of failure, she will remember the short sentence: "*Jesus autem tacebat,*" [141] and she too will be silent, keeping all her strength for the Lord—the strength we draw from silence. When she is abandoned, forsaken, in such anguish as drew from Christ the loud cry: "Why hast Thou forsaken Me?" [142] she will remember the prayer: "That they may have my joy filled in themselves." [143] And, drinking to the very dregs the chalice given by the Father, she will find a heavenly sweetness in its bitterness.

Then, after having repeated again and again: "I thirst" [144]—thirst to possess Thee in glory—she will sing: "It is consummated," [145] "Into Thy hands I commend my spirit." [146] Then the Father will come to take her into His heritage, where "in Thy light we shall see light." [147] "Know ye also that the Lord hath made His holy One wonderful," [148] sang David. Yes, in the case of such a soul, God's holy One is made wonderful indeed, for He has destroyed all else to clothe it with Himself, and it has conformed its life to the words of the Precursor: "He must increase, but I must decrease." [149]

* * *

[137] *John* VIII, 29.
[138] *Luke* VI, 12.
[139] *Heb.* XIII, 15.
[140] *Ps.* CXLIV, 6.
[141] *Mark* XV, 5.
[142] *Mark,* XV, 34.
[143] *John* XVII, 13.
[144] *John* XIX, 28.
[145] *John* XIX, 30.
[146] *Luke* XXIII, 46.
[147] *Ps.* XXXV, 10.
[148] *Ps.* IV, 4.
[149] *John* III, 30.

Fifteenth Day
"Janua Coeli"

After Jesus Christ, of course, and as far away as the infinite is from the finite, there exists a created being who was also the great "Praise of Glory" of the Most Holy Trinity. She corresponded fully to the divine vocation of which the Apostle speaks; she was always holy, unspotted, blameless in the sight of the thrice-holy God.

Her soul is so simple, its movements are so profound that they cannot be detected; she seems to reproduce on earth the life of the Divinity, the simple Being. And she is so transparent, so luminous that she might be taken for the light itself. Yet she is but the mirror of the Sun of Justice: *Speculum Justitiae*.

"His Mother kept all these words in her heart." [150] Her whole history can be summed up in these few words. It was within her own heart that she dwelt, and so deeply did she enter it that no human eye can follow her. When I read in the Gospel that Mary "went into the hill country with haste into a city of Juda," [151] to perform her charitable office to her cousin Elizabeth, I picture her to myself as she passes—beautiful, calm, majestic, absorbed in communion with the Word of God within her. Her prayer, like His, was always: "*Ecce*—Here I am!" Who? "The handmaid of the Lord," [152] the last of His creatures, she, His Mother!

Her humility was so genuine! For she was always forgetful of self, unconscious of self, delivered from self. So she could sing: "He that is mighty hath done great things to me; henceforth all generations shall call me blessed!" [153]

The Queen of Virgins is the Queen of Martyrs too, but it was within her heart that the sword transpierced her,[154] for with her everything took place within her soul. Oh, how beautiful she is to contemplate during her long martyrdom, enveloped in a majesty both strong and sweet, for she has learned from the Word Himself how they should suffer who are chosen as victims by the Father; those whom He has elected as associates in the great work of redemption; "those whom He foreknew and predestinated to be made

---
[150] *Luke* II, 51.
[151] *Luke* I, 39.
[152] *Luke* I, 38.
[153] *Luke* I, 49, 48.
[154] *Luke* II, 35.

conformable to His Son," crucified by love. She is there, at the foot of the Cross, *standing* in her strength and courage, and my Master says to me: "*Ecce Mater tua.*"[155] He gives her to me for my Mother! And now that He has returned to the Father, that He has put me in His place on the Cross, so that I may "fill up those things which are wanting of the sufferings of Christ for His Body which is the Church,"[156] Mary is there still, to teach me to suffer as He did, to tell me, to make me hear those last outpourings of His soul, which only His Mother could catch.

When I shall have said my "*Consummatum est,*" it will be she again, *Janua Coeli,* who will usher me into the eternal courts, as she utters the mysterious words: "*Laetatus sum in his quae dicta sunt mihi, in domum Domini ibimus!*"[157]

* * *

Sixteenth Day

"*In the Bosom of the Tranquil Trinity*"

"As the hart panteth after the fountains of water: so my soul panteth after thee, O God. My soul hath thirsted after the strong living God; when shall I come and appear before the face of God?"[158] Yet, as "the sparrow hath found herself a house, and the turtle a nest for herself where she may lay her young,"[159] so, while waiting to be taken to the holy city of Jerusalem, "*Beata pacis visio,*"[160] *Laudem Gloriae* has found her retreat, her beatitude, heaven beforehand, where she already begins her life of eternity.

"In God my soul is silent, it is from Him I expect my deliverance. Surely He is the rock where I find salvation, my citadel, and I shall be moved no more!"[161] This is the mystery to which my lyre is tuned today. My divine Master has said to me, as to Zaccheus: "Make haste, and come down for . . . I must abide in thy house."[162] Make haste and come down, but where? Into the inner-

[155] *John* XIX, 27.
[156] *Col.* I, 24.
[157] *Ps.* CXXI. 1.
[158] *Ps.* XLI, 2-3.
[159] *Ps.* LXXXIII, 4.
[160] Vespers, *Office of the Dedication of a Church.*
[161] *Ps.* LXII, 2-3. (d'Eyragues.)
[162] *Luke* XIX, 5.

most depths of my being, after having left self, separated from self, stripped myself of self—in a word, without self. " I must abide in thy house." It is my Master Who says this; my Master Who desires to abide in me with the Father and His Spirit of Love so that, in the words of the Beloved Disciple, I may have " fellowship " with Them. " Now therefore you are no more strangers and foreigners; but you are . . . the domestics of God,"[163] as St. Paul says. I think that to be a domestic of God is to abide in the bosom of the tranquil Trinity, in the innermost depths of myself, in the invincible fortress of holy recollection described by St. John of the Cross.

David sang: " My soul longeth and fainteth for the courts of the Lord."[164] Such, I think, should be the feeling of every soul when it enters its inner " courts " to contemplate its God and keep in closest contact with Him. It faints in a divine swoon before this all-powerful love, this infinite Majesty which dwells within it. It is not that life forsakes it, but the soul itself disdains this natural life and withdraws from it. Feeling such life to be unworthy of a spirit raised to such dignity, it dies to this life and flows into its God.

How beautiful is the creature thus stripped and freed! It is then " disposed to ascend by steps, in the vale of tears," that is, to pass from all that is less than God, to the " place which he hath set,"[165] that " large place "[166] sung by the Psalmist which, so it seems to me, is the unfathomable Trinity: " *Immensus Pater, immensus Filius, immensus Spiritus Sanctus.*"[167] It rises, ascending above the senses, above nature, above self. It passes beyond all joy and all sorrow, passes through all things, never to rest until it has penetrated *within* Him Whom it loves, Who will Himself give it the Psalmist's " repose of the abyss "—God, the unfathomable Trinity. And all this will be done without leaving the " holy fortress." The Divine Master has said to it: " Make haste and come down."

Nor will the soul leave it when at last it lives, like the immutable Trinity, in an *eternal present*, adoring God eternally for His own sake, and becoming, by a gaze ever more simple, more unifying, " the brightness of His glory,"[168] or, in other words, the ceaseless " Praise of Glory " of His adorable perfections.

[163] *Eph.* II, 19.
[164] *Ps.* LXXXIII. 3.
[165] *Ibid.*, 6-7.
[166] *Ps.* XXX. 9.
[167] *Athanasian Creed.*
[168] *Heb.* I. 3.